DEBRIS OF BATTLE

Also by the author:
REBELS FROM WEST POINT

DEBRIS OF BATTLE

The Wounded of Gettysburg

Gerard A. Patterson

STACKPOLE
BOOKS

Published by
STACKPOLE BOOKS
5067 Ritter Road
Mechanicsburg, PA 17055

Portions of South After Gettysburg: Letters of Cornelia Hancock, 1863–1868, *edited
by Henrietta Stratton Jaquette, copyright 1956, have been quoted with the kind permission
of HarperCollins Publishers.*

Map of Gettysburg designed by George Skoch.

Printed in the United States of America

10 9 8 7 6 5 4 3 2 1

FIRST EDITION

Library of Congress Cataloging-in-Publication Data

Patterson, Gerard A.
    Debris of battle : the wounded of Gettysburg / Gerard A. Patterson. — 1st ed.
      p.   cm.
    Includes bibliographical references (p. 233) and index.
    ISBN 0-8117-0498-X
    1. Gettysburg (Pa.), Battle of, 1863.   2. United States—History—Civil War,
1861–1865—Medical care.   3. United States—History—Civil War, 1861–1865—
Civilian relief. I. Title.
E475.53.P28   1997
973.7'75—dc21
                                                        97-4996
                                                           CIP

To my wife Diane,
our sons, Eric and Marc,
and their families

Contents

Acknowledgments

The unfairness in acknowledging the aid received in researching a book of this sort is that so much invaluable assistance comes from conscientious and knowledgeable persons on the staffs of libraries and historical groups around the country whose names one never learns.

While apologizing for unintentional omissions, I would like to cite particularly Charles H. Glatfelter and Elwood W. Christ at the Adams County Historical Society, headquartered on the Lutheran Theological Seminary campus; D. Scott Hartwig, supervisory park historian, Tom Desjardin, and Winona R. Peterson, historians at Gettysburg National Military Park. I am also thankful to Dr. Richard J. Sommers at the U.S. Army Military History Institute, Carlisle Barracks for acquainting me with so much useful information, but never leading me to conclusions. Those I arrived at on my own.

The work could not have been completed without the generous help of the staff of the National Archives and the Library of Congress in Washington, D.C.; the Virginia Historical Society, Richmond; the Vermont Historical Society, Montpelier; the Bailey/Howe Library, University of Vermont, Burlington; the Carnegie Library in Pittsburgh; and my local library, Mt. Lebanon Public Library.

The presentation has been much enhanced by the map-making skill of George Skoch, and the time given in reviewing the raw manuscript by such kind individuals as Keith and Mary Bowman.

The interest demonstrated by William J. Miller, the editor of *Civil War Magazine,* who published an article of mine on the wounded of Gettysburg in his November 1995 issue, is much appreciated.

I am most grateful for the encouragement and guidance of two special people at Stackpole Books—William C. Davis, editor, and Michelle J. Myers, managing editor—and for the continued support, in ways too varied to describe, of my wife Diane.

I cannot delay to pick up the debris of the battlefield . . . My wounded, with those of the enemy in our hands, will be left at Gettysburg.

—*Dispatch from Maj. Gen. George G. Meade,*
commander of the Army of the Potomac,
as he started in pursuit of Lee's army.[1]

Some of the Confederate dead. *Library of Congress.*

Introduction

When it was over the army, as if trying to conceal some vile repugnant act in which it had been engaged, barred all approaches to Gettysburg. It seemed to be seeking an interval of privacy to assess its losses and prepare to face the curious and the sympathetic who would come, attracted by the awful din that had been generated there the three previous days.

Among the first to encounter the barricades blocking the many roads leading into the now quiet arena on the Sunday after the fighting ended was an odd delegation of clergy in a carriage and an omnibus creeping along the road from Emmitsburg, Maryland, nine miles distant. The caravan halted in front of a treetrunk obstacle and a priest climbed down from the carriage. He left behind fourteen nuns in their stiff, butterfly-like white bonnets. They were the Sisters of Charity, a nursing order.

Trying to reassure the taut soldiers that they were not Southern sympathizers attempting to infiltrate Northern lines, Father Francis Burlando attached a handkerchief to the tip of his cane and hoisted it overhead as he approached the guards. He explained that they had come from St. Joseph's Provincial House with medical supplies and were ready to help if needed. The party was permitted to pass and soon began to encounter what was being kept, for the moment, from outsiders.

There were numerous soldiers on horseback in the trampled fields but all was strangely quiet. One of the nuns observed that the soldiers were "as silent almost as the dead that lay by the hundreds on the ground."[2]

"We were compelled to drive cautiously to avoid passing over the dead," related Father Burlando, chaplain at St. Joseph's. "Our terrified horses drew back or darted forward reeling from one side to the other. The further we advanced the more harrowing the scene; we could not restrain our tears."[3]

When they finally reached the town, they were taken aback by the appearance of the inhabitants, most of whom had huddled in the cellars for safety during the fighting.

"Tension was depicted on every countenance," a sister observed. "All was confusion."[4]

To Mother Ann Simeon Norris, the residents appeared as "frightened ghosts, so terrified had they been during the fearful battle."[5]

By the time the sisters arrived, every church pew in Gettysburg had already been given over to the wounded. The schools, meeting halls, and warehouses had been turned into hospitals. Any large open areas where a number of casualties could be concentrated and attended collectively by the medical personnel were considered prime locations. With or without invitation, many of the private dwellings in the community of 2,500 people had been occupied by the hurt of both armies, their blood forever staining carpets, mattresses, sofas, and books as remembrances of their stay.

The dazed townspeople wandered aimlessly about their once tidy streets or congregated along the red-brick sidewalks to quietly discuss with neighbors the dreadful storm that had just passed through and to view the damage.

Strewn everywhere about were knapsacks, broken muskets, filthy rags, paper cartridges, bits of food, crinkled letters, battered caps, and other discardings of transient soldiers. Shattered window panes and bullet holes lined the walls of the low rowhouses, particularly along those on streets leading up toward Cemetery Hill, recently occupied by sharpshooters. Here and there a body in dusty blue or tattered gray, as well as the swollen carcasses of horses with their stiffened legs grotesquely raised, awaited removal with infinite patience.

Fannie J. Buehler, emerging from her house on Baltimore for the first time since being confined inside with her six children for the duration of the battle, was mesmerized by the sight of the dead soldiers and their belongings "all lying in the streets, so far as we could see, either up or down."[6]

Another resident, fifteen-year-old Tillie Pierce, gazed at the transformation in her familiar surroundings and was left with the feeling that this was not the place where she belonged. She felt she had somehow found herself "in a strange and blighted land."[7]

The awful quiet was what also struck a correspondent of the *Philadelphia Public Ledger* when he arrived that Sunday aboard a wagon he had managed to rent in York.

"Entering the town, I found a guard, which offered no hinderance," he wrote that night. "A woman emerged from an alley way, a step or two, looking up and down the streets, with a kind of vacant look; soldiers whispered to each other at the street corners, and did sentry duty from corner to corner.

"Further on, a barricade had been erected, the centre of which was broken, and through it was coming a regiment of cavalry, dirty and jaded, seemingly to the last degree, yet with high resolve stamped on every brow and every lip full of firmness and triumph. When I saw them, I knew we had won."[8]

The scene in the town was but a fragment of the devastation evident over the twenty-five-square-mile area in which the battle had been waged. The thousands of wounded in the residents' midst—mainly men of the Union First and the Eleventh Corps who had been there since the first day of the fighting and during the Confederate occupation of the town—were only a fraction of all those on the field in need of attention.

When all the wounded were gathered from the Wheatfield and the Peach Orchard, Cemetery Ridge and Little Round Top, the Devil's Den and Culp's Hill, and all the other bloody sectors, there would be more than 14,500 Union soldiers to be treated.

The retreating Confederates left behind some 5,500 men so badly hurt they could not even be transported. These were in addition to the 1,800 wounded Rebs taken prisoner during the battle.

There were dead men everywhere to be buried. Some 7,000 had been killed and few of the nearly 4,000 Confederate dead had been interred. The Rebels had assumed the offensive role and were generally slain during unsuccessful assaults. Their bodies lay out of reach of their comrades and were left to await final resolution of the combat before they could be given any attention. There were also more than 3,000 dead horses and mules that somehow had to be disposed of.

Millions of dollars of government property littered the field—muskets, blankets, sabers, knapsacks—and had to be gathered up before it was lost to battlefield looters.

The civilian population was in dire need of provisions, for the food supply in the region had been all but exhausted by the two huge armies foraging there. Wells had been drained dry for miles around. The Union soldiers, waiting for marching orders, hadn't been issued rations in days.

Dealing with all these problems at once was a staggering task, one far too great to satisfy with the resources at hand. The misery that would have to be endured during the attempt led one medical officer who witnessed it all to conclude that "the period of ten days following the battle of Gettysburg was the occasion of the greatest amount of human suffering known to this nation since its birth."[9]

Despite the desperate situation that existed, the town was isolated, in part by the military's exaggerated concern for security, but mainly because the singletrack railroad serving Gettysburg had been broken up by the invaders. Mail delivery was halted and telegraph lines were down. The three local newspapers suspended publication and the residents, oddly enough, were kept woefully ignorant of the scope and historic importance of the event that had transpired about them.

As word got out about the state of affairs at Gettysburg via eye-witness accounts provided by soldiers fresh from the field or by appeals from the pulpit, a national response began to grow.

The government in Washington, embarrassed by its inability to cope, gave no official encouragement whatsoever. From here and there, doctors, nurses, and ministers started for Gettysburg to offer assistance. Wives and mothers came to sit by and care for their loved ones, determined that their needs not be overlooked in such a great mass of distress. Those with no special healing skills accumulated supplies of every description that they perceived might be in demand, and consigned their offerings by whatever means possible to this town in Pennsylvania few recognized by name.

Gradually, the reaction swelled to such enormous proportions that merely channeling all that was donated became, in itself, an awesome job of sorting and distribution.

The effort was made all the more remarkable by the fact that it was all voluntary and unorchestrated, with no one individual or group in overall charge to prioritize and guide. It was an operation conducted in support of, but separate from, the army and its generals. Help came from myriad sources, including many unlikely contributors. Were it not for the early arrival of the superbly organized United States Sanitary Commission, dogging the army with provisions in anticipation of just such an emergency, thousands more would have surely perished. The United States Christian Commission, the other major civilian relief agency, which addressed spiritual needs as well as corporeal, was of immeasurable assistance to the wounded soldiers of both sides.

Also significant were the efforts of individuals like Lydia Smith, a black woman who lived in Gettysburg. She was free but impoverished, and felt such compassion for the wounded abandoned on the field, Union and Confederate alike, that she rented, with her meager funds, a ramshackle wagon and an old horse that was just a "pile of bones." It had been rejected by every dismounted cavalryman trying to rejoin his unit, but with her pathetic rig, Lydia canvassed the countryside for small donations of food to take back to the famished soldiers. She distributed what she had garnered indiscriminately, without regard for the color of their uniforms.[10]

A few inherited pivotal roles in the aftermath of Gettysburg. Railroad genius Herman Haupt, who by sheer coincidence was a former Gettysburg resident thoroughly familiar with the area, was chosen to get the vital rail line back into operation. Dr. Henry Janes, a thirty-one-year-old Vermont physician practicing but a few years, suddenly found himself responsible for the scores of field hospitals the Union army hastily set up on the battlefield. And because of a fateful decision by the army's high command he had but a fraction of the medical personnel needed to staff them.

While hosts of people came to Gettysburg to relieve suffering, there were many on the scene who sensed an opportunity for profit—the scavengers, the morticians preying on relatives hoping to take home remains for burial, and the wagon owners who demanded exorbitant fees from wounded and helpless soldiers to transport them to evacuation points.

It was not until November 20—twenty weeks after the battle, and the day after President Lincoln came to town to deliver a few appropriate remarks at the dedication of a national soldiers cemetery there—that the last of the wounded were removed from Gettysburg.

When they were all gone, it marked the end of a singular exercise in disaster relief with aspects as dramatically gripping as the battle itself and, in different ways, as heroic. This is what took place at Gettysburg after the last shot was fired.

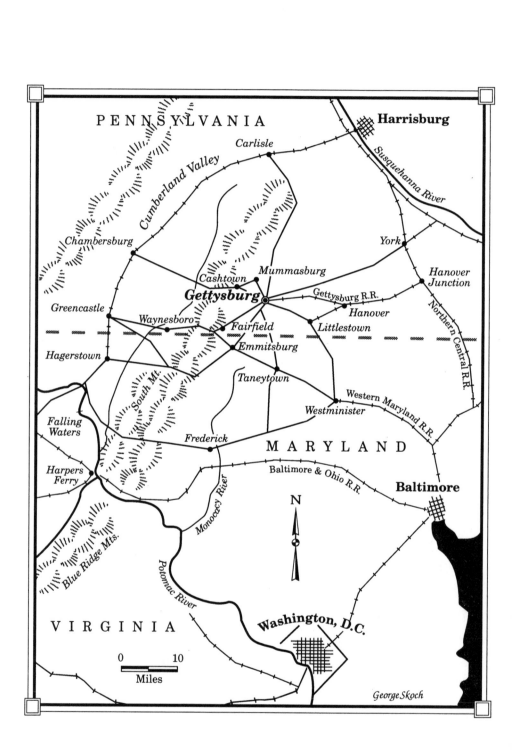

PENNSYLVANIA

Harrisburg

Carlisle

Cumberland Valley

Susquehanna River

Chambersburg

York

Cashtown   Mummasburg

Hanover
Junction

Gettysburg   Gettysburg R.R.

Greencastle   Waynesboro   Fairfield   Hanover

Littlestown

Northern Central R.R.

Hagerstown   Emmitsburg

South Mt.   Taneytown

Western Maryland R.R.

Falling
Waters   Westminister

Frederick   M A R Y L A N D

Harpers
Ferry   Baltimore & Ohio R.R.   **Baltimore**

Monocacy River

N

Blue Ridge Mts.

Potomac River

V I R G I N I A   **Washington, D.C.**

0   10
Miles   George Skoch

"Without Proper Means"

From the time the battle ended, Dr. Jonathan Letterman could see that his revolutionary field hospital system was not functioning as it should, and he was well aware of the reasons why.

It was almost precisely one year before that the thirty-nine-year-old regular-army surgeon had become medical director of the Army of the Potomac, then under Gen. George B. McClellan. Almost immediately, he began to use his exceptional organizational skills to devise a more efficient method of giving the wounded prompt attention on the battlefield. It was a quest driven by the chaotic scenes he had personally observed during the Peninsular Campaign before Richmond in 1862. Surely, he reasoned, modern medicine could salvage more from the carnage of warfare.

He brought much experience to the task. The son of a Canonsburg, Pennsylvania, physician, Letterman had entered the army in 1849, right after he graduated from Jefferson Medical College in Philadelphia. Accompanying troops in the field on numerous campaigns against the Seminoles, Apaches, Navajos, and Utes over a period of twelve years had taught him much about treating wounds of every description. He understood the dangers and difficulties of transporting those in need of attention any great distance.[1]

The system Letterman organized involved not only field hospitals but a fully-equipped ambulance corps to serve them. The wounded were to be no longer collected in haphazard fashion by litter-bearers with no clear instructions about how and where to convey them. Each regiment now had its own ambulances and every brigade, division, and corps had officers specifically responsible for ambulance service. Three privates were assigned to each ambulance with carefully defined duties in camp, on the march, and in battle. In addition to the ambulances, each brigade was assigned its own medicine and supply wagons.

The hospital arrangement was designed not only to provide prompt attention to the wounded, but to see to it that any major operations were performed by the most skillful and responsible surgeons available in the army.

To effect this, the medical director had each division establish a field hospital in the rear of the unit, out of danger, yet easily within reach of the ambulances before an engagement. At each of these division hospitals, three surgeons—selected solely on the basis of operating ability rather than rank—were designated to perform or oversee all major procedures. Three other medical officers were detailed to assist them and a medical officer was assigned to each regiment. These regimental doctors situated themselves at dressing stations directly to the rear of their respective units during the fighting, where temporary aid to the wounded could be provided before they were forwarded to the division hospitals. So detailed was Letterman's plan that there were officers responsible for setting up cook tents and organizing food, water, fuel, and other supplies at the hospitals. Others handled administrative details, such as preparing patient lists.

Letterman's approach, as elaborate as it may have seemed, had been put to the test the previous December during the slaughter at Fredericksburg and, more recently, in the Chancellorsville campaign. It proved so effective, that other Union armies swiftly adopted it. The medical director, a dark taciturn man with a "sad calmness" about him, had labored hard to revamp the army's medical procedures and should have been well satisfied with his accomplishments.[2] But now, with the end of the fighting at Gettysburg the wounded were being brought in to the spreading field hospitals in staggering numbers. The conscientious surgeon with a face "worn in the cause of suffering" recognized more keenly than anyone else how unprepared his medical staff was.[3]

The number of doctors available—almost 650 in all—seemed adequate, at least for the Union wounded, though those assigned to the corps that had incurred the heavier casualties would be far more pressured than those attached to units lightly engaged.

But what of their supplies? Where were they? The field hospitals were being set up as they should have been to accommodate the casualties, if

Jonathan Letterman, medical director of the Army of the Potomac, who revolutionized battlefield treatment. *Library of Congress.*

only in barns and groves that required a red flag to identify them as such. However, the wagons with the blankets, tents, cooking utensils, basins, and other basic items the hospitals needed to function were nowhere in sight.

Much to his anger and disgust, Jonathan Letterman knew all too well where they were. On June 19, the medical director had protested vainly when the number of medical supply wagons was ordered reduced by Maj. Gen. Joseph Hooker, then the commanding general. Hooker, in order to facilitate the more rapid movement of the army pursuing the invading Confederates up from Virginia cut the supply wagons from six per division to two.[4] Letterman, who knew from long army service how to maneuver around unwelcome orders, tried to compensate somewhat for this loss by cannily creating a reserve supply train of twenty-five wagons in Washington. When summoned by Letterman, Medical Purveyor Jeremiah B. Brinton, in charge of the reserve unit, managed to bring it up as far as Westminster— twenty miles from Gettysburg—on the eve of the battle. But when Maj. Gen. George G. Meade, the army's new commander, arrived on the field, the problem Letterman thought he had eased was only compounded. As soon as the fighting broke out, Meade, naturally cautious and not sure that he would be able to hold his position, ordered that corps commanders send to the rear all their trains, excepting ammunition wagons and ambulances.

Despite Letterman's vigorous complaint, Meade insisted that, to avoid capture, the conveyances be parked between Union Mills and Westminster, in the vicinity where Brinton waited. During the second day of the battle, with his position in peril, the commander ordered the wagons moved even farther back. Finally, following the repulse of Lee's last assault on Cemetery Ridge, Meade, "after much persuasion," relented and permitted Letterman to bring up half of his supply wagons.[5]

The question was, when could they be expected to arrive and how long would it take to distribute the contents to units scattered over such a wide area? With storm clouds forming, Letterman knew his helpless wounded were in for a hellish time. "Without proper means, the Medical Department can no more take care of the wounded than the army can fight a battle without ammunition," the earnest, incessantly smoking medical director wrote of his predicament. "The Medical Department had these means, but military necessity deprived it of a portion of them, and would not permit the remainder to come upon the field."

Had control of the supplies been solely in his hands, the doctor said bitterly, he would have "run the risk of their capture, than that the wounded should suffer for want of them. Lost supplies can be replenished, but lives lost are gone forever."[6]

The canvas tents were particularly missed, hundreds of which were packed away in the absent supply wagons. Without them, those wounded who could not be crowded into the homes and barns in the area—that is the bulk of the casualties—had to lie on the wet muddy ground with no cover save the branches of trees and no concealment from the sight of the misery and suffering swelling to ghastly proportions around them. The surgeons had to perform their work in the open air with no protection from sun or rain for themselves or their patients.

With no tents, the men were left to improvise shelters, haphazardly rigging blankets above the heads of the wounded with sticks, tarps, and whatever else was at hand, and creating in the process a motley display of disarray disgustingly offensive to a man of Dr. Letterman's standards.

In no sector were conditions worse in regard to exposure than in the rear of Cemetery Ridge, near Rock Creek, where the hospitals of Gen. Winfield Scott Hancock's Second Corps were established. Here, the casualties of the Confederates' climactic attack on the Union center on the last day of the battle were received. Not only were the losses enormous from the advance by parts of three Rebel divisions and the earth-shaking cannonade that preceded the attack, but there were few dwellings in that section of the field that could be turned into hospitals.

As it happened, it was to this area that a young woman named Cornelia Hancock innocently ventured, one of the first women to appear on the scene. It was her first view of a battlefield.

Cornelia's journey to Gettysburg had come about almost on impulse. A devout Quaker from Hancock's Bridge, New Jersey, she was twenty-three-years old and unmarried. She had inconspicuously set off for the battleground after learning from a relative that there was an opportunity to help. She had no nursing skills but thought she might at least comfort the soldiers by writing letters for them. So limited a contribution did she expect to make that, as she was leaving her home and happened to encounter some friends on their way to church, she said "I hid myself down in the carriage lest I should be stopped to be bidden good-bye or saluted by any of the formalities they might wish to indulge in." Least of all did she want to hear the admonition, "Why, Cornelia, thee is too young to go."[7]

On her arrival, after an arduous trip by train and wagon, she learned that there were men from the 12th New Jersey at the Second Corps hospitals outside of town. She set out next morning in that direction "expecting to find some familiar faces."

Cornelia, carrying her supply of stationery, pencils, and postage stamps, reached the field hospital situated in a little woods, soon saw "a collection of semi-conscious but still living human forms, all of whom had been shot through the head, and were considered hopeless. They were laid there to die and I hoped that they were indeed too near death to have consciousness." Looking about, she was dismayed to find that "there was hardly a tent to be seen" and that the "earth was the only available bed during those first hours after the battle."[8]

The lack of shelter was the feature of the landscape that appalled others far more accustomed to the battlefield than she. Andrew B. Cross, a United States Christian Commission delegate, arrived Sunday and attested: "There were a few tents, some little shelter coverings, some gum cloths spread on two rails, with any cloth or covering they could get, but the great mass had no cover or shelter."[9]

Though it isn't clear what precise sector she was describing, Mary C. Fisher from York, Pennsylvania, who reached the field two days after the battle, saw a crowd of about 500 wounded men "lying upon the ground, some of them literally half buried in mud. There was no shelter."[10]

Conditions were much the same at all the so-called hospitals to the rear of the fishhook-shaped Union position where doctors and attendants cursed whoever was responsible for the breakdown that deprived them of their basic supplies.

An exhausted Michigan surgeon with the Fifth Corps, Dr. Cyrus Bacon Jr., noted in his journal on that first night after the battle, "having no tent, I sleep on the lid of the operating table." When the rain became too much for him, the doctor said he crawled into an ambulance where he was able to "find room to sit at its foot bent up so as to be packed."[11]

On July 5, at the Jacob Schwartz farm the Third Corps, which connected with the Second on the Union line, set up a hospital. William Watson of the 105th Pennsylvania performed fourteen amputations without leaving the table, realizing full well while he worked that the sort of recovery facilities to which his patients would be consigned would be inadequate. "Most of [the wounded] are lying on the wet ground without any shelter whatsoever," he said.[12]

Capt. A. H. Nickerson of the 8th Ohio was shot through the lungs and one arm. He was among those at a Second Corps field hospital when the skies, disturbed by the awful thunder created by the armies, responded with a sustained and inescapable downpour. He was better off than most. A black body servant named Jerry dutifully trailed Captain Nickerson about the field with a haversack and rubber coat, just as so many of the Confederate officers were followed by slaves brought from distant homes. Finding his master lying unprotected in the rain, Jerry threw the coat over him. But "it would only cover a small portion of my person," the captain remembered.

"Inadequate as it was, it was more than many of my comrades had. The rain poured down in torrents, saturating the exposed portions of my clothing until, with the aid of a shallow pool that formed where I lay, it permeated the whole and I was thoroughly drenched."[13]

For some doctors, the workload under such abysmal conditions was more than they could bear. A division commander in the Eleventh Corps, Gen. Carl Schurz, told of visiting a hospital at a farm and seeing "long rows of men lying under the eaves of buildings, the water pouring down upon their bodies in streams."

The surgeons stood in pools of blood as they amputated arms or legs in heaps. After laboring for hours, the general observed that one "put down his knife, exclaiming that his hand had grown unsteady, and that this was too much for human endurance, hysterical tears streaming down his face."[14]

The only exception to the suffering was found at the Twelfth Corps. There, the director of the unit on the Union right flank that had beaten off repeated Rebel assaults on Culp's Hill, had failed to obey orders. The corps' medical supply wagons had not been sent to the rear. Whether Meade's directive wasn't followed due to a communications lapse or willful disobedience, the medical director of that corps, Dr. John McNulty, made no apology. Almost defiantly, the doctor reported to Medical Director Letterman. "It is with extreme satisfaction that I can assure you that it enabled me to remove the wounded from the field, shelter, feed them, and dress their wounds, within six hours after the battle ended and to have every capital operation performed within 24 hours after the wound was received."[15] Such an assertion only underscored the degree of misery that might have been avoided throughout the bleeding army if all its supply wagons had been closer at hand.

Until additional medical supplies came up and could be distributed, the physicians had to work with what they had when the battle erupted.

The doctors treating the hundreds of wounded from the Union First Corps that filled the Lutheran Theological Seminary were perhaps worst off because the retreating Confederates—sorely pressed for medical instruments—confiscated most of the surgeons' tools and left them all but helpless.

During this time, the most mundane items became priceless. What surgeon Abraham Haines of the 19th Indiana needed was a lamp. When one couldn't be provided, he left his First Corps wounded on the seminary grounds and went out to look for one. Noticing a deserted house nearby, he simply broke in. In the kitchen he found some lard and filled a can with it. Then he went into a bedroom, yanked a sheet from a bed and tore off a strip to serve as a wick, stuffed it in the can, and he had his lamp to dress wounds that night. When he ran out of bandages, the doctor made another midnight requisition. He walked toward town and burglarized another empty house. He pulled some fine sheets from the beds which were promptly converted into bandages and lint for his patients.[16]

Dr. Cyrus Bacon showed similar initiative in setting up a Fifth Corps hospital near Little Round Top. After commandeering a stone farm dwelling, the 7th Michigan surgeon "ransacked the house and secured operating tables, clothes for dressing, etc." Some of his assistants joined him in the effort to make up for the shortage of medical supplies, emptying the closets and bureaus of apparel, including "a neatly worked lady's chemise." When the young woman from whose wardrobe the garment had been taken noticed it being used as a resting place for Dr. Bacon's surgical instruments, she demanded it back. "Only if you substitute another piece of cloth," the harried physician insisted. "She gladly supplied its place," he said.[17]

Back at Westminster, Medical Purveyor Brinton was well aware of how badly supplies in his reserve train were needed. When ordered up by Letterman (who may not have even told Meade of his ploy to compensate for Hooker's reduction of medical transportation), Brinton wasted no time getting to Gettysburg. His heavily laden wagons, wheels mudcaked by the heavy rain, rolled into the area on the evening of July 4. Most likely, darkness had already fallen, and his teamsters would have been guided, perhaps, by the lanterns and campfires that burned throughout the night, providing an effect that under other circumstances might have been taken for a glorious Independence Day celebration, but now would have seemed as somber as a rack of flickering church candles.

Welcome as they were, the materials in Brinton's train hardly began to answer the enormous need that increased by the hour. Help on a grand scale was needed—help far beyond the army's ability to furnish, even when all its medical and supply wagons were brought up. The losses were greater than had ever been encountered. Where in the world would help come from, and when, when?

As desperate as were conditions on the scene, the office of Surgeon General William A. Hammond in Washington—through which medical help must come—was apparently not being promptly informed of the state of affairs.

On July 5—two days after the battle—Hammond wired his friend Letterman: "I have no reports from you. I presume therefore you have what you need. Is this so?"[18]

The craving for food was even more pressing than the need for shelter. The first day after the battle, the army's chief commissary was able to issue some 30,000 rations, the first provisions distributed since the army had arrived. But there were thousands who got not a scent of this food, and hunger—deep, gnawing hunger—set in without the distraction that fear and tension of combat afforded.

As strenuously as he had to work, a Third Corps surgeon wrote that he had "nothing but two hard crackers for three days" and was "nearly starved."[19]

Delegate Cross of the U.S. Christian Commission had only two boxes of hardtack in his wagon when he reached Cemetery Ridge on the Sunday after the battle. He may have been reminded of the miracle of the loaves and fishes as he broke up the biscuits in smaller and smaller bits and distributed them to the famished Second Crops wounded. As he did so, some equally hungry soldiers of the Third and Fifth Corps made their way over to his wagon for some small share.

"Think of two boxes of soda crackers in a hospital of over 3,000 wounded men who had not anything to eat for three days . . . It was all we had.

"The scarcity of everything was exceedingly great, no army provisions of any kind having yet come, and the men having been without food in many cases for three days."[20]

At some of the aid stations, the men just couldn't wait for the government to provide. William Baird of the 6th Michigan Cavalry was given a horse and cart and sent out into the country for whatever supplies he could find for the hospital. Without disclosing how the transactions were arranged, Baird said he "met with the best of success in the way of Bread, Butter, Eggs and Fruit as well as sheets for Bandages . . ."[21]

When young Cornelia Hancock noticed wagons of bread and other food arriving on July 6, she needed no suggestions on how to make herself useful.

"I helped myself to their stores," she wrote, and sat down with a loaf in one hand and a jar of jelly in the other.

"It was not hospital diet but it was food, and a dozen poor fellows lying near me turned their eyes in piteous entreaty, anxiously watching my efforts to arrange a meal. There was not a spoon, knife, fork or plate to be had that day, and it seemed as if there was no more serious problem under Heaven than the task of dividing that too well-baked loaf into portions that could be swallowed by weak and dying men."[22]

Mary C. Fisher undertook to feed some of the hundreds of wounded she found in a barn on July 6 with food she had brought from York. She recalled that "many had to be fed like infants," and that she would never forget seeing "the tears of gratitude run down the cheeks of men who would have died in the ranks without flinching as they received the food we so gladly gave."[23]

Scattered moans and cries came intermittently from out of the darkness of the vast open field over which Pickett's charge had been made, and reminded the exhausted Union soldiers seeking sleep on the crest of Cemetery Ridge that there were hundreds, if not thousands, of Rebels still out there, desperate for attention.

It was after sunset when Lt. Edward F. Rollins of the 15th Massachusetts and his men were sent forward to establish a picket line along the Emmitsburg Road intersecting the field. As they ventured forward into the blackness, the men stumbled over dead bodies and were exhorted by the wounded, "For God's sake don't step on us," or to give them a drink, or simply turn them over. Though strict orders were given to pay no attention to the enemy wounded, because stretcher bearers would come for them later, "flesh and blood could not refuse these offices," the lieutenant said.

Bordering the road was a rail fence that presented the final obstacle the Rebels had faced in reaching Federal guns after crossing nearly a mile of open ground. And it was here that the casualties were particularly heavy. Rollins and his men came upon what he called "a pile of dead and wounded, struck as they exposed themselves in clambering over the fence during the charge."

It was not until eleven o'clock that night that a detail of surgeons and assistants came out from the Federal lines, "giving the wounded, as far as I could learn, not much but morphine," Rollins said.[24]

When daylight came and parties went out to help the now-visible Confederates writhing on the field, they found themselves being fired upon by a strong Rebel picket line set up to mask the army's withdrawal. Only the soldiers in blue clearly associated with ambulances were let alone. Anyone else was looked upon as attempting to reconnoiter and test their lines. Consequently, it was the men of their very own regiments who were responsible for prolonging the agony of the Southerners caught in this no man's land.

Despite the risk—or perhaps unaware of it—Col. Charles Wainwright wished to make a tour of the historic battlefield to impress the details on his mind. He rode out between the lines on horseback and soon encountered the weak calls of the Rebel wounded pleading to be moved.

"For this I was powerless," the artillery officer said. When he returned to his lines, he appealed to some regimental surgeons to do something for the men but they "objected that they did not belong to their regiment."

"I fear that I should be very hard on such fellows if I had the power," he said in disgust. "As a rule, the wounded of both sides are treated alike by our surgeons."[25]

After awhile, some members of the 14th Connecticut couldn't stand the sight of unattended Confederates "lying there in hundreds, moaning or shrieking in their pain—as indeed we had heard them all through the night previous." Taking a chance on getting shot themselves, they went out and brought in as many as they could.[26]

When one fallen Southern officer saw a Yankee ambulance passing him by on the field, he supposedly offered the driver $500 to stop and take him away.

It wasn't until Sunday, July 5, after the armies had disengaged, that Lt. John Dooley of the First Virginia Infantry, shot through both thighs during the assault, was finally brought in. The rain poured down as he was carried to a field hospital that he found "differs from the battlefield only in this respect, that we have some kind of medical attendance and rations of crackers and substitute coffee.

"But the accommodations are the same, viz., the wet, muddy hillside, sans tents, sans blankets, sans fires, sans water, sans everything relating to exterior comfort," he said.[27]

Dooley was among the more than 900 Confederate wounded taken prisoner and conveyed to the Second Corps hospitals after the attack, there to join some 2,300 Union soldiers deposited by the ambulance attendants on the sodden ground in a grove bordering Rock Creek without anything to lie on or to cover them. Many were stripped almost bare of their clothing, their drenched garments given up as bandages to stop the bleeding.

Responsibility for the selection of the site had, oddly enough, been entrusted to nineteen-year-old Thomas L. Livermore, who on June 30, had been named Chief of Ambulances for the corps, a function he knew little about.

After riding around looking for a place "removed from the range of projectiles," as instructed, the Illinois youth thought he had found an ideal location by Rock Creek.

"At this point it was of sufficient volume to afford water for all necessary purposes," Livermore said in listing the advantages of his choice: "The left bank was a hillside, and the right was level and low and perfectly accessible from the road leading from the field of battle, and both hillside and level were clothed with trees nearly free from under-growth."

The youth was quick to add that "my selection met with the approval of the medical director" of the corps.[28]

But it was not Livermore's expectation that the wounded would actually be placed on the level side of the creek; that was to be simply an unloading area for the ambulances. With no one directing them otherwise, however, the litter bearers soon began depositing their loads in the vicinity of the vehicles rather than carrying them across the narrow creek to the crowded hillside. Obviously, no one had calculated the ferocity of the rain that continued throughout the night of July 4 and into the next day.

As the stream rapidly rose, the hundreds of disabled soldiers along the low-lying marshy banks began to realize they were in danger of being carried away by the angry waters. Attendants scurried to drag or carry the screaming patients to higher ground but there were far too few carriers for the task.

The overflow was probably not over two feet in depth around where Captain Nickerson of the 8th Ohio lay "but to men who could not raise their heads, this, like Mercutio's wound, was enough—it sufficed. The few attendants there worked like Trojans, but it was impossible to save all, and quite a number of the more helpless ones were drowned within the range of my limited vision."[29]

Someone else noted that at a point where some two hundred Rebels were clustered, a "shallow stream had in a few hours swollen to such a torrent as actually to sweep away beyond recovery, several wounded men who lay, thoughtless of any new peril, asleep upon its banks.[30]

How many soldiers who thought they were going to survive their wounds were instead drowned by the flash flooding became a matter of controversy, with one source putting it as high as twenty and the surgeon in charge of the hospital insisting that none of his patients actually drowned. But some of the wounded were so shaken by the ordeal that even after they had been moved to safer parts of the quagmire, were heard "cursing, praying, begging their visitors to put an end to their suffering."[31]

When young Livermore learned what had befallen the men lying on the level part of the hospital site he had selected with such satisfaction, he could only say, "they ought not to have been there."[32]

Probably at no time had the people of Gettysburg longed for the spiritual comfort of gathering for Sunday services and joining hands and voices in communion as much as on that first Sabbath after the battle.

But that emotional balm was kept from them. Both Catholic and Protestant sanctuaries were filled with hundreds of wounded sitting or lying in the pews the churchgoers customarily occupied. Even the little aisle doors of the benches had been ripped away for more convenient access or converted to tables. The Blessed Sacrament was, under the circumstances, removed from the altar of St. Francis Xavier Roman Catholic Church on West High Street, though one wonders when its presence could have been more appreciated. Passersby, instead of the accustomed strains of organ music coming through the stained-glass windows of the churches, heard a ceaseless dirge of mournful moaning.

A Philadelphia woman, staying at a home in town while she nursed at the hospitals, said that at night, "I buried my head in my pillow to shut out the sounds which reached us from a church quite near where the wounded are lying."[33]

But congregations of wounded in the churches were only one of many anomalies to be observed in the community. The new Adams County Court House was also crowded with wounded. Much of the furniture rested in haphazard heaps around the building where it had been thrown out the windows onto Baltimore Street to make room. Bleeding soldiers were scattered about on the bare wood floors and the administration of justice was suspended while the courtroom was used as an operating theater. When passing the place, Fannie Buehler confessed, "I stopped my ears that I might not hear the groans of those poor unfortunate men whom I could not relieve."[34]

One sound that helped to drown out the cries for a time was the music of a regimental band that began to play patriotic airs in front of the makeshift hospital every afternoon.

The main building of little Pennsylvania College, established in Gettysburg thirty-one years before, served two purposes during the Confederate occupation. The four-story structure was perhaps the largest in the town and could shelter a large number of wounded once all the students' trunks and other personal belongings were gotten out of the way (with the president's office becoming the main depository.) But the roof also provided an ideal signal station as well as an observation point to scan Cemetery Hill, Culp's Hill, and other features of the Union line looming in back of town.

Classes were still in session at the Lutheran-affiliated institution (many of whose graduates went on to study at the theological seminary) when the battle began along the Chambersburg Pike less than a mile away. Members of the army signal corps noisily mounted the cupola of the main building to make observations while professors were delivering their lectures. So distracted were the students that President Henry Louis Baugher told the group he was trying to teach, "we will close and see what is going on, for you know nothing about the lesson anyhow."[35]

After the Federals were driven through the town, the Confederates began bringing their wounded to the college, (from which at least eight of the Southern soldiers had graduated) and filled every room and corridor. In the library, books were removed from the shelves to serve as pillows for soldiers lying on the hard, uncovered floors. In addition to the College Edifice, or "Old Dorm," neighboring Linnaean Hall was occupied and eighteen wounded men from the Union First Corps were taken into the house of Dr. Baugher, a man who had lost a son at Shiloh the year before.

In all, there were more than 700 wounded Rebels on the campus with a few of their own doctors left behind to attend them. There were so many Rebels there, in fact, that the college was soon being referred to as "the Confederate Hospital."

The two-story public school on East High Street became another unlikely treatment center and, just as the pupils were divided in classes, the wounded soldiers delivered there were segregated. The Union soldiers were placed on the first floor and the Confederates upstairs.

This wasn't usually the case. A Christian Commission delegation from Baltimore reported that "in nearly all the hospitals which were located in the churches and other buildings and private houses scattered over the town, the Union and Rebel wounded were lying side by side, and each was taken charge of and ministered to by the attendants without distinction or discrimination," adding:

"There was evidently no difference of feeling among the sufferers."[36]

Little was unchanged about the atmosphere in the town, which usually numbered about 2,500 residents. Gettysburg was considered, as someone from a neighboring community enviously put it, "a right smart place," lively and prosperous, benefitting from agriculture as well as carriage-making and other light manufacturing.[37]

For one thing, a good many of the residents, particularly the merchants, had fled before the battle. They took with them almost all their wares to Philadelphia, Baltimore, or whatever area they deemed a safe distance from the invading Rebels. Government workers at all levels had also hastily departed, with responsibility for the protection of official documents their primary excuse. Predictably, the empty dwellings were quickly identified by the Rebels and ransacked with impunity. Most of the 300 or so black freemen in the area, terrified of being dragged into slavery, disappeared. All the funds were removed from the Bank of Gettysburg on York Street and the empty vault became a refuge for about twenty women and children during the battle. The three local newspapers, the *Adams Sentinel,* the *Gettysburg Compiler,* and the *Gettysburg Star & Banner,* suspended publication, with the latter experiencing a particularly difficult time getting back into print because some angry Rebs had deliberately scattered its type before departing.

Townspeople who remained were overcome with a sense of isolation, and were certain that no one was even aware of what conditions were like there since the battle. It was an understandable attitude because no mail was being delivered. The postmaster—Fannie Buehler's lawyer husband—actually left town with the correspondence in his possession, though it meant his wife would be on her own with six children to protect. The single-track Gettysburg to Hanover Junction Line Railroad link with the outside world, had been put out of service a week before by the Confederates. If indeed anyone was concerned about Gettysburg's post-battle plight they could only reach the community by horse, and then expect a difficult time in convincing Union road guards that they had not come to loot or aid the Confederate wounded to escape. This was perceived as Copperhead country—an area populated by Northern Democrats opposed to Lincoln's war policy—and the soldiers were wary of the loyalties of anyone circulating in the area.

Quite naturally, the locals, once more free to circulate, gravitated to what they called "the diamond," the center of town where all the roads converged: the Chambersburg Pike, the way to Carlisle and Mummasburg; the Baltimore Pike; the Emmitsburg Road; and the York Road. There were eleven roads in all coming together at or just before the square, to give the town its special commercial and, more recently, military importance. It was here, around the large open square (where until 1858 the old court house had stood) that information—official or rumored—could be gathered and disseminated.

It was here also that activity and movement could be most effectively monitored. For that reason, the Federal officers charged with winding up affairs at Gettysburg soon moved down from the army's general headquarters on Cemetery Ridge to set up their own command posts in various buildings facing the square. They included the provost marshal, who was concerned with security, the processing of prisoners, and basic traffic control; the chief quartermaster, who was responsible for supplying the army as long as it remained in the area and for collecting all the salvageable government property discarded on the field; and the medical director, who was trying somehow to administer to the needs of scores of hospitals hastily set up in and around the town.

Though the interests and missions of all who were drawn to the community core were different, collectively they contributed to a scene of noisy, frantic, and discordant activity that grew by the hour.

There was the cursing teamster on a supply wagon trying to determine which of the maze of roads led to his destination; the bewildered relative, with carpetbag in hand, searching for a loved one; the self-important courier seeking somehow to escape the congestion; mobs of disarmed and sullen Confederates being herded into captivity; harried housewives carrying trays and bundles of things from their homes to the hospitals; canvas-walled ambulances laden with those wounded who were able to be moved; and an extraordinary number of skulkers from both armies—men who had usually left ranks under the guise of assisting a wounded comrade and were in no hurry to get back to their units and further danger. There were, as well, the members of the normal everyday society—the curious young-sters and elderly idlers who enlivened the square.

Everything at Gettysburg, now that the Rebels had been dislodged, was again radiating from the diamond.

One of the first strides toward order came with the arrival of the calm skilled band of Sisters of Charity, whom Father Burlando deployed in pairs to the church hospitals. After doing so, the priest heard confessions, and then quickly returned to Emmitsburg to arrange to have additional nuns sent to Gettysburg from Baltimore, where they were treating other wounded and sick soldiers.

With quiet efficiency, the sisters scurried about, letting orderlies and the volunteering townspeople know how they could be most useful—even if the function was not in any way related to dressing a wound, but simply involved heating a huge pot of nourishing soup or ripping up bed linens for bandages. At the end of their first day's labor, the exhausted nuns returned to McClellan's Hotel at the square, where they spent the night on the floor of the foyer, for there were no beds available for them.

"Needless to say, they did not sleep very much," someone observed.[38]

Sixteen-year-old Liberty Hollinger, who lived on York Street, remem-bered the "many instances of their kindness and usefulness as I watched them sit by the hospital cots, moistening the parched lip, fanning the heated brow, writing a letter to the loved home-folk or reading and praying with the wounded and dying. No wonder the men learned to admire and love them."[39]

Rev. Francis Burlando,
among the first to come to
Gettysburg and offer help.
*St. Joseph's Provincial
House Archives.*

Mother Ann Simeon
Norris, who, as a Sister
of Charity, provided
skilled nursing hands.
*St. Joseph's Provincial
House Archives.*

Taking care of wounded soldiers was a strange role for the women of the town who, until now, had thought of the war as being remote. For them, battles were only topics of newspaper articles and tales from soldiers on furlough.

Salome "Sallie" Myers, a twenty-one-year-old schoolteacher living with her family on Baltimore Street, showed how quickly the townspeople were able to adjust to the upheaval around them and meet the challenges presented to them, however horrific they may have appeared. On the first day of the battle, a surgeon of the 143rd Pennsylvania pounded on the door of her home while Sallie was with her mother and three sisters.

"You must come up to the churches and help us," he exclaimed, "the boys are suffering terribly!"

Sallie, who "had never been able to stand the sight of blood," went into the Catholic church to find men lying on the pews and the floors.

"The groans of the suffering and dying were heartrending," the young woman said. "I knelt beside the first man near the door and asked what I could do. 'Nothing,' he replied, 'I am going to die.' I went outside the church and cried."

But summoning her courage, Sallie soon returned and had the man— Sgt. Alexander Stewart of the 149th Pennsylvania, wounded in the lungs and spine—removed down the street to the Myers home. There, with shutters and windows closed, she sat all night in the stifling July heat fanning her first patient, as his life slowly slipped away.[40]

Though the townswomen were untrained to dress wounds, they could help nourish the men—though even those with the largest families had never been challenged on the most festive occasions to prepare food in the quantities being unceasingly required of them.

Despite their own plight, the women baked bread for the hospitals from the time they were set up on the first day and they continued until their hands ached and blistered and the last of their flour and yeast was gone.

With Union medical and quartermaster officers largely unaware of the whereabouts of the assortment of hospitals set up in town and how many men were being treated at them, no system existed for supplying these facilities. Their occupants were totally dependent on the townspeople, whose provisions had already been almost decimated by the two armies foraging in the region for so long. Residents of neighboring communities were still ignorant of the situation. A hungry fifteen-year-old boy in town wrote that after the fighting stopped "people that knew us came to see if we were alive or not, but never thought of bringing anything to eat with them."[41]

Cassie Cunningham returned with her family on July 3 to their place near Marsh Creek, and before she had even removed her bonnet she set yeast for baking when she saw how famished the soldiers were. For six weeks she baked "all the bread the big brick oven would hold every day," consuming the family's entire 1862 crop of twenty-five barrels of flour (even though it was evident the armies trampling their property had already destroyed what would be their 1863 crop.) She remembered, "Every wounded man who could walk found his way to the house when the odor of baking bread floated out the oven."[42]

In town, Fannie Buehler set up a table on her front porch that was covered with food for the taking, free of charge, for whoever came by. "The kitchen fire never went out, the tea kettle was never without plenty of boiling water, and a large wash boiler never emptied of oat meal or corn meal gruel, the same of coffee or soup," she related. She did this despite the fact that she had so many children of her own to feed.[43]

One thrifty housewife, who noticed a Rebel commissary set up in rear of her house, cutting up and distributing beef to a cavalry unit quartered nearby during the battle, went further than just emptying her own larder. She boldly approached the wasteful butcher and solicited the beef bones left on the ground and had them conveyed to her kitchen where they were washed, cut up, and quickly converted into about one hundred gallons of nourishing soup that was distributed at the different hospitals, with no one aware of the source.[44]

Lydia Smith, a poor black woman in town, was not willing to simply wait until help arrived. Walking beside a tottering old horse and ramshackle wagon she had rented, she went off into the countryside in search of food and clothing for the wounded soldiers. She deliberately headed toward the farm section around Bendersville, an area that was not as heavily traversed by the armies and more likely to have supplies to spare.

When the farmers wouldn't donate to the incongruous load she was accumulating, despite her heartfelt descriptions of the plight of the soldiers, Lydia used the last of her money to buy from them. When it came to distributing what she had gathered to the Union and Confederate wounded, often lying side by side, Lydia showed no bias whatsoever, giving equally to all. Of the initiative she had taken, Lydia would only say: "I thank the good Lord that put it into my heart to try to do something for these poor creatures."[45]

Just having something useful to do was as important to relieving the anxiety of the residents as it was to those being helped. Contributing to the tension were the frantic reports that the Rebs were going to shell the town as a parting gesture. Sporadic sniping continued throughout the uncelebrated Fourth of July holiday, causing people to hug the walls of buildings if they ventured on the sidewalks, and to flit quickly across streets when trying to reach the hospitals. It was not until Sunday that people finally felt that they were no longer in danger, that Lee's army had actually gone away.

There were six private physicians practicing in Gettysburg at the time, and even though they were largely unskilled in treating war wounds, all offered their services. Dr. Theodore Tate was placed in charge of the Confederates housed at the public school. A more likely designee for that assignment would have been Dr. John W. C. O'Neal. O'Neal had come back that spring from Baltimore to set up practice in Gettysburg, where he had attended the college. The forty-two-year-old doctor was originally from Fairfax, Virginia, and must have been amazed to have been discovered in this little Pennsylvania town by so many people from his earlier life.

On the day before the battle started, Dr. O'Neal rode up the Chambersburg Pike on his old horse to make a sick call when he encountered Confederate infantrymen headed toward town. They were from Gen. J. Johnston Pettigrew's North Carolina brigade in quest of the shoes that were reported to be had in Gettysburg. The physician was taken before the general and questioned at length about the presence of Yankees. O'Neal told him that he knew of none but added, lest his Southern drawl convey the wrong idea about his sentiments, "General, if I did have any matter of information I couldn't give it to you for I'm a medical practitioner and not an informant."

He was also asked by Pettigrew if he had any newspapers, apparently a primary source of intelligence for the invading force, and what led the Rebs to believe that there were shoes to be found in the town ahead of them.

While detained by the Confederates, Dr. O'Neal was pleased to discover among them a Dr. Montgomery, whom he had known in Baltimore and "who took charge of me and we fell back to Cashtown." There O'Neal arranged for them, and another Rebel surgeon, to have dinner with one of his patients, though it was risky for the doctor since his loyalties were already regarded with suspicion by his neighbors. It was not until the Southerners gained control of Gettysburg the next day that O'Neal was able to make his way back to his family, paying a bottle of whiskey as a bribe to be escorted home.

The following morning when he went out to make his rounds, the doctor took the precaution of tying a white handkerchief around his arm and carrying his medicine bag with him at all times.[46]

Of the routine he fell into, Dr. O'Neal said, "I'd leave my house around 7 o'clock in the morning, go to a hospital, work there until 12 o'clock, come home, eat lunch, go out again and work steadily until darkness fell. I suppose the most that wandered in were sick from exposure. Many were in a terrible condition. They came through the town, their faces haggard, nearly famished, caricatures of men."[47]

While the shortage of tents was one of the major problems of the medical staff, the lack of tools was the foremost concern of the burial details. The order came down that each regiment of the army, resting in place while the high command was contemplating the next movement, was to clear the area in its front of bodies, Union and Confederate. But there were few implements to work with. Most were stored in the supply wagons that had been sent away, and the task of interment was one that, in the intense July heat, could not wait. It was an effort further hampered by the annoyance of Rebel snipers reminding the laborers that the Confederates had not yet vacated the area. Some of the Union corpses had been on the field since the first day of the battle—men who had fallen on Oak Hill and Seminary Ridge within what became the Confederate front lines, and had been ignored after being stripped, as was customary, of all valuables. The now barefoot bodies, pockets turned out, were blackening and swelling.

"The greatest want I experienced was tools," one medical officer trying to provide resting places for those who died at his field hospital noted. "I had not a shovel or a pick with which to construct sinks, or bury the dead, and no axes. I was compelled to send a foraging party to the farmhouses, who, after a day's labor, procured two shovels and an ax."[48]

Manpower was no problem; the suddenly idle army could provide all that was needed, albeit without enthusiasm for the grim task. In addition, there were thousands of Confederate prisoners of war being held in pens who if they could be given something to work with, could be pressed into service to take care of their own dead, at least.

With so few tools and some 7,000 soldiers to be covered as rapidly as possible, those involved in the exercise progressively resorted to more and more extreme economies of effort. The first Union dead to be put under were respectfully covered but, as the rate of progress slowed, shallower graves were dug until, at the scenes of the bloodiest fighting, as soon as a rain came body parts would begin protruding.

By and large, there was some attempt to mark each Federal grave, if only with a board from a wooden ration or ammunition case, on which a name and regiment number had been lettered in chalk. That is, if there happened to be someone present who could still identify the dead soldier. (The difficulty of establishing positive identification at a time when soldiers didn't wear tags around their necks is clearly indicated by the fact that of the 3,000 Union dead interred, almost one-third were unidentified.)

When it became the Rebels' turn, there was no great effort made to provide or mark individual graves. Great shallow trenches were opened up, into which bodies were arranged like railroad ties. They were covered over lightly with some scribbled message nearby that might have read "75 Rebels buried here" or "54 Rebs there."

It was all rather impersonal. The soldiers involved viewed their work as simply an unpleasant duty assignment that had to be carried out. The level of their emotional concern was indicated by one of the Sisters of Charity when she happened to notice that next to a pit where some fifty Confederates had been dumped "one little group of soldiers was sitting by a fire trying to cook their meat."[49]

There was no attempt to sort by rank or social class; the rigid forms, still but for their hair fluttering about in the breeze, were simply picked up in order of their proximity to the hole and deposited therein.

In one of these ditches was casually tossed the indistinguishable body of a brigadier general, who had died in Pickett's charge. That this was the way they were capping the military career of West Point graduate and regular U.S. Army Capt. Richard B. Garnett was a thought that surely never entered the minds of the sweating men holding the arms and legs of the riddled corpse as they swung the body in among the rustics that "Dick" Garnett of Virginia had chosen to lead. After his body had been stripped of mementos, including his brass-buttoned gray tunic with its fancy gold knots embroidered on the sleeves, those disposing of it probably didn't even recognize him as the Reb leader who had made himself a conspicuous target by going into the disastrous charge on horseback. He had made it as far as the Emmitsburg Road with his men. Further indignity was to come when the general's sword was discovered after the war in a Baltimore pawnshop, apparently hocked by someone who had pilfered it, making identification of the remains even more difficult.

Perhaps Garnett's was one of the bodies interred by the burial detail of the 12th New Jersey. Captain George A. Bowen and his men were ordered out on Sunday, two days after the battle, to bury the dead in front of the Second Corps position on Cemetery Ridge and to send the wounded Confederates to the nearest place of treatment.

He acknowledged that, "We found few living as they had laid out there since Friday afternoon in the broiling sun and in the rain of Saturday."

The hardness and rockiness of the soil in that vicinity made the digging strenuous work and there was little time to spend on it. Consequently, Bowen admitted, "they got but very shallow graves."

The trenches were dug very near the bodies so they would have to be carried as short a distance as possible. As grim and repugnant as was the assignment they were on, the captain couldn't help but remonstrate when he saw one of his men callously break the stiff extended arm of a dead man with his shovel so that it would take less dirt to cover him. In response to the admonition, the grave digger argued that the man was dead and what he had done "would make no difference to him."

Coming upon another Reb, wounded in a dozen places but still breathing faintly, the party prudently paused to dig a hole for him because "we expected him to die at any moment."[50]

"The dead were buried everywhere," said one chronicler of the hodgepodge being created by Bowen's and other's details. "The whole ground around Gettysburg became one vast cemetery."[51]

There was supposed to be some method to it all, but systems broke down in the face of actual conditions on the field.

"When they could conveniently be brought together, they were buried in clusters of ten, twenty, fifty or more," Bowen said, "but so great was the number, and so rapid the decomposition in those who had lain for days in the hot sun, that many could not be removed. In gardens, fields, woods, or by the roadside, wherever found lying, shallow ditches were dug, the bodies placed in them, and covered as hastily as possible."[52]

The bodies buried during the days immediately following the fight were, of course, the more visible and accessible. There were hundreds being overlooked. Many had carefully concealed themselves in a tree on Culp's Hill or wedged themselves between boulders in the foreboding Devil's Den to preserve their lives. Having failed in that effort, they were not easily found. The rising odor of the abundant cadavers was strong enough to discourage the grave diggers from looking any further for additional work.

In addition to the dead horses and mules on the field—most of them artillery horses struck down near the guns they pulled, but some cavalry mounts and those of officers reckless or courageous enough to ride during the fight—there were hundreds aimlessly staggering about with severe wounds. Special details had to be created to deal with this problem as well, and for days the intermittent firing of the luckless soldiers assigned to this work could be heard as they sought out these disabled animals and put an end to their misery.

Burying the fallen soldiers was enough of a problem with the scarcity of tools at hand. Interring the carcasses of several thousand horses and mules was out of the question. With ropes and chains, they were dragged by teams into mounds and cremated by farmers anxious to reclaim their land. The smoke and smell of these pyres soon became so commonplace that they were paid little notice. Everyone knew the source.

When, almost a year before, Secretary of War Edwin M. Stanton had summoned Herman Haupt to Washington to persuade him to take control of the army's chaotic transportation system, the forty-six-year-old engineer confidently and candidly stated his terms. "I have no military or political aspirations, and am particularly averse to wearing the uniform; would prefer to perform the duties required without military rank, if possible, but if rank is essential as a means to aid the performance of duty, I must acquiesce.

"Pay I do not require or care about. If I take the position you have so kindly offered, it will be with the understanding that I can retire whenever, in my opinion, my services can be dispensed with, and that I will perform no duties on the Sabbath unless necessity imperatively requires it, and of that necessity I must be the judge, so far as may be consistent with military subordination."[53]

While receiving the rank of brigadier general, Haupt was careful not to accept a commission (or the pay) so that he remained free to carry on his personal business.

The pragmatic Stanton was willing to agree to such unorthodox demands for two reasons. He was a man with a mammoth problem on his hands, and he realized he was dealing with perhaps the foremost railroad and bridge engineer in the country.

The aversion Herman Haupt had for uniforms developed, no doubt, at West Point from which he had graduated in 1835 at the remarkably young age of eighteen, only to resign from the army three months later to pursue a railroad engineering career. The next year, already the principal assistant engineer for the state of Pennsylvania, Haupt found himself in the town of Gettysburg, seeking to locate a railroad route across South Mountain to Hagerstown. He would remain there for ten years, marry, and build a home on Seminary Ridge (Confederate General James Longstreet would one day place one of his batteries in Haupt's front yard.) During this time, Haupt, a native of Philadelphia, also served as a professor of mathematics and civil engineering at Pennsylvania College in Gettysburg and while teaching there was able to complete a book entitled *General Theory of Bridge Construction,* regarded as one of the most valuable works on the subject. Haupt later became general superintendent of the Pennsylvania Railroad and doubtless never expected to be involved with Gettysburg again. By the time the war broke out, he had had a hand in the construction of six major railroad lines.[54]

The rapid results that Haupt was able to achieve in righting the army's rail supply system after accepting Stanton's entreaty (and maintaining the operation in face of constant enemy attempts to disrupt) were astonishing. Perhaps the most impressive feat was Haupt's construction of the Potomac Run Bridge in May 1862 which, after viewing the span during a visit to the army, President Lincoln proclaimed "the most remarkable structure that human eyes ever rested upon.

"That man Haupt has built a bridge . . . about 400 feet long and nearly 100 feet high, over which loaded trains are running every hour,

Herman Haupt, transportation chief responsible for restoring the rail line to Gettysburg. *Library of Congress.*

and, upon my word, gentlemen, there is nothing in it but beanpoles and cornstalks."[55]

What added to the achievement was that the bridge—containing more than two million feet of lumber cut from nearby woods and not even stripped of bark—had been constructed under Haupt's direction in just nine working days by ordinary, inexperienced soldiers.

An incident that occurred during the brief period that the pompous John Pope commanded the army provided an indication of the importance of Haupt's services. Pope had no appreciation for Haupt's function and all but ignored him before deciding to put transportation of army supplies where he thought it belonged, under the management of the quarter-master's department.

Haupt, a man extremely jealous of his professional reputation, reacted by deciding to exercise his peculiar option and simply leave the army and go home to Cambridge, Massachusetts, where he had an important project under way. Within a few days, he received an imploring telegram from the War Department: "Come back immediately; cannot get along without you; not a wheel moving on any of the roads." His role was never challenged again.[56]

On June 28, Haupt happened to be in Washington at Secretary Stanton's office when he learned that his old academy classmate, George Meade, had been promoted to commander of the Army of the Potomac. While professing to be anxious to join the new commander, Haupt—given the geography—adopted a strange, circuitous route for doing so. After sizing up the situation, the independent-minded citizen/soldier "concluded that the most efficient service that I could render would be to go to Harrisburg, ascertain the condition of affairs in Pennsylvania—especially the numbers and position of the forces that had been raised [to meet the Confederate invasion]—and then make my way across the country on foot, or horseback, and give General Meade all the information I could gather."[57]

Discovering the North Central Railroad, the most direct connection between Washington and Harrisburg to be "badly injured," Haupt detoured east and approached the Pennsylvania capital via Philadelphia and Reading, and arrived late on June 30 to find the threatened city in a state of "much confusion and excitement." Pressing every harried official he could stop for details of the enemy's movement, Haupt accurately concluded that, even though Lee had pulled back from the Susquehanna, he was not retreating, but concentrating his widely dispersed army.

The way Haupt (who, despite his protestations, seemed to enjoy playing the general) had it figured out, "Lee had just received the intelligence that Hooker had been relieved and Meade put in command. He knows that our Army Corps are scattered, and that Meade cannot get the reins in hand for some days, at least, and he has formed the design to concentrate with all possible expedition and fall, with largely superior force, upon our Army Corps and overwhelm them successively. We are in the most critical condition we have been in since the war commenced. . . ."

Feeling quite at liberty to do so, the confident transportation chief got off a telegram to General in Chief Henry W. Halleck that night warning, "Lee is falling back suddenly from the vicinity of Harrisburg, and concentrating all his forces. York has been evacuated. Carlisle is being evacuated. The concentration appears to be at or near Chambersburg. The object, apparently, a sudden movement against Meade, of which he should be advised by courier immediately."[58]

Having done what he could as an intelligence officer, Haupt returned to his primary role to see to the state of the rail lines as Lee, with overwhelming superiority of numbers, was clashing with the Union First and Eleventh Corps at Gettysburg, as Haupt had predicted.

On reaching Westminster, twenty miles from Gettysburg, but the farthest point to which rail service could still be provided to the army, Haupt discovered "everything in great confusion, hundreds of wagons waiting, and the officers clamoring for supplies." No trains were arriving along the Western Maryland Railroad spur from Baltimore or anywhere else.[59]

Besieged by the quartermasters, Haupt said, "I asked them to give me a few minutes to think, and to escape the crowd I crept into a covered wagon and hid myself." When he emerged, he had a plan to restore service and get supplies to at least that point, as distant as it was from where the army was in position.

First of all, the civilian superintendent of the railroad was "relieved at his own request." Then, with his own force of 400 railroad men, brought up from Alexandria, Virginia, with a train of split wood, lanterns, buckets, and other necessary items, Haupt took over the operation of the twenty-nine mile, single-track line himself. Without any storage tanks along the way, the buckets were used to scoop water for the locomotives from streams along the way and wood was brought along, cut and split, and ready to burn. With no adequate sidings or turntables on the road, Haupt arranged to get maximum use out of the single track by running trains in convoys of five or six with sufficient guards along for protection from the perceived danger of Rebel sympathizers destroying the numerous bridges along the route. Almost overnight, Haupt had thirty trains per day moving over a line on which only three or four had previously been accommodated and, if nothing else, the army's steady supply of rations was assured as far as Westminster.[60]

But a stopgap supply system that was welcome for the delivery of provisions during the battle suddenly became woefully inadequate when the fighting ended and there were tens of thousands of wounded on the field to be evacuated. Ferrying them in ambulances a few at a time from the field hospitals to the Westminster railhead over two roads was painfully slow, and the more serious cases couldn't undertake the journey at all— even if there had been sufficient ambulances available to promptly move such an enormous number of casualties.

Once more the army looked to Herman Haupt to deal with the transportation crisis. The answer lay in somehow getting the one line that directly served Gettysburg back in service. Just twenty-five miles long, the spur connected at Hanover Junction with the main Northern Central Railroad line to Baltimore, York, and other points where the wounded could receive proper hospital treatment.

But Confederate Maj. Gen. Jubal Early's men, in the vanguard of the invading horde, had not only torn up much of the line and burned three key bridges along the way but destroyed the telegraph line running parallel to it, thus cutting off the town's communication as well as its vital rail transportation.

If Haupt needed any prodding in meeting his responsibility, a dispatch from Secretary Stanton that arrived at midnight on July 3 provided ample. "Spare no efforts to send trains to bring in the wounded," the secretary ordered. "If transportation by rail cannot be had, provide it in any other practicable mode."[61]

What had delayed repairs of the line that Haupt knew so well was, of course, the presence of the Rebels. Nothing could be done until the battle was decided and, in Haupt's words, "we have full and undisturbed possession" of the right of way. Now, with the danger of interference gone, Haupt set to the task with vigor.[62]

The day after the fighting ended, Halleck heard reassuringly from Haupt: "I am now at Hanover Station. A bridge is broken between this place and Littlestown. I will proceed at once to repair it, and commence to send off wounded; then return and take the Gettysburg Railroad and commence repairing it. It will be well to make a good hospital in York, with which place I expect in two days to be in communication by rail. Until then, temporary arrangements can be made for the wounded. I learn that the wire is intact for nine miles toward Gettysburg. I will have it repaired, and communicate any information of importance that I can obtain."[63]

At 11 P.M., the general in chief got another wire from the indefatigable Haupt stating that "night has overtaken me at Oxford, seven miles east of Gettysburg. We have been at work on a large bridge near this town, which is considerably damaged. It will require two hours tomorrow to finish it, when we will proceed to Gettysburg. A portion of the track is torn up . . . about a mile of the telegraph wire is down and wire carried off. I have sent my engine to junction for men and material to repair it . . ."[64]

As demanding as was the task of opening the line, Haupt showed how splintered he viewed his role in the army by abruptly changing the subject and closing his wire to Halleck by asserting, "persons just in from Gettysburg report the position of affairs. I fear that while Meade rests to refresh his men and collect supplies, Lee will be off so far that he cannot intercept him."[65]

Even later that night, Haupt recorded that the construction corps had reached the last bridge on the road to Gettysburg. "It was dark and rainy, and the men were required to do their work by the aid of lanterns, but at such a time personal convenience was not consulted. After getting the work properly started, I walked to Oxford, 10 miles from Gettysburg, and passed the night at the house of a friend."[66]

The next morning, Herman Haupt, a man so much identified with modern, engine-powered rail transportation, arrived back in Gettysburg riding in a buggy. It was Sunday and, as a rule, he did not labor on the Sabbath, but this was destined to be one of the busiest days of his life.

At the diamond, Haupt encountered another academy classmate, Brig. Gen. Marsena Patrick. The provost marshal was an irascible man who had suddenly found himself burdened with the myriad responsibilities of processing thousands of Confederate prisoners, protecting government property from civilian pilferers, and weeding out Southern sympathizers he thought might attempt to interfere with the Federal army. Together the two went up to Meade's headquarters off the Baltimore pike.

Finding the newly victorious commanding general with his cavalry commander, Alfred Pleasonton, Haupt informed them that "by noon that day they would be in communication with Washington, both by rail and telegraph, at which more surprise and gratification were expressed, as it had been understood that the destruction of the bridges had been so complete that two or three weeks would be required for their renewal."[67]

Amazing! Haupt had done it! Federal authorities had every reason to believe that the line could be put back into operation the next day and the removal of the wounded could begin.

There was, however, just one nettlesome snag. The track wasn't clear all the way into the Gettysburg depot. The damaged bridge over Rock Creek more than a mile outside of town was proving more difficult to restore than expected. The heavy rains had literally washed away much of the struggling construction crew's efforts. In addition to the span itself, the workmen had to deal with the tangled mess created by the Rebs who had set six or seven freight cars ablaze and then had run them off the tracks into the creek where the bridge had been. For the moment, service could only be provided to a point just beyond the crossing. The distance may not have been great but the gap meant that the line would be operating for a time without the facilities of the depot and the Adams Express Company next to it. Moreover, it meant that the wounded would have to be carried an additional mile or so to the clearing across the creek where the trains were being halted. No matter. Train service to Gettysburg had basically been restored and the evacuation of the wounded in sizeable numbers could finally get under way. Hurrah for Haupt!

Thinking that he had relieved Meade of his transportation worries at Gettysburg, Haupt turned his conversation with the commander to the direction in which Meade planned to move in pursuit of Lee so that new supply lines could be arranged. He was shocked to hear Meade say that "he could not start immediately; the men required rest."

"As a class-mate of General Meade at West Point, I did not hesitate to express my opinions freely without fear of offense." Haupt said of his efforts to persuade Meade to move. "I could not, however, remove the idea from General Meade that a period of rest was necessary."[68]

But a man of Haupt's energy was simply not going to let Meade remain idle. In a rather bizarre fashion, he seemingly forgot his place and decided to appeal directly to General Halleck to urge Meade "to more prompt action than he appeared to contemplate." Boarding his own locomotive at Oxford around midnight, he ordered the no doubt incredulous engineer to steam to Washington where early the next morning Haupt—with little or no sleep—made his argument to the general in chief.[69]

In dashing off to the capital, Haupt apparently felt free to leave the Gettysburg scene. His work was completed and he had left the civilian operators specific instructions on how to get maximum use out of the single track line that was so vitally needed to get the wounded out and supplies in to the Gettysburg area. All depended on maintaining a tight schedule and wasting not a minute loading and unloading the trains. But these were experienced railroad operators accustomed to following a timetable. There was nothing to be overly concerned about.

The second day of the battle, when Union medical personnel were already feeling the effects of their commander's orders for holding supply wagons far in the rear, two wagons appeared on Cemetery Ridge with the inscription "U.S. San. Com." on their sides.

A surgeon standing not five hundred yards to the rear of the line of battle and surrounded by wounded, exclaimed when he noticed the vehicles, "Thank God, here comes the Sanitary Commission; now we shall be able to do something."

His excitement was justified for both conveyances were laden with sponges, chloroform, beef soup, brandy, lint, bandages, and other badly needed items.[70]

Here was just one more instance of this unique relief organization being on hand when and where it was most needed, which was by no means an accident or a coincidence. The U.S. Sanitary Commission was known to demonstrate a system and planning that put government providers to shame.

If ever the name of an agency was misleading as to its aegis and function, it was that of the U.S. Sanitary Commission. The official connection of this private enterprise with the federal government was merely the authority it had been given by Congress to investigate and report upon the state of sanitation at army camps and hospitals. But the organizers of this service had managed to expand their influence to a point where, two years after the commission's formation in June 1861, it had become a catalyst for more than 7,000 relief societies throughout the country. The organization channeled its donations of everything from books to blankets to the troops on such a massive scale that it was sometimes difficult to discern which was the army's primary source of supply, the U.S. Government or the Sanitary Commission.

The agency's concern with sanitation had broadened to the extent that its feared "medical inspectors" were poking into every aspect of care of the soldiers, from the quality of food being served them to the serviceability of the clothing they were issued. Assistance was given by the commission to the families of soldiers in the field. Lodges for recreation and relaxation were erected and operated in the camps. Medical texts reflecting the latest treatments for wounds and sickness were prepared and distributed by physicians associated with the commission. Vegetable gardens were planted around hospitals to improve the diets of patients. A claim office and a pension agency were established to help soldiers secure their bounties. The commission also meticulously maintained a hospital directory that recorded the condition and whereabouts of more than 600,000 men for the benefit of their relatives and friends, information even the government was often unable to convey.

To support all these services and maintain the flow of supplementary supplies to the army, the commission arranged huge fundraising fairs in dozens of major cities that would be remembered in the way world expositions are recalled. These events yielded gigantic sums and helped the commission to further reinforce its standing with the army. People donated not only cash to the effort but their watches and jewelry, and even prized livestock for auction. Famous people made contributions of their autographs for sale by the commission fund-raisers.

The Sanitary Commission had become so powerful and influential that no officer could retain or aspire to high rank in the medical department without the commission's approval. Indeed, the present surgeon general of the army, William A. Hammond, owed his appointment to the determined lobbying of the Sanitary Commission. In gross understatement, Mary Livermore, the wife of a Chicago newspaper editor who was one of the relief organization's mainstays, said "the commission did a more extensive work than was at first contemplated."[71]

The commission had its genesis in the determination of Northern women not to have their sons and husbands who had gone to war fall casualty to neglect.

This refusal "to release their hold on the men of their households, even when the government had organized them into an army," as Mrs. Livermore put it, resulted from the worldwide publicity given only a few years before to the shocking toll the British army had suffered from diseases related to camp conditions during the Crimean War and the measures the legendary Florence Nightingale had taken to alleviate them.[72] Although American women were active in thousands of local aid societies throughout the nation, their work lacked cohesion. A concerted effort was needed to impress upon the government their commitment to doing all in their power to make sure that their loved ones did not suffer needlessly from conditions that were avoidable and correctable. One group, the Women's Central Association of Relief, made up of members of some of New York City's wealthiest and most influential families, found an eager standard bearer in the intellectual pastor of All Souls Unitarian Church, the Rev. Henry W. Bellows. It was he who conceived the creation of a government-sanctioned civilian sanitary commission. He led a delegation to Washington in May 1861 that represented not only the women's groups but also the medical profession. "The [War] Department regarded us as weak enthusiasts, representing well meaning but silly women," Bellows stated.[73]

Undeterred, the group persevered and soon managed to gain approval from members of Congress and President Lincoln for the formation of an official commission (which, ironically, included not one woman.) Even if the body seemed to duplicate the work of the medical department and, in the president's words, appeared to be "a fifth wheel to the coach," the idea of inviting more civilian participation in the war effort was appealing. Both the president and the legislative branch had other more pressing matters to address, what with the conflict erupting in earnest.[74] Besides, the bureaucratic reasoning went, the panel was being given no real authority and would be operating strictly in an advisory capacity, so how threatening could it be?

But the farsighted Dr. Bellows, who was by no means overly modest, had something grander in mind for his creation. It wasn't long before he, as president, was expressing the view that all "local, state and other efforts of a benevolent sort are . . . mere trifles, ephemeral and inconstant efforts without method or philosophy as compared with our plan.

"Our plans have a breadth and height and depth," he would assert, "which no similar military philanthropic undertaking ever had, since the world began."[75]

However carried away the forty-seven-year-old clergyman had gotten with the possibilities of his undertaking, the primary beneficiaries of its expansion were the common soldiers, who were coming to regard the awesome auxiliary as the first place to turn for help in areas their government had neglected.

What was particularly impressive about the commission's performance was that it did not merely respond to the army's needs; it anticipated them. The organization's strategists in Washington followed the movements of the army as closely as the enemy commanders did, trying to estimate when and where the next encounter might occur so that supply depots could be set up within reach and aid would be available if required. To provide this help, some 500 Sanitary Commission agents were in the field, accompanying or trailing the army, marching when it marched but always leaving some of its members behind to attend the casualties of the last engagement.

The commission, following a policy that incensed even many of the agency's most avid supporters, made its provisions available to Union and Confederate soldier alike. Because of the well-known nondiscriminatory posture of the commission toward those in need, its agents' treatment when they returned from Gettysburg to Frederick, Maryland, to refill their two wagons was difficult to understand or condone.

The agency's supplies at its forward depot at Frederick had been carefully concealed in case the invading Confederate army suddenly changed course and moved in that direction. Once reloaded, one wagon immediately headed back by way of Westminster. About three miles from Gettysburg, the agents aboard stopped and set up a distribution center in the White Run schoolhouse on the Baltimore pike near several field hospitals. The other wagon, however, a four-horse vehicle accompanied by Dr. Alexander McDonald, the commission's general superintendent with the Army of the Potomac, started out on July 4 along the direct road to Gettysburg, thirty miles away. There they encountered a cavalry element of the retreating Rebel army. The fact that the supplies being ferried were destined for wounded Confederates as well as Yankee soldiers didn't impress the intercepting troop. For some reason, Dr. McDonald, a civilian, was taken away to Richmond and thrown into Libby Prison, where captured Union officers were held. Wherever the confiscated cargo ended up, it is doubtful that it reached any place in as much need as existed around Gettysburg at that time.

Either unaware of or undeterred by Dr. McDonald's fate, the next day the commission sent five more wagons with supplies from its Frederick cache while, at Gettysburg, its agents sought a location from which to operate. With their shelves bare and all their merchandise having been sent away, Samuel and Ed Fahnestock, proprietors of a general store and warehouse at the corner of Baltimore and Middle streets near the diamond, told the commission it was free to use their facilities, probably never realizing the inventory that was to arrive there would have made their usual operation seem a petty enterprise.

Sensing the crisis, Dr. Bellows quickly made his way to the field for a personal evaluation of the situation at Gettysburg. He immediately messaged Frederick L. Olmsted, the landscape architect who had left the design of New York City's Central Park to accept the position of general secretary of the commission in Washington:

> No energy you can use in forwarding by every possible chance can equal the demand here. If I were to spend a week, I could not fitly describe the horrors and suffering of our wounded men. The dead are not yet buried; hundreds are yet undressed of their wounds; thousands have not food. The country is stripped bare of ordinary supplies; there is not food for the well, and they will not sacrifice much for the sick. Indeed there is nothing to be had for love or money.
>
> Forage is very scarce; forward it for our use . . . . Beef is the only thing of which there is enough at the hospitals.
>
> The men want succulents; not so much spirits as usual.[76]

Faced with such a challenge, the relief agency began as quickly as it could to communicate by messengers, newspapers, personal letters, and the pulpit to activate all its ladies aid societies and other support groups to rush help to this obscure town in Pennsylvania. Appealing to the very heart of the nation, the commission was itself somewhat overwhelmed by the response that began to build.

Even as it issued its summons, the commission was as yet unaware of just how much reliance was to be placed upon it as the result of an incredible decision then being made, under extreme pressure, by Gen. George Meade with the apparent concurrence of his medical director, Jonathan Letterman.

Maj. Gen. George G. Meade. *Library of Congress.*

"God Pity Us!"

The combat-dazed soldiers of the Army of the Potomac welcomed the order to prepare to march. They had had more than enough of Gettysburg, now permeated with the scent of death and decay. They had achieved their victory at a fearful cost and were ready to relinquish the ground that a few days before they had fought so fiercely to defend. They had buried their dead and done what they could for their wounded comrades; it was time to move on to some other yet undisturbed field. Their thoughts were fixed on somehow overtaking the beaten Confederates and perhaps, if they could muster the strength, put an end to things. They would prefer any activity to "lying around and doing nothing but see the sickening sights and smelling the miserable smells," as one Second Corps member put it.[1]

As George Gordon Meade, strongly prodded by Washington, started out in pursuit on July 6, he fully expected "in a few days to have another battle at some distant point." He felt, therefore, that "it was absolutely necessary that I should carry away the greater portion of my Surgeons and medical supplies."

This meant, the commanding general realized, "the wounded at Gettysburg were, in a measure, dependent upon such extra assistance as the Government could hastily collect" and the generosity of private relief groups.[2]

But in the eyes of Dr. Jonathan Letterman there was really no crisis. If the medical director had any problem with Meade's decision he didn't voice it as vociferously as he had earlier when the transportation and flow of medical supplies were curtailed. His surgeons had been operating virtually around the clock since the battle ended, and were in a state of utter exhaustion when the order came to put away their scalpels and join their units on the march toward Virginia. By Letterman's assessment, "the greater portion of the surgical labor was performed and what remained to be done was to attend to making the men comfortable, dress their wounds, and perform such secondary operations as from time to time might be necessary."[3]

Of the 650 doctors attached to the army, only 106 were left behind. Just 106 doctors to treat more than 14,000 Union wounded. When Meade spoke of taking "the greater portion" of the medical staff with him what he meant, in fact, was that fully 85 percent of the doctors were being removed.

In Letterman's view, the number that remained would be ample for the work to be done. He was not even expecting the vacancies left by the departing surgeons (many of whom were more than anxious to leave the nightmarish scene) to be filled by civilian doctors. Few regarded private physicians with more disdain than Letterman when it came to military service.

"No reliance can be placed on surgeons from civil life during or after a battle," he asserted. "They cannot or will not submit to the privations and discomforts which are necessary, and the great majority think more of their own personal comfort than they do of the wounded."[4]

And as Letterman departed, he seemed more concerned about replenishing his own medical ranks than the staffing at Gettysburg. On July 7, he wired the surgeon general's office to have fifty medical officers meet the army at Frederick, ready for immediate duty, "to make up, as far as possible, the deficiency of medical officers existing in consequence of the large detail from this army left at Gettysburg."[5]

Almost as an afterthought to his requisition, Letterman asked Hammond, "also if possible send twenty surgeons to report Surgeon Janes at Gettysburg."[6] Just two days later, a group of forty-seven skilled army surgeons, hastily assembled at various Washington hospitals, joined the Army of the Potomac at the place designated. There was no trace, however, of the twenty surgeons supposed to have been sent to Gettysburg.

What was the actual state of the field hospitals that Dr. Letterman could so confidently strip the staffs of five out of every six doctors, including most of the operating surgeons? Had he actually seen for himself how the wounded were faring? On whose estimate was he relying? Was he simply bending under pressure from the cautious Meade to have a maximum number of medical personnel on hand if and when he intercepted Lee and precipitated another battle?

The stunned reaction from a number of sectors to the surgeons being ordered to leave would indicate that the high command had little appreciation for how hard-pressed the medical staff was, or for the number of cases awaiting attention.

"What! Take away surgeons here where a hundred are wanted, and where, if the men have not immediate help, hundreds must die for want of that attention!" a Christian Commission volunteer exclaimed at the news that "all the surgeons that could in any way be spared were ordered forward with the army."[7]

"My heart grew sick when I saw men, some officers among them, feverish or bleeding or weak almost to death because there were not then surgeons enough to operate upon the vast multitude in time to save them all ere gangrene set in, for the regimental surgeons had to join their commands on the march," lamented one physician from Philadelphia who had offered his services.[8] He was among many who would dispute that the major operations had been all but completed by July 6 when Letterman left.

"Every surgeon in the hospital was kept busy nearly a week amputating limbs, probing for and removing bullets, or sewing, bandaging and dressing the wounds of those who were too badly mangled and shattered to be aided in any more hopeful manner," he remembered.[9]

Dr. Letterman's assertions to the contrary, five days after the battle, Cornelia Hancock would be writing her sister that "there is a great want of surgeons here; there are hundreds of brave fellows who have not had their wounds dressed since the battle."[10] Cornelia had no overall view of the medical scene at Gettysburg but she could tell what she personally observed. She spoke of a long table in the woods around which were constantly gathered a group of surgeons and attendants.

"This was the operating table, and for seven days it literally ran blood," she related. "A wagon stood near rapidly filling with amputated legs and arms. When wholly filled, this gruesome spectacle withdrew from sight and returned as soon as possible for another load. So appalling was the number of the wounded as yet unsuccored, so helpless seemed the few who were battling against tremendous odds to save life, and so overwhelming was the demand for any kind of aid that could be given quickly that one's senses were benumbed by the awful responsibility that fell to the living."[11]

Someone far more experienced than Cornelia, Mrs. Ellen Orbison Harris, secretary of the Philadelphia Ladies Aid Society, who had been to

Antietam and other battlefields to nurse, wrote almost in despair to her physician husband on July 9. It was six days after the battle at the Second Corps field hospital where she, too, was laboring: ". . . Am full of work and sorrow. The condition of things here beggars all description. Our dead lie unburied, and our wounded neglected. Our wounded in numbers have been drowned by the sudden rising of the waters around, and thousands of them are still naked and starving. God pity us! God pity us!"[12]

The day after the medical staff departed, a Third Corps surgeon, William Watson, calculated that he himself had by then taken off more than fifty limbs but said "there are many operations yet to be performed."[13] Even after two more days of surgery, Watson started a letter home with the apology, "I have time to write but a few lines. We have eight hundred wounded in our Division Hospital and only eight medical officers to attend them."[14]

Sarah M. Broadhead, a public school teacher, walked every day from her home on the Chambersburg Pike to the First Corps hospital at the Lutheran Theological Seminary to assist with the wounded in any way she could. She heard one exhausted doctor say after most of his colleagues left that he was afraid "that many would die from sheer lack of timely attendance. . . . There were not enough surgeons," she was told.[15]

The Committee of Maryland's Christian Commission delegation added its testimony to the shortage of doctors in the field. While the hospitals in town were generally sufficiently staffed, thanks particularly to the number of housewives who volunteered to assist, "in a number of the farmhouses and barns, and tents of the groves and fields the face of neither a chaplain nor a surgeon had been seen, and it was then the third day after the last, and the sixth after the first of the battle."[16]

Incredibly while thousands were crying for attention, the surgeon general's office in Washington (obviously unaware of the situation that existed at the battlefield) was casually turning down numerous offers of medical assistance from the private sector.

The day after the battle ended, Gov. Andrew G. Curtin of Pennsylvania wrote to Surgeon General Hammond to say "our people over the State are exceedingly anxious to render assistance to the wounded at Gettysburg" and inquired about "how many volunteer surgeons I may send."[17]

Hammond advised the governor of the Medical Department's plans the next day: "Five thousand vacant beds in Philadelphia, which have been ordered, will be first filled. We have plenty of hospital room prepared where the wounded will be more comfortably cared for than in any extemporized hospitals.

"The Medical Director of the Army of the Potomac has plenty of surgical aid," Hammond stated confidently to Curtin.[18]

On July 6, three days after the end of the fighting, Hammond's office responded to another offer of help from "the medical men in the hospitals of Philadelphia" by saying that "if their service should be needed they will be thankfully called upon. It is believed that at present there is sufficient hospital accommodations and that tents are not needed."[19]

On the day the army left with so much of the medical staff, a brief private dispatch was written for inclusion in the *Pittsburgh Gazette* addressed to the secretary of the Pittsburgh Sanitary Committee. The message stated: "The only way of getting to Gettysburg is by horses and carriages. Do not send any more surgeons."[20]

The source of this imperative instruction must certainly have been Jonathan Letterman himself. His views had already been made plain to the major general in command at nearby Baltimore, Robert C. Schenck, who was another man anxious to help. Not one to be deterred, Schenck, as he was wont to do, took it upon himself to advise the highest authorities in Washington of the situation and of his plan to assist. On the day the fighting ended, he advised Secretary of War Stanton:

> I learn that the suffering near the battle-field at Gettysburg and beyond is terrible, in the want of sufficient medical attendance, food and other help. The food we can supply, but I understand that the medical director of the Army of the Potomac has objected, and perhaps very properly, to civilian surgeons being indiscriminately admitted.
>
> Cannot I authorize my medical director or purveyor to organize and employ a corps of 10 or 12 able loyal surgeons from civil life to go up and give their services? Barns, houses and yards are full of these sufferers. Pennsylvania is not taking care of them, notwithstanding the Governor's notice to the public that she would.[21]

In fairness, while Letterman may have woefully miscalculated how much work was left to be done when estimating how many surgeons would be required, he never expected the wounded to remain at Gettysburg as long as they did. The idea was to evacuate them quickly to regular hospitals in Philadelphia, Washington, and other major cities.

Yet, as will be seen, it was the medical director himself who was to have an important influence on the prolongation of their stay by a related decision he would make before leaving: to take all but thirty of the army's more than 1,000 ambulances with him.

Supplies weren't any more abundant than manpower at the time Letterman rode away with Meade. The medical director was satisfied that after Dr. Brinton's caravan arrived and the commanding general released the supply wagons, the hospitals were at least being sufficiently supplied with drugs and bandages. However, a Second Corps doctor unlucky enough to have been left behind, gave a relief worker a list of what he had on hand "when the army commenced its pursuit of the rebels—a few stretchers, eight pounds of chloroform, one box of bandages, sixteen rolls of plaster and three pounds of lint; and sixteen hundred wounded."[22]

Although the supply wagons had begun arriving on July 5, it was after Letterman left that Dr. Justin Dwinell, also of the Second Corps, saw any of the contents.

"It was an important circumstance that our Hospital wagons containing tents, blankets, cooking utensils, provisions, shovels, axes, and Medical Stores could not follow the army as usual," he observed. "They did not arrive so as to be available until the seventh. As soon as we got the tents up, we were able to put every wounded man under shelter.

"Nothing but to gain victory should ever prevent these wagons from following the ammunition train," he admonished the decision-makers ranking him.[23]

An administrative detail Letterman also addressed before leaving the scene with General Meade was to deposit responsibility for dealing with the colossal mess at Gettysburg on Dr. Henry Janes.

In placing the wounded "under the general charge" of Janes, Letterman was turning to a thirty-one-year-old physician from Waterbury, Vermont, who had been in the army only two years, and who had been practicing medicine but eight.[24] Janes had studied under a local doctor and attended medical lectures at Woodstock College before going to New York to attend the College of Physicians and Surgeons.

Henry Janes, the young Vermont physician left in charge of the wounded at Gettysburg. *Vermont Historical Society.*

After earning his medical degree, he stayed in the city a year as house physician at Bellevue Hospital. Later, he returned to Waterbury and started a private practice. Then the war began.

In 1861, he went off with the 3rd Vermont Volunteers as a regimental surgeon and, after the battles of South Mountain and Antietam, he was in charge of hospitals at Burkettsville and Frederick, Maryland. At Chancellorsville, Janes supervised a Sixth Corps division hospital after having been promoted to surgeon of the U.S. Volunteers. During the battle at Gettysburg he was appointed medical director for the First Corps, a post he had barely assumed when Dr. Letterman made him the man responsible for somehow treating all the wounded at Gettysburg.[25]

What led to Letterman's selection of such a young man as Janes to handle this great responsibility? It may well have been Janes' quickly-earned reputation for hospital organization.

In addition to his "great skill as a surgeon and physician," Brig. Gen. W. T. H. Brooks, a 6th Corps division commander, said of Janes, "I doubt if any [hospital] in the army excelled his in good order and neatness and general comfort of its patients.

"His administrative abilities caused him to be selected more than once to establish and take charge of general hospitals for the Brigade and Division."[26]

A graphic description of the situation was provided to Janes by George K. Johnson, a medical inspector the surgeon general had dispatched to Gettysburg for an appraisal. The wounded, Johnson discovered to his astonishment, were everywhere:

> There were some in churches, some in barns, some in tents among the fruit trees, some in tents in the fields, some under such shelter as a farmer would be ashamed to show for his cows.
>
> Some were under blankets hung over cross-sticks, and some without even so much shelter as that. There were some scattered groups of men outside the hospitals. It sometimes appeared as if an experiment had been made to see how many wounded could be crowded into a given space in a house.[27]

A correspondent for the *Philadelphia Public Ledger* capsulized the situation by stating to his readers that, "This town, and the vicinity with a space of country surrounding it of eight or ten miles is literally one vast and over-crowded hospital."[28]

It was the very fact that the wounded were dispersed in so many relatively small clusters over a wide area that compounded the task of attending them with Janes' remaining skeletal staff. He did not even know where many of them were to be found. If the young doctor initially felt flattered by his designation, once he fully realized the conditions across the vast battlefield, he doubtless would have been glad to see the honor bestowed on someone else.

Contributing to the soldiers' desire to leave this part of Pennsylvania was the feeling of disgust they were developing over the attitude of many of the local farmers. While the troops might have expected an overwhelming show of gratitude for the effort they had made in turning back the Rebel invaders, what they were observing was nothing of the sort.

Most of the thrifty, compulsively orderly farm families of German ancestry had, until now, viewed the sectional conflict with indifference, a struggle over issues that were foreign to their interests. When, after two years, the war finally intruded itself upon their lives, it entered with a destructive force few parts of the country had yet experienced. For miles about, their carefully tended fields had been stripped of laboriously built post and rail fences, all the grayed wood having gone to fires or barricades. There was not a grazing animal to be seen. The low stone walls dividing the properties in the area, products of countless plowings by generations of frugal farmers, had been broken down by shot and shell. Once rich fields of wheat and grain had been trampled to worthlessness by masses of farm-boys-turned-soldiers who could fully appreciate the extent of the damage they were doing. The ground itself was furrowed and scarred by the wheels of caissons and gun carriages. Once symmetrical orchards had been made incongruous: some trees had been reduced to stumps while on others fractured limbs with crumpled dead leaves hung limply.

Regardless of what high principles the Union soldiers may have been fighting for on their soil, they were being regarded by some of the ruined farmers as the source of financial devastation, and they were not anxious to comfort the soldiers in any way. The farmers would submit to having their houses, with their shattered window panes and emptied barns, taken over for the wounded but would do little to assist the occupants. In fact, if they could recoup some of their losses in the process, some were all too willing to try.

Capt. Benjamin Thompson of the 111th New York, at a Second Corps field hospital, said it this way: "The patriotism of the neighboring farmers did not shine very brightly. A well-to-do farmer near us refused us straw for our men . . . not a man or woman in the vicinity offered a hand to help or drop of milk for the poor sufferers."[29]

Surgeon Watson, laboring to near collapse at a Third Corps hospital, observed, "I have yet to see the first thing brought in for the comfort of the wounded. Some farmers brought in some bread which they sold for 75 cents a loaf. The brave army that has protected this State surely deserves better treatment."[30]

"While many of the people cheerfully did all in their power to mitigate the sufferings of the soldiers," James L. Bowen, another wounded man, recorded, "truth compels the statement that others saw in the necessities of that horrible hour an opportunity to earn a sizeable penny and improved it to the utmost."[31]

The morning after the epic struggle for Little Round Top, a committee of farmers trudged to the summit and confronted a major of the 155th Pennsylvania to complain that their straw and hay had been taken away to field hospitals for the wounded. They demanded payment and were promptly ordered off the hill by the outraged officer, with the admonition that if they did not leave immediately he would have his battered regiment destroy their farms and have them arrested "for their disloyalty as well as their inhumanity."[32]

The next day other farmers visited field hospitals where amputations and burials were taking place, interrupted the blood-smeared surgeons in charge to demand payment for the straw upon which their patients were lying.

"The people seem to consider us lawful prizes, and are not only extortionate but give to us little real sympathy," a Michigan doctor noted. One peddlar was circulating about his hospital with bundles of straw to sell, another small loaves of bread.

"Such items make one indignant for the honor of his country," said the physician in disgust.[33]

Further avarice was seen along the road to Westminster where thousands of hungry and weak, wounded soldiers were attempting to walk the twenty miles to the nearest railhead for transportation to some point where they might be able to receive better medical attention. Many residents lining the route offered food and water to help the pathetic procession of walking wounded. But there were some who were actually charging fifty cents to a dollar for their bread.

Perhaps the meanest offenses were being committed by the farmers who removed the handles and buckets from their wells to prevent the soldiers from reaching water.

Probably none of the departing soldiers was as furious with the demeanor of the civilian population as artillery Colonel Wainwright. As far as he was concerned, "Gettysburg may hereafter be classic ground, but its inhabitants have damned themselves with a disgrace that can never be washed out . . . I should rejoice had it been levelled with the ground."[34]

What particularly offended him were the hundreds of people who had come "in their wagons to see the sights, to stroll over the ground, and gaze and gape at the dead and wounded.

"But not one lifted a finger to help the tired soldiers remove the one or bury the other," the colonel noticed. "One man was found selling pies at 25 cents to the poor fellows . . . I think that Meade might and should have seized every able-bodied citizen he could get his hands on, and forced them to do all the burying."[35]

Wainwright, of course, had not been exposed to the conduct of people who resided in the town who, in marked contrast, were freely opening their small homes and their larders with no thought of charging anyone. But the sad fact was that the abuses that had been observed, as ugly and unfeeling as they might have been, were just a prelude to what was to transpire after the army was gone.

When the cautiously pursuing Union army began to traverse the areas evacuated by the Rebels, one grim discovery after another was made. Usually identified by a yellow cloth of no uniform shape or shade, they were the Confederate hospitals west and north of the town, twenty-four camps in all, filled with soldiers too seriously wounded to travel with the two trains of ambulances winding tortuously back to Virginia. Some were set up in barns and inns along the route the blue infantry columns followed. Most were concealed in patches of woods. All were in dreadful condition.

A Sixth Corps surgeon moving along the road to Fairfield said, "Never had we witnessed such sad scenes as we were passing through. The Confederate surgeons were doing what they could for their wounded but they were destitute of medicines and surgical appliances and even food."[36]

The Rebs had been virtually living off the land for a month, operating far beyond their regular supply lines so there were few provisions accumulated to give to those being left behind. Theirs was also an army in which only the highest-ranking officers were provided with tents; the foot soldiers slept in the open on a blanket and perhaps a patch of oil cloth or carpeting that was rolled up and slung over the shoulder on the march. Even the wounded could expect nothing better for cover until the Yankees took them into captivity.

A Sanitary Commission agent who canvassed the camps noted, "The wounds were in a large proportion of cases very severe; amputations and resections were frequent.

"The corps of surgeons are as a body intelligent and attentive," he found, but added, "I cannot speak favorably of the camp police. Often there is a deplorable want of cleanliness, especially in barns and outbuildings; vermin and putrid matter are disgustingly offensive."[37]

The explanation for the latter was simple; there were few able-bodied men being left behind to attend to such matters. There were only convalescents or men without shoes whose feet were so bruised they could not make the trek home.

A surgeon of the Union Eleventh Corps reported as late as July 9 that "we find daily large collections of their wounded in a wretched condition a few miles out and left without Surgeons or Supplies. We are doing all we can for them."[38]

When all was tallied, it was determined that Dr. Janes would have some 5,400 more Confederate wounded to care for than the 1,800 or so the Union forces already had in their hands: those nearly 1,000 who had been collected after Pickett's charge and the 800 crowded into the Pennsylvania College buildings in town. Most of these men came from Maj. Gen. Harry Heth's Third Corps division, hurt at the unexpected start of the battle, and from Lt. Gen. Richard Ewell's Second Corps who had been arriving there during every day of the fighting.

As the Confederates' squalid aid stations were uncovered, the weekly *Adams Sentinel,* back in print, published a page-one article under the compelling heading "Inhumanity and Poltroonery of the Rebel Surgeons." The piece declared that the "infamy and cowardice of the Rebel surgeons in deserting the men of their army wounded at the battle of Gettysburg is without parallel in the war." The wounded, according to the *Sentinel,* were left with "neither surgeons, stores nor nurses but literally abandoned to their fate.

"These men complained bitterly of the cruelty of their surgeons in thus forsaking them, but bore up patiently under their sufferings for many days until they could be attended to by some of our own surgeons, most of whom had at once to hasten forward with their own regiments to other fields."[39]

The account (reprinted from the *New York Times*) was, of course, much exaggerated. General Lee, with some 8,000 wounded in transit and in need of close attention, had nevertheless left a number of surgeons behind with attendants. In fact, in proportion to the number of wounded, he had probably left more doctors than General Meade.

There were eight Southern surgeons functioning at Pennsylvania College alone. Both Maj. Gen. Robert Rodes of the Confederate Second Corps and Maj. Gen. Lafayette McLaws of the First Corps ordered ten doctors to remain at Gettysburg, suggesting that was the number each of the army's nine infantry division commanders was expected to assign.

In Rodes' case, the ten physicians were responsible for 760 wounded men, and in McLaws' division, 576. In addition, Rodes said he left ninety-seven attendants and (he being better supplied for having been in the vanguard of the invading army) ten days' rations, while McLaws provided seventy nurses and cooks for his men who were congregated near the Hagerstown Road in back of Seminary Ridge. Curiously, McLaws, whose command had suffered heavily in the Peach Orchard and the Wheatfield on the second day, had elected to transport nearly two-thirds of his wounded back to Virginia, whereas Rodes, whose brigades were badly cut up during the first day of fighting around Oak Hill, was abandoning half of his to the enemy.[40]

In addition to a lack of personnel, the Confederate aid stations were also short on medical supplies. If the Rebels thought the Yanks would have a bountiful amount to share with them, they were in for a huge disappointment. Until they got more, there was little the Yanks could do to relieve the misery of the men in their charge. While they waited, it was a fair question as to who was better off, those Southerners who had fallen into Federal hands or those in their own hospitals.

At the Union hospitals, it generally meant a long wait for surgical attention, often days, but—preferences for operations aside—the Rebs could expect somewhat equal treatment from their captors.

Though suffering intensely from his two leg wounds, Lieutenant Dooley of the First Virginia took a judicious view of the treatment he was getting at the Union Second Corps hospital behind Cemetery Ridge:

> The whole ground for miles around is covered with the wounded, the dying and the dead. Confederate and Yankee are often promiscuously thrown together, although the officials separate us generally as much as is convenient. The Yankees are nearly all comfortably quartered, having tents and blankets and many little comforts which they have of course received from their comrades. This is only natural and none of our boys expect to receive attentions in preference to the enemy's wounded.[41]

In that area, according to Cornelia Hancock, as long as there were Union soldiers in need of surgical treatment "the rebels lay in a dying condition without their wounds being dressed or scarcely any food." After viewing their suffering day after day, Cornelia could only say, "if the rebels did not get severely punished for this battle, then I am no judge."[42]

Where on the field the wounded Confederate was captured was also a factor in how promptly he received attention. At a hospital of the well-supplied Union Twelfth Corps, a member of the 4th Texas with the picturesque name of Decimus et Ultimus Barziza (because he was to be the last of ten children) found "our wounded were generally well treated, and were put side by side with the enemy's."[43]

Six days after the battle, a tired Third Corps surgeon wrote: "I still have a few operations in my own Division when I will turn my attention to wounded Rebels. There are about 100 of them in a Barn near us in a most distressing condition."[44]

Though it was the U.S. Sanitary Commission's rigid policy not to discriminate between blue and gray in distributing its supplies, even the head of that agency, Henry Whitney Bellows, accepted the principle of the Union wounded being given surgical attention before the Confederate. Having observed the proprieties being followed on the field, Bellows said after his tour:

> The rebels, as was just, had to wait their turn for having their wounds dressed, or their limbs amputated till the Union men had been cared for. They were treated with equal kindness and

attention. Many after six days were looking forward as to an unspeakable blessing, for the amputation of their shattered limbs. The terrible destitution of many of the rebels will not bear description."[45]

The longer the wounded Confederate prisoners were neglected, the more repugnant they became to treat and it took a great deal of compassion to even approach them. To these "limp, grimy fellows," said one volunteer nurse, "a wash was as essential as powders or salves.

"Many of those who fell into our hands were almost loathsomely dirty," she elaborated. "One felt a desire often to get between them and the wind; and probably, had we followed our inclinations, we should never have performed, in a single case, the process of ablution." Somewhat satisfying, however, was the fact that the "rebel wounded displayed the warmest appreciation of the efforts in their behalf," the nurse noted.[46]

Anna Morris Holstein of Upper Merion, Pennsylvania, had, with her husband William, been nursing in the army since Antietam. She shared many of the same observations about the condition of the Southern prisoners at Gettysburg, men who had been through a long, arduous campaign that afforded little opportunity to clean body or clothing. For a week they had precious little water to drink never mind any to squander on washing. Mrs. Holstein found that "though attended by their own surgeons, they neglect them so shamefully that it was an act of common humanity to provide better treatment for men helpless and suffering—prisoners as they were." Nevertheless, the compassionate woman had to admit that "their condition was when captured so filthy that the task of waiting upon them was a revolting one."[47]

The degree to which Northern nurses devoted themselves to the Rebel wounded was often a touchy proposition. The line between simple humanity and sympathizing with the enemy had to be carefully observed lest the nurse fall into the unpleasant situation that Clarissa Jones found herself in.

After offering her services to the Christian Commission, the twenty-eight-year-old schoolteacher on summer vacation from Germantown, Pennsylvania, started off for Gettysburg, bringing with her "eight barrels of the finest Drugs from the druggists of Philadelphia." When she arrived at the Second Corps hospital, she noticed that "when all the Blues were furnished with nurses the rest fled to Gettysburg" and there was no one to see to the Confederate soldiers picked up from the field of Pickett's charge.

"Upon a call for volunteers, I was the only one to offer myself," she discovered.

Though she was a woman alone among the hundreds of Rebs lying in a section of a wheatfield by Rock Creek, Clarissa said, "I never heard one word out of the way," and felt her work was so appreciated by the long-ignored men that "it would not have been safe for any man to say a rough word to me."

The first casualty she had sought to help was a young Virginian suffering intensely from lockjaw. His brother had let himself be taken prisoner to take care of him and when Clarissa arrived "was bathing the boy's wounds with a piece of paper" for he did not have even a handkerchief to use. Eventually, the devotion the young woman was showing the helpless Confederates began to annoy some of the Union solders nearby. She sensed a coldness developing toward her. When she confronted a group and asked what was the trouble, she was asked pointedly, "Are you a Rebel sympathizer?"

She responded that she most decidedly was not, and then decided to have a heart-to-heart talk with the men, telling them of the sufferings of the Rebels and "how desperately they needed the affectionate care of a woman, just as much as they did." Later, one of the Federal soldiers, upon reflection, said to Clarissa by way of authorization: "Miss Jones, you do all you can for those Johnnies; they're not such a bad sort, after all."[48]

Among the doctors in McLaws' division detailed to remain with the Southern wounded was Dr. Simon Baruch, a young man launching in the most horrific manner, what would be a brilliant professional career. After emigrating with his family from Schwersen, Germany, he had studied in Charleston, South Carolina, and at the Medical College of Virginia. Receiving his degree in 1862 at the remarkably young age of twenty-two, Baruch immediately offered his services to the Confederate army and was assigned to Brig. Gen. Joseph Kershaw's South Carolina brigade as assistant surgeon. He would later joke that he had not yet even lanced a boil.

By the time the Pennsylvania campaign began, Baruch was already a seasoned campaigner, well accustomed to ministering surgical treatment in the field. When his brigade went into action on the second day at the Peach Orchard, Baruch "set up operating tables, constructed of doors laid upon dry goods boxes and barrels" at the Black Horse Tavern on the

Hagerstown Pike, and awaited the arrival of casualties. He and two other surgeons had 222 seriously wounded men on their hands when they were informed that the army was retreating and they were to be left behind.

It was no new experience for Baruch, young as he was, because the previous September—after Antietam—he had been in charge of a field hospital at Boonsboro, Maryland, when similar orders arrived for him to remain when the army withdrew. "On that occasion having had six weeks of the most agreeable period of army life," Baruch recalled, "I regarded this order into captivity with much more complacency than did my colleagues."

As they awaited the enemy's appearance on the now quiet and tranquil battlefield, "the demands of hunger claimed paramount attention, for we had not eaten a meal in three days," said the young doctor. Describing the less than ceremonious moment of his second capture, Baruch remembered looking up and observing that "as far as the eye could reach, the summit of the hill was covered by a line of cavalry whose weapons shimmered in the brilliant July sun. The suddenness of their appearance lent awe to the scene."

For some reason, the ranking officer at the hospital turned to Baruch and directed the accented immigrant to go out and meet the blue troop "because you understand these Yankees," as if he assumed that they, as Baruch, were foreigners.

With the brazenness of youth, Baruch said, "I hastily donned my gray coat and green sash and sauntered toward the advancing line." Approaching a burly fellow with pistol drawn, Baruch perfunctorily announced, "I surrender; where is your commanding officer?" The cavalryman, in turn, called out, "Say, cap, here's a Reb wants to see you."

In such fashion, Kershaw's wounded officially became a shared responsibility.[49] If Baruch did not take his predicament too seriously,

Simon Baruch, Confederate surgeon accustomed to being left behind. *Confederate Veteran.*

it was because he fully expected to be released and sent back to the Confederate lines as soon as the wounded in his charge were taken over by the Union medical staff. After all, wasn't that what always took place with the doctors of both sides after a battle?

There was one other obvious detail that General Meade had to take care of before he left Gettysburg.

"A considerable number," as he put it, of Confederate dead remained unburied. He thought the best way of getting the job done was to contract with some civilian in town to take on the task a matter he entrusted to Provost Marshal Marsena R. Patrick to arrange.[50]

"Had a great deal of difficulty in getting hold of Some respectable parties to do any thing with, the people being nearly all Copperheads," Patrick noted later, revealing in the process the disgust he too was developing over the patriotic fervor of the local populace.

Finally, Patrick said, "I called together the leading citizens [Union]" at a private home, "made the necessary arrangements and Set a man at work."[51]

That man was Samuel Herbst, but as the slowness of his progress would show, it was not going to be easy to find the necessary help at the height of the harvest in this agricultural region with so many hands off to war. By now, the able-bodied Confederate prisoners had been sent to camps. The authorities did not want to have them loose in the area, given the political climate.

The burial problem was just one more element of the residue of the battle that no one in authority seemed to have any clear idea of how to address. It seemed to grow messier and messier.

After the battle of Spotsylvania, in May 1864, Provost Marshal Patrick humiliated the thousands of prisoners that had been taken from Maj. Gen. Edward Johnson's Confederate division by calling off their brigade names and regimental numbers, and ordering the disarmed men to fall in with their units. Thus, they were made to look as if they had given up as a cohesive force and were marched off to prison camps under their own officers. Patrick felt quite smug about having had the chance to display his thorough knowledge of the Rebel's organizational structure, information he personally gathered by interrogating prisoners who had little sense of military security and freely provided whatever information was asked of them.

At Gettysburg, Patrick made a point of letting the nearly 5,000 un-wounded Confederates in his hands know who was in control.

A Mississippi lieutenant, one of nearly 2,000 Rebs taken in the break-up of Pickett's Charge, remembered being "turned into the pen with a balance of the herd," under guard in a large open field after the failed assault. Toward nightfall, General Patrick decided to address his captives:

> Prisoners, you are here now in my charge; quite a large number of you; I guarantee to you the kindest treatment the nature of the case will permit, so long as you conduct yourselves in a becoming manner. If, however, there should be any attempt, upon your part to escape me, woe be unto you. My splendid cavalry is at hand, armed & ready for action, & in numbers almost equal to your own, & in case of any disturbances among you, they shall be ordered to charge you, cutting & slashing, right & left, indiscriminately." That's the way the Rebel lieutenant remembered Patrick's threats.[52]

The provost marshal could have saved his dire warnings, for there were not many Rebs in his holding area in any mood to attempt an escape. A few slipped away, either during the night or en route to the rail depot at Westminster the next day. But the greater majority was ready to accept imprisonment, the meager rations, the rough bunks, and the boredom they could expect at Point Lookout, Johnson's Island, or some other prison camp. They felt that even that would be preferable to the hardships they faced in the Rebel ranks, particularly now that they had seen their final all-out effort to secure a decisive victory at Gettysburg so completely crushed on Cemetery Ridge. That they had had enough was evident to all those who studied the seemingly unending procession of tatterdemalions shuffling away from the scene of their defeat.

Confusion became the first passenger when the Gettysburg railway finally resumed service as far as the outskirts of town on July 7.

With Haupt off on his mission to the capital, no one was in charge, and everything backed up. A train would arrive at the point where service suddenly terminated and sit untouched on the track next to a hill of food, clothing, and other badly needed supplies deposited on the open fields on

The railroad depot at Gettysburg, from which the wounded were transported to various hospitals. *Stewart Collection, Adams County Historical Society.*

a previous run. No one knew what was to be taken where. Worse, wounded soldiers were arriving in droves, the most serious cases by ambulance but most limping along on their own, trying to flee the ghastly field hospitals. They would surround a train stalled on the tracks but could locate no one in authority who knew when the cars might depart again. No doubt they also had to listen to a chorus of angry cursing from the civilian locomotive engineers, supply officers, and ambulance drivers over the state of affairs. Eventually, the trainmen, sensing that they were falling far behind schedule and seeing no attempt by army personnel to unload their cargo, simply got up steam and chugged back to Hanover Junction with the vital supplies undelivered—without a single wounded soldier aboard.

So bad was the start-up of service that Henry Bellows of the Sanitary Commission observed that "a train of cars loaded with wounded was necessarily detained on the tracks . . . for 24 hours; 600 of them must have suffered the pangs of hunger as well as the faintness of wounds without our succor."[53]

The assistant that chief quartermaster Rufus Ingalls left in charge was Capt. W. G. Rankin, a man with a serious drinking problem. He was somewhat overwhelmed by the chaotic situation, and wired his superior: "There has been great difficulty here in regard to the road . . . and many vexatious delays, owing to a want of men and management. It had not been under my control."[54]

Lt. Col. Edward P. Vollum, who had been sent from Washington specifically to take charge of the transportation of the wounded, took two days to get to Gettysburg due to the erratic rail lines. When he finally arrived about 7 P.M. on July 8, Vollum, a medical inspector attached to Surgeon General Hammond's office, was shocked to find "about 2,000 slightly wounded men collected without food, shelter, or attendance for the night."

The thirty-six-year-old doctor subsequently learned that the day before three trains destined for Baltimore had managed to get off with a total of 822 wounded Union soldiers. But that day wounded were taken away on only one train, 640 men, in all.

"No system has as yet been adopted for the transportation of the wounded, nor had this been possible in the deranged condition of the railroad," Vollum acknowledged.

"The railroad authorities were perplexed, and deficient in motive power and rolling stock," the inspector determined.[55]

Clearly the first order of business was to do something for the men who had been left behind that day and forced to wait until the next to be moved. But how? They couldn't go back to the various hospitals and homes from which they had come.

The U.S. Sanitary Commission prided itself on its ability to step in and meet the needs of the soldiers at the point where government ceased to function. That line was never more clearly drawn than at the spot where the railroad abruptly came to a halt outside Gettysburg, but which might as well have been in the middle of nowhere.

In the midst of this chaotic scene, several long tent poles began to rise above the throng and canvas walls grow taut. Minutes later, the smoke of cooking fires drifted from the vicinity of the tents and the aroma of hot soup and coffee filled the air. Hungry men soon followed a trail toward the source—finally, someone was doing something for them.

In the center of this activity, two women of obvious refinement, a mother and her grown daughter, stirred steaming kettles, poured fresh milk from pitchers, and led the wounded into the tents.

It was no new experience for Georgeanna M. Woolsey, or "Georgy," as she was called. She had just returned to the comfort of her New York City townhouse (a staid structure enlivened by the chattering of seven daughters) from Virginia where she had nursed the wounded after Chancellorsville. A letter from Frederick Law Olmsted, the Sanitary Commission executive secretary with whom she had worked closely since the war began, made her think, however, that she must immediately go to Gettysburg. She was joined by her widowed, sixty-three-year-old mother who had the added incentive of seeing to the well-being of her only son, Charles, an officer on the staff of General Meade. What was ordinarily a four-hour journey between Baltimore and Gettysburg took the ladies twenty-four hours, so clogged were the rail lines. When they finally stepped off one of the first trains to arrive at the battle site, they realized they need go no further to be of help. Immediately after getting settled, they pitched in at the Sanitary Commission's relief lodge and feeding station.

Of the routine they fell into, Georgy said, "as soon as the men hobbled up to the tents, good hot soup was given all round and that over, their wounds were dressed—for the gentlemen of the commission are cooks, or surgeons, as occasion demands—and, finally, with their blankets spread over straw, the men stretched themselves out and were contented till morning, and the next train."[56]

While the commission labored to relieve those being made to wait, the military authorities tried to unsnarl the mess that had been created. Chief Quartermaster Ingalls had advised his superior, Quartermaster General Meigs, that the main thing lacking at Gettysburg was "a dispatcher with full power." He couldn't have hoped for a more effective one than the man who arrived back on the scene on July 9, absolutely furious at the way things had gone awry in his absence—Herman Haupt.[57]

"Find things in great confusion," Haupt immediately wired Meigs. "Road blocked; cars not unloaded; stores ordered to Gettysburg, where they stand for a long time, completely preventing all movement there; ordered back without unloading; wounded lying for hours, without ability to carry them off; all because the simple rule of promptly unloading and returning cars is violated."[58]

Georgeanna Woolsey, a volunteer who fed thousands of wounded awaiting evacuation trains. *Massachusetts Commandery, Military Order of the Loyal Legion, U.S. Army Military History Institute (MOLLUS–MHI)*

The solution was clear to him; he took over the line from the indifferent civilian operators and in a matter of hours he was able to notify Meigs: "We are about straight again at Gettysburg; I have put the road in the charge of our own men." Haupt meant Inspector Vollum.[59]

No one could have been more pleased with Haupt's arrival than the inspector, who had the responsibility for getting the wounded out of Gettysburg in any fashion he could. Already he had acquired an absolute antipathy for the attitude of the commercial railroaders. He would say bitterly:

> The railroad companies, who got the only profit of the battle, and who had the greatest opportunities of ameliorating the sufferings of the wounded, alone stood aloof and rendered no aid. Their trains were allowed to go off without a single individual attached to them in any way authorized to minister to the wounded. There was no check-line or means of stopping the train in case of necessity; no way provided for passing from car to car. The cars—ordinary stock and freight cars—were always unclean; no one connected with the companies to clean them; the dung of cattle and litter from freight often remaining to be removed by any extemporized means at hand. There was no water, or vessels to contain it, no lanterns, no straw—absolutely nothing but the bare cars, filthy from the business of transporting freight and cattle. The only agents of the railroad companies that appear upon the memorable scene were those sent especially to look after their pecuniary interests. . . .[60]

With the army in full control, not only was a semblance of a schedule maintained, but every train went off with a medical officer aboard. Instruments, dressings, stimulants, and other items were furnished the attending surgeon, and he was instructed to announce his coming by telegraph so that the train was properly received at its destination. When the army found itself lacking, the Sanitary Commission provided each car with a sufficient quantity of hay, tin cups, bedpans and urinals.

The same day that Haupt was assuring the fretting Meigs that things had been set right, Captain Rankin wired Ingalls to confirm that the situation "is now corrected, and the road today working under military authority . . . General Haupt has just been in my office, and railroad matters to this point are arranged so that there will be no confusion hereafter."[61]

As far as the railroad was concerned, there wouldn't be any more confusion. The problem that remained, however, was getting the wounded to those trains. And it was in that regard that Jonathan Letterman's other major decision before leaving was to become pivotal.

Letterman, in extending still another pittance to his stand-in, Dr. Janes, had decided that six ambulances and four wagons per corps would be adequate to convey the wounded from their hospitals to the railroad depot and to other hospitals. The army would need all the rest of the vehicles if another major battle took place. But when actually inventoried, Janes' fleet only amounted to thirty ambulances for more than 20,000 wounded!

In explaining his decision, Letterman said, "I was informed by General [Rufus] Ingalls that the railroad to Gettysburg would be in operation on the 6th, and upon this based my action. Had such been the case, this number would have been sufficient. As it proved that this was not in good running order for some time after that date, it would have been better to have left more ambulances. I acted on the best information that could be obtained."[62]

But what did Letterman actually mean by that? Even if the railroad had been restored completely on July 6 and regular service provided directly from the depot, rather than from outside of town, thousands of wounded would still have had to be transported from the hospitals far behind Cemetery Ridge, Lutheran Theological Seminary, and other points well beyond litter-bearing distance. How were they to get there if not in ambulances? Perhaps the medical director was suggesting that because of the irregularity of the service and the confused scene at the boarding area, the ambulances were taking longer per trip than was expected, and therefore fewer men could be delivered. But there seems little doubt that a gross misjudgment had been made about the number of conveyances that would be required to effect such a massive evacuation. As a consequence, countless soldiers were forced to remain longer than necessary at the woefully inadequate field hospitals. Who knows how many more died simply for lack of better treatment available elsewhere.

Another medical inspector at the scene, Lt. Col. John M. Cuyler, had to acknowledge "our means of conveying the wounded from the field hospitals to the railroad were inadequate." The veteran regular army surgeon was quick to add "I am satisfied that as many ambulances were left by the Army of the Potomac as could possibly be spared."[63]

Even the surgeons responsible for the field hospitals recognized that the men would be better off anywhere else. They actually went among their patients telling them that if they could possibly reach the trains on their own, they were free to leave. But they couldn't count on an ambulance to take them. "Any of you boys who can make your way to the cars, can go to Baltimore," a doctor would say as he went up and down the rows of wounded under his charge. Each of the men would then test his strength and speculate whether or not to try the trek that day or wait until the next. What spurred them more than anything else was the sight of so many dead being removed each morning. At the Second Corps hospital alone, of the 3,200 patients being treated, 437 wouldn't survive: one out of nine Union soldiers, one out of every five Confederates.[64]

Christian Commission delegate Louis Muller provided another indication of the casualty rate when he reported stopping at a barn on the night of July 11 that was crowded with wounded of the Union Third Corps. "The next morning I visited it and found six men dead, who died during the night. Ten or twelve die every day, out of three hundred patients."[65]

Once on the roads into town, the motley parades of wounded—made up of marchers leaning on crutches, sightless ones holding on to a comrade's empty sleeve, and others weak and white-faced with fatigue—fell victims to a new species of vulture. They were the Gettysburg civilians who happened to own a wagon and team, and would gladly pick up the wounded soldiers and carry them to town—for a price. Of this practice generated by the army's failure to provide, Georgy Woolsey wrote in utter dismay:

> Hundreds of fellows hobbled along as best they could in heat and dust, for hours, slowly toiling, and in many hired farmers' wagons, as hard as the farmers' fists themselves, and were jolted down to the railroad, at three and four dollars the man.
>
> Think of the disappointment of a soldier, sick, body and heart, to find at the end of this miserable journey that this effort to get away, into which he had put all his remaining stock of strength, was useless; that 'the cars had gone,' or 'the cars were

full,' that while he was coming down others had stepped down
before him, and that he must turn all the weary way back again,
or sleep on the roadside till the next train 'tomorrow!'[66]

A Lancaster nurse told of five wounded men who, "after lying three
days without anything to eat and suffering great agony from their wounds
. . . were charged $25 (all they had in the world) for bringing them two
miles into Gettysburg in an uncovered wagon without springs, whose
every motion they thought would put an end to their sufferings." The next
day, three of them died.[67]

Charles Muller, a wounded member of the First Minnesota, a man who
labored with the language, remembered how on July 11 "a farmer came
around whit his farmer wagon and said for a dollar each he would take us
to the Rail Road Station. I put up my dollar and in company of eight others
we were hauled to the Station about 2 miles away.

"On going through Gettysburg we wanted to buy some Bred," he
recalled, "but they toll us that they wont sell any to the Yankies." Regardless of how often the passengers were told such a thing and no matter by
whom, they were not ready to accept it as fact and consequently "we had to
go to Baltimore whit a growling empty stomach."[68]

Capt. Benjamin Thompson of the 111th New York added to the chorus
of complaints against the avaricious farmers, relating that he had employed
one of them to take the men of his company to the depot and was "charged
$20 for the service." Sanitary Commission President Bellows, after his
inspection tour, acknowledged, "transportation for the wounded from
worse to better quarters, and of supplies, was necessarily very scarce, and
was a chief source of distress."[69]

What had been annoyance with the farmers over their whining about
the damage the battle had caused to their property now turned to deep disgust as the army became aware of the coldhearted way the farmers had
found to profit off the wounded. Artillery Colonel Wainwright was pleased
to see at least one of the profiteers put out of business. The man had
charged $20 for bringing a dozen wounded cavalrymen some seven miles.
"Fortunately, the quartermaster to whom he applied was not weak," the
colonel asserted, "and instead of paying him the money took his horses for
government use, and left him to walk home."[70]

Lest Jonathan Letterman be unaware of just what was going on in the army's rear while his attention was focused on future needs, a plainly-worded wire he received on July 9 at headquarters at the Rappahannock probably gave him cause to reflect.

Rather than complaining in tone, the dispatch seemed more of an attempt to simply get things on the record so that the situation was clearly understood by those in authority. It read in part:

"The number of wounded here probably exceeded 20,000. We have been short of nurses, surgeons, and transportation, both ambulance and railroad. . . ." The report was signed "HENRY JANES, in Charge of the Hospitals."[71]

As it happened, the very same day that Janes was informing his direct superior of his shortages, another telegram was being sent by the Surgeon General's office to one of its medical inspectors who had just arrived at Gettysburg.

"Unofficial reports are received that many supplies are needed at Gettysburg," informed the missive. "Nothing official confirms these reports. Please answer at once. Do you need anything, ambulances or supplies?"[72]

Bad enough that Janes had been left so ill-prepared by Medical Director Letterman; it now appeared that Washington wasn't even being informed— almost a week after the battle—of the deplorable conditions at the scene so that resources could be mustered to remedy the situation.

While other details were busy collecting the wounded and the dead, corps commanders had been directed to assign parties to pick up all the discarded arms and accoutrement in the vicinity of their lines, and turn them over to the ordnance officers.

A soldier of the 148th Pennsylvania so engaged estimated that "four thousand muskets were gathered up in wagons from the field of Pickett's charge and fight, and ranked up like cordwood."[73] In one section, the discarded weapons were picked up and stuck in the ground, bayonets first, until someone observed that "there were acres of muskets standing as thick as trees in a nursery."[74]

As the collection work was going on, a wounded staff officer, Frank Haskell—a man with a keen sense of history—took a final tour of the battleground to further establish the details in his memory. He noted:

Numbers of civilians and boys, and some girls even, were curiously loitering about the field, and their faces showed not sadness or horror, but only staring wonder or smirking curiosity. They looked for mementoes of the battle to keep, they said; but their furtive attempts to conceal an uninjured musket or an untorn blanket—they had been told that all property left here belonged to the Government—showed that the love of gain was an ingredient at least of their motive for coming here.[75]

One such youngster, thirteen-year-old Jacob Taughenbaugh, said he and his playmate were careful not to "go over to where the Union troops were. They were still camped in their position, and we were afraid they would take away the revolvers we had found. One of us boys had hid them away in the pocket of his hunting coat."[76]

Such souvenir hunting may have appeared harmless enough, but a *New York Herald* correspondent hanging about to wrap up the story of the great battle observed that many who came were "bearing away any and everything that they consider of pecuniary value."

"Here in this orchard I find a country man engaged in cutting the harness from one of the dead battery horses, and preparing to carry it from the field. Another has collected a dozen blankets, dropped by soldiers in the heat of the engagement. Another walks past me with three of the best muskets he can find on the battlefield."[77]

A writer for the rival *New York Times* also reported the wholesale pilfering of government property. "The battlefield for miles around is covered with rifles, bayonets, blankets, cartridge-boxes, clothing, etc. and thousands of dollars worth of it are being carried off daily by those visiting the scene of the conflict."[78]

Provost Marshal Patrick noted angrily that people were coming from the countryside "in Swarms to Sweep & plunder." There was little sensitivity observed. One man told of having "picked up a letter from a boy to his father evidently stained with his father's blood contents very interesting . . . also one from a girl to her lover."[79]

With few guards posted to control the stripping of the field, organized efforts at stealing began. One operation involved "a number of nondescript scavengers of mixed nationalities" from Spring Forge, York County, who made their living by selling rags to a paper mill. Their interest was not in gathering weapons but garments and they came in teams, day and night, to load up loot. "They even resurrected corpses from the shallow entombment in the hope that some valuable might be found on the festering body," one resident said of the ghoulish plunderers.[80]

All the weapons and other equipment that the army did manage to collect were deposited in a great pile near the railroad depot for eventual shipment to Washington. But there was no establishing how much property had been stolen. Few were more incensed over the level of looting going on at Gettysburg than Rufus Ingalls. The chief quartermaster took infinite professional pride in the fact that not a single ambulance or wagon that was his responsibility during the campaign had been lost to the enemy. He was not someone who would tolerate the unauthorized removal of a single cartridge from the field. Before he had to leave with the army, Ingalls notified his superior in Washington, Quartermaster General Meigs: "I saw citizens carrying off arms, and doubt not it will require coersive steps to recover them."[81]

As it happened, Meigs had two men in mind ideally suited to deal with such a situation, and almost immediately after receiving Ingalls' disturbing intelligence, he had them en route to Gettysburg. The town would soon know when they arrived.

Dr. John H. Brinton, curator of the newly created Army Medical Museum in Washington, had been dispatched to Gettysburg by Surgeon General Hammond after the battle. His task was to assist the surgeons and to collect specimens of battle injuries that might be useful in developing more effective techniques for treatment.

Brinton had been sent on such missions before. Part of his responsibility was to show other surgeons what sorts of bone samples would be particularly instructive and to encourage them not to simply discard the limbs after surgery, but to ship them off to the museum. "Many and many a putrid heap have I had dug out of trenches where they had been buried, in the supposition of an everlasting rest, and ghoul-like work have I done, amid surrounding gatherings of wondering surgeons," he confessed.[82]

Gettysburg was a treasure trove for a man of Brinton's interests (though it was said that with Dr. Janes in charge, amputations were being minimized at the hospitals and viewed as a last resort), but the prize specimen he came away with was actually an object designed to prevent injury.

"One of my men on this occasion took from the body of a Southern soldier, a breast plate of soft steel, in two halves, intended to be worn under the coat or vest," he related. "One ball had struck it and indented or bent it without perforation. Another, however, had passed through in the region of the liver, causing the death of the wearer."[83]

The vest was the only example of defensive armor that Brinton had come upon during the war. Although the Confederate soldier who wore it was probably deposited namelessly in a mass grave, his odd apparel was placed on prominent display at the army museum for future generations.

After a few more steamy days, there was no longer a need for milestones or signposts to indicate Gettysburg's proximity. A strange smell permeated the heavy summer air. It was an odor a veteran soldier would have instantly identified but was repugnantly mysterious to the civilians who had never experienced such a sensation. It intensified until the droves of people approaching the town by rail and wagon to assist the wounded or locate relatives gagged and retched, and were forced to cover their nostrils while their senses strained to adapt to the obnoxious assault.

"As we drew near our destination, we began to realize that war had other horrors than the sufferings of the wounded or the desolation of the bereft," Cornelia Hancock remembered of the culmination of her journey from New Jersey. "A sickening, overpowering, awful stench announced the presence of the unburied dead, on which the July sun was mercilessly shining, and at every step the air grew heavier and fouler, until it seemed to possess a palpable horrible density that could be seen and felt and cut with a knife."[84]

Mrs. Edmund A. Souder, arriving from Philadelphia after foregoing the sea breezes of Cape May, where she usually vacationed at that time, was similarly affected: "Long before we reached the town, the odors of the battlefield were plainly perceptible."[85]

Few were as intimately exposed to the source as Sgt. Thomas P. Meyer of the 148th Pennsylvania Volunteers who headed a burial detail on the field. "The stench on the battlefield was something indescribable," he wrote. "It would come up as if in waves and when at its worst the breath would stop in the throat, the lungs could not take it in, and a sense of suffocation would be experienced." To combat it, he said, "we would cover our faces tightly with our hands and turn the back toward the breeze."[86]

The civilians who once boarded up their houses against Rebel intruders now tried to seal them against the odiferous invasion. "When you would open the windows for the morning air," recounted attorney William McClean, "you would be assailed by the foul odors which arose all over the field. We citizens became gradually acclimated to it. But some visitors coming from a pure atmosphere into this, were poisoned and went home and died."[87]

How true this was is difficult to say, but schoolteacher Sally Broadhead was also among those convinced that the air had been rendered toxic by the unburied or inadequately interred bodies of men and animals. "I fear we shall be visited with pestilence," she averred, "for every breath we draw is made ugly by the stench."[88]

Young Nellie Auginbaugh had her own theory. It was that "the only thing that saved our town from an epidemic" were the heavy rains that followed the battle.

Various measures were tried to cope with the pervasive smell. "The only disinfectant known there was chloride of lime and it was used so freely that it did not seem natural when we smelled it no longer," said Nellie.[89]

And was it ever spread about! Not only were the sidewalks covered with chloride but "the state of the hospitals was much improved by the same means," Mrs. Souder noticed. Still, she warned, "camphor and cologne or smelling salts are prime necessaries for most persons, certainly for the ladies."[90]

Others went about with bottles of pennyroyal or peppermint oil to sniff when conditions became too unbearable. People in the town were hard pressed to even compare what they were smelling. A child of twelve, Mary Elizabeth Montfort, would only say it was something worse "than the time we found a dead rat behind the loose boards in the cellar."[91]

Sufficiently alarmed, army authorities published several appeals in the local newspapers for horses, wagons, and manpower to "bury the dead and to cleanse the streets in such a thorough way as to guard against pestilence."[92]

So repulsive was the scene that it detracted from a true appreciation of what had taken place there. How could one dwell on thoughts of noble and heroic deeds when so many of those who had given their lives in the struggle were now reduced to insect-covered, swollen heaps, stripped of all dignity and as offensive as an enemy? "The deadly, nauseating atmosphere," sensitive Cornelia Hancock lamented, "robbed the battlefield of its glory, the survivors of their victory."[93]

Perhaps later a better image of the place would emerge. But, at present, only the deepest of compassion could sustain anyone for any more than a cursory visit.

With the battle decided, a squabble of a different sort began to erupt in the town: a conflict between neighbors centering on who was the more loyal—the more patriotic.

Henry J. Stahle, the editor and proprietor of the staunchly Democratic weekly, *The Compiler,* was perhaps the most notable casualty of this fray, though many found themselves ostracized. Stahle should have been aware of the trouble he was in. The day after the battle ended, victorious Union forces re-entered Gettysburg and he "saw fit to put out in their honor the American Flag" at his two-story residence-office-printshop on Baltimore Street. Before long, some "miserable wretch wearing a United States uniform at the instigation of more miserable wretches" ripped down the banner, declaring that "it was a Copperhead flag and should not float in the breeze."

The next day, it was not the soldier who tore down the flag, but Stahle who was under arrest on a charge of "lack of loyalty." He was carried off to a cell at Fort McHenry.[94]

It seems that on the first day of the battle a wounded Union officer, Lt. Col. William W. Dudley of the 19th Indiana Infantry, had been carried into Stahle's home and placed on a couch in the dining room. A neighbor sought to clean his leg wound while Stahle rushed over to the Adams County Court House, now in the possession of the Rebels, to find a Confederate surgeon willing to come and see to the colonel.

One of Stahle's political foes, a prominent Republican lawyer named David McConaughy, would seize upon the incident to accuse the newspaper editor of disclosing to the enemy the hiding place of Union soldiers. He carried his complaint to an all-too-willing listener, Provost Marshal Patrick, a man admittedly "thoroughly disgusted with the whole Copperhead fraternity of Gettysburg & the country about."

Patrick wrote in his diary that he had promptly disposed of the matter: "A Copperhead Editor, confined for pointing out the refuge of Union

Marsena Patrick, the Union army's provost marshal. *Library of Congress.*

Soldiers to Rebel officers, was brought before me & Affidavits substantiating the fact presented, to Accompany him to the Baltimore prisons. . . ."[95]

Stahle was not the only one turned upon as residents began to evaluate the patriotic fervor of their neighbors during the recent crisis. A Philadelphia woman newly arrived on the scene observed: "There is a strong feeling of indignation against the men here who betrayed the Union soldiers who were concealed. Many persons think they are entitled to be hung without trial."

She and the delegation of ladies she accompanied were much attuned politically to the prevailing sentiment there. She noted, for example, the arrival of a "distinguished Copperhead from New York," and questioned his mission. "I dare say he has looked after the New York soldiers, but he has taken special pains to find some one to look after the rebels . . . The ladies said they had no refreshments for Copperheads and he should get nothing from them."[96]

Although only sixteen at the time, and hardly politically aware, Liberty Hollinger observed what was going on: "Most of our people were occupied as we were, helping whenever opportunity offered. True, we had a few people in our town who were dubbed 'copperhead' because they did not ring true blue."[97]

These political frictions had their effect, however, on even the very young. "There were many Democrats who wouldn't admit their sympathies," recalled thirteen-year-old Jacob Taughenbaugh. "I had some fights with Democrats' sons, because I wouldn't stand to have them call me a nigger, as they did."[98]

John C. Wills and his family, who owned the Globe Hotel twice occupied by Rebels, once during their foray before the battle and again during, got a full taste of the bitterness. "We know we were censured for entertaining Confederates," he asserted, and said in their defense, "It was our business and we entertained them the same as we did the Union soldiers."

When visited by the provost marshal about their activities, Wills said, "we told him as the spirit of feeling was high between the two political parties this charge was brought against us through political enmity."[99]

Those accused of disloyalty were convinced that their political enemies were taking advantage of the existing martial law to attack them. Said *The Compiler* angrily in one edition:

> The Federal officer who was impelled by the urgent solicitations of several fanatical Jacobins to search several houses in town for rebel soldiers, expressed himself very honestly and as a gentleman soldier would do, by declaring that those who requested him shared little of his respect, none of his praise. No doubt he was acquainted with the grand structure of spite work, which is raising its columns by lying informations and scandalous fabrications in our christian town.

The paper predicted that the soldiers who remained in Gettysburg would find themselves "used as 'cats paws' to promote party interests and called upon by the fomented colors of Abolitionists to strangle any who may have incurred the displeasure of those blatant politicians."[100]

While General Patrick tended to couple the plundering of the battlefield with Copperhead sympathies, they were actually unrelated. The scavengers were basically apolitical. Their behavior had nothing to do with secession, states' rights, or anything remotely associated with the issues of the day. It was purely a marriage of larcenous proclivity and opportunity. But Patrick was hardly the only one to ascribe outrageous acts to anyone whose loyalties he suspected. The Civil War may have moved on from Gettysburg, but the political fratricide boiling over seemed, for those caught up in it, almost as acrimonious.

THE GREAT BATTLES.

Splendid Triumph of the Army of the Potomac.

ROUT OF LEE'S FORCES ON FRIDAY

The Most Terrible Struggle of the War.

TREMENDOUS ARTILLERY DUEL.

Repeated Charges of the Rebel Columns Upon Our Position.

Every Charge Repulsed with Great Slaughter.

A Great Outpouring

The newspapers proclaimed in line upon line of bold type highlights of the signal victory at Gettysburg. Little was left unstated by the time the reader reached the body of the dispatches. It was from the pulpits, however, that most of the populace learned of the unfinished state of affairs. It was through the churches that the relief agencies mustered the quickest response possible to the needs of their agents at the scene.

The appeals were two-fold in nature and equally desperate in tone. One was for food, clothing, and medical supplies. The other, with the army moving on, was for volunteers to come and offer direct assistance. All prejudice against civilian doctors was suddenly suspended by their exhausted military colleagues at the Gettysburg hospitals. The situation was made too dire by the sheer volume of wounded and the army's inability to move the casualties more quickly. Military surgeons were ready to accept all the help they could get from anyone who could apply a suture. In response to the appeal, scores of private physicians left their practices to offer their skills. Nurses, experienced on the battlefields, visualized the need and presented themselves for duty. Clergymen in large numbers received the call.

While the volunteers packed their valises and hastily arranged their affairs for an indefinite absence, the accumulation of supplies began at thousands of different locations throughout the North. Donations were based on perceived rather than specifically stated needs. Predictably, it resulted in a super-abundance of some items and a dearth of others.

One member of the congregation of the Ascension Church in Philadelphia remembered:

> In place of a sermon, the clergyman had brought a sewing machine; instead of Sabbath day finery each woman wore the more royal ornament of plain working apparel.
>
> In every available niche a sewing machine was shrined; even the pulpit desk was removed and a brood, noisy as so many canaries, clustered and chattered upon the platform. Here were some preparing lint; there were others cutting shirts, drawers, bandages; while in another place others were sizing rags—of all things on a battlefield most necessary and useful. Now and then young men staggered in under great burdens of material contributed at the houses in the vicinity, or poured into the treasury the gifts of friends and neighbors. The scene was a picture of war-time. Christian love and sympathy shone through it and over it like a benediction. There was a heart beat in every click of the needle.[1]

This feverish activity produced tons of supplies of infinite description—blankets to bandages and candles to fans—which were stuffed into barrels and crates. But burlap sacks and bundles would be of no use whatever unless they could be transported to the scene.

The Sanitary Commission had already delivered five wagonloads of supplies from its "flying depot" at Frederick. Surrounding communities were sending in wagonloads of hastily gathered provisions, particularly the towns of Lancaster and York, Pennsylvania, even though the latter place had itself only been recently sacked by the Rebels. Sallie Broadhead, the teacher who had made the Lutheran Theological Seminary up the Chambersburg Pike her nursing station, daily made her way there "with as much food as we could scrape together, and some old quilts and pillows." She remembered with delight when she found "that a wagonload of bread and fifty pounds of butter had arrived, having been sent in from the country."[2]

Fannie Buehler recalled how her friends in the vicinity, "knowing that I was on the ground, sent me many boxes and barrels of supplies . . . wine and pickles, oranges and lemons, sugar, tea, coffee, beef tea" for distribution. But it was not until the railroad was reopened that a regular flow of provisions could be instituted on the scale that the destitute soldiers and civilians at Gettysburg required. Once that spigot was turned on, however, the outpouring became difficult to control. Just sorting and distributing all that was arriving was proving to be a major logistical challenge.[3]

Predictably, the very first train that arrived included two cars chartered by the Sanitary Commission. One was a car cooled by a ton of ice that contained several tons of fresh eggs, butter, mutton, chickens, fruit, milk, and other provisions purchased by the commission in Philadelphia. The second car carried several large campmeeting tents and a lot of miscellaneous furniture that had been bought in Baltimore, and for which commission agents anticipated a need. Both transactions were arranged by Secretary Olmsted, who was orchestrating the commission's relief effort from Baltimore. "I have arranged to receive and take care of about forty tons of supplies a day, for the present, if the people supply them, as I think they will," Olmsted wrote his wife of his preparations on July 7.[4]

To receive all that was expected to arrive in Gettysburg, commission agents accepted the use of Fahnestock Brothers' empty mercantile store on Baltimore Street. The proprietors of this, the largest store in town, had sent

Supplies are heaped in front of the U.S. Sanitary Commission's depot on Baltimore Street. *Gettysburg National Military Park.*

virtually all their merchandise away for safekeeping when the Rebels approached. (The owners, in fact, actually maintained their own car at the railroad depot to expedite the removal of their wares whenever the enemy was even rumored to be in the area.)

Before long the building became an overstuffed mishmash of odd-shaped containers into which its custodians would simply seem to disappear. "Carload after carload of supplies were brought up to this place, till shelves, and counter, and floor up to the ceiling were filled, till there was barely a passageway between the piles of boxes and barrels till the sidewalk was monopolized and even the street encroached upon," a commission agent said of the scene.[5]

Many of the donations that arrived and were sorted carried little messages from the givers that together conveyed how broad was the base of support for the relief effort and how heartfelt was the need to contribute.

"These stockings were knit by a little girl five years old and she is going to knit some more, for mother says it will help some poor soldier," a note attached to a pair of wool socks read.

"This blanket was used by a soldier in the war of 1812—may it keep some soldier warm in this war against traitors," read another.

A small bundle of bandages included something of an apology: "This is a poor gift, but it is all I had," the message read. "I have given my husband and my boy, and only wish I have more to give, but I haven't."[6]

Each morning uniformed soldiers and army wagons arrived at the crammed storehouse from the various hospitals to receive the food, clothing, and medical supplies the government of the United States had been unable to provide. All drove away laden with bread, eggs, fish, ice, meat, furniture, and an endless variety of other items that had been systematically purchased by the commission from its treasury or randomly donated by the thousands of ordinary citizens who viewed the agency as a conduit for their gifts. "If the articles needed one day were not in our possession at the time, they were immediately telegraphed for," an agent explained.[7]

Dr. Bellows, a man an admiring associate said "likes to see his usefulness made manifest in newspapers," detailed in a report to the *New York Times* the commission's routine since rail service was restored.[8]

"Every day since Tuesday, a car-load of delicacies, costing $2,000 in Baltimore and containing 1,000 pounds of mutton, 1,000 pounds of chicken, 1,200 dozen eggs, 1,500 loaves of soft bread, with condensed milk, beef stock, etc. had been ordered forward and distributed."

Rev. Henry W. Bellows, president of the U.S. Sanitary Commission.
Library of Congress.

He added, that those at home should know, that "ceaseless wagon-loads" of hospital clothing were coming in.[9]

In just the first week after the battle, the commission spent $20,000 on its effort—about as much as arrived in contributions—but by July 23, so much money was going out of the organization's treasury that it was down to $75,000. Dr. Cornelius R. Agnew, a commissioner, appealed to the agents in charge at the scene, "to take in sail."[10]

The commission's generosity wasn't restricted to the Federal facilities. The agency was actually going out of its way to invite the surgeons at the Confederate hospitals to draw on its stores. Dr. Simon Baruch, the young physician left behind at the hospital of Kershaw's South Carolina brigade on the Hagerstown road, was more than a bit surprised when two days after his capture the white-bearded figure of Dr. Gordon Winslow, a Sanitary Commission inspector, appeared at the flap door of his tent. The "face beamed with kindness" and offered to furnish him with some supplies. "Tears started to my eyes and a lump arose in my throat as I realized for the first time in my life a practical demonstration of the precept, 'love thine enemy,'" the desperate doctor said of the gesture by Dr. Winslow, who had taken upon himself responsibility for the twenty-four Confederate hospitals in the twelve-mile area.[11]

Baruch's reaction was not singular. Everywhere Winslow visited, he made his offer to the Southern doctors. "The astonishment and gratitude of these officers were expressed in no measured terms."[12] They eagerly availed themselves of the opportunity and, subsequently, someone observed, "one of the strangest of the many strange and wonderful sights of which the Commission's depot at Gettysburg was the scene after the battle, was the mingling in the busy crowd of friend and foe, National uniform and Confederate uniform, Union army wagon and rebel army wagon, all engaged in the common work of helping the suffering . . ."[13]

To obtain the proffered provisions for his unit, Dr. Baruch rode into town with an orderly "who had hired two horses by paying a shoulder of bacon." At the commission's cluttered warehouse, a clerk had Baruch state the location of his hospital, the names of the surgeons and the number of wounded and told him he would have to wait until a wagon became available to haul his supplies. The doctor idled away the time by reading a copy of the *New York Herald* and noted, "this was the first Northern newspaper I had seen in two years and the first news I had read of the outside world."

In a short time, a wagon was loaded with a mouth-watering array of provisions, including a keg of tamarinds, a barrel of eggs packed in sawdust, a lemon box, a large slab of butter covered in ice, and other things he had not seen in ages. Adding to his good feeling, as he accepted all these sumptuous rations for his hospital, was the sense that he had been treated "as courteously as if I were a merchant purchasing goods."

While in town, Baruch was advised to apply also at the office of the medical director of the army for medical supplies and, in so doing, he chanced to meet Jonathan Letterman just before the latter went away. Baruch was much impressed. He found Letterman "a true soldier, magnanimous to his enemy, and a true physician, considerate of the wounded." Despite Letterman's other concerns, Baruch related that the medical director took the time to personally hand him a blank requisition, instructed him how to fill it out, approved the application, and sent it to the medical purveyor for execution.[14]

In observing the sensitive, sad-faced medical official's attentive handling of this one individual request, it is difficult to imagine his being the very same man who would, in but a few hours, leave the scene under the sort of condition he dictated.

The headquarters and distribution center of the United States Christian Commission, an organization that had become the Sanitary Commission's arch rival as a vehicle for the home front's charitable support for the men in uniform, opened in Schick's storeroom at the southwest corner of the diamond.

Although the distance between the two stations was only a stone's throw, the groups that occupied them could not have been further apart philosophically in their approach to disposing of the donations presented to them.

The Christian Commission was an offspring of the Young Men's Christian Association and had grown out of a concern for the spiritual welfare and moral protection of the members of the association who had gone off to war. It had strong support, naturally enough, from the clergy and Christian literary interests.

The main objective stated in the commission's charter was "the spiritual good of the soldiers of the army, and incidentally, their intellectual improvement and social and physical comfort." To achieve its goals, the

Philadelphia-based association sent what it called "delegates" into the field for varying lengths of time—usually clergymen—to distribute Bibles and other religious works and preach sermons to all those willing to listen. It set up tents for reading and provided stationery to soldiers so they could write home. The commission paid the postage as a way to keep the men under the moral constraints of wives and mothers.

At the same locations, the commission passed out enormous quantities of soap, needles, socks, towels, mosquito nets, and canned foods, as well as wines and liquors for medicinal purposes. If not intended as a lure to get the men to listen to the commission's religious messages, the material amenities being disseminated made the soldiers all too willing to come back to have their spiritual needs addressed.

Because it came into being in November 1861, after the Sanitary Commission had been firmly established as the army's primary adjunct, it was not an easy task for the Christian Commission to attract attention and gain support. It was difficult for the giving public to understand the new commission's role and purpose. There was no animosity directed toward it—only indifference.

At the governmental level, however, the Christian Commission found itself far more quickly accepted than the Sanitary Commission, because it was not perceived to be as threatening. After all, it was not concerned about the way medical treatment was being administered and did not criticize and supervise the performance of the army's commanders and their medical staffs. As far as the military brass was concerned, whatever influence the Christian Commission could assert over their men that might serve to inhibit their drinking or prevent their contraction of diseases from the camp followers was a benefit that could only be welcomed. In fact, the army was all too willing to provide the transportation to move around the commission's delegates and their familiar box tents, tons of Bibles, and supplies.

While the commission gave relief to both sides in the war, its leaders showed their bias by alluding in one publication to their support "of the brave men now in arms to put down a wicked rebellion."[15]

The Sanitary Commission, however, viewed the growing influence of the Christian Commission with mounting concern. It wasn't that its officers didn't appreciate the value of the religious work the Christian Commission was involved in (the head of the Sanitary Commission himself being a prominent minister). But there was a fear that the Christian Commission's activities might undercut the "Sanitaries" as the main channel for support from the private sector. Local churches were the key centers for the work of the ladies' aid societies around the country and any preference expressed by their ministers could work against the Sanitary Commission. The Rev. Henry Bellows privately predicted of the interlopers: "We have made the word commission a human word; add Christian to it, and the two will be invincible."[16]

But George Templeton Strong, the prominent New York lawyer who served as treasurer of the Sanitary Commission, was far more jealous of his organization's standing and was unrestrained in his contempt for the other group. He referred in his diary to its chairman, the Rev. George H. Stuart of Philadelphia, as "that evangelical mountebank and philanthrope." The officials of the Christian Commission he encountered in Washington were classed by Stone as "an ugly-looking set. . . . Some were unctuous to behold, and others vinegary; a bad lot."[17]

At a meeting just that April to discuss working in concert, Strong said of the Christian Commission's representatives:

> There is an undercurrent of cant, unreality, or something else, I do not know what, in all their talk, that repels and offends me. This association, calling itself a 'commission' when it is no more a commission than it is a corporation, or a hose company, or a chess club, or a quadratic equation, and thus setting out under false colors and with a lie on its forehead, seems to me one of the many forms in which the shallowness, fussiness, and humbug of our popular religionism are constantly embodying themselves.[18]

However, the Christian Commission was firmly entrenched with the Army of the Potomac in the spring of 1863 whether the Sanitary Commission liked it or not. So much so that when its field agent sensed something astir at the army's camps around Falmouth, Virginia, in early June, he had no difficulty obtaining advance word of a major movement in order to prepare. He had only to ask the quartermaster there: "When will you require our tents?" When he was told, before five o'clock, the delegate replied, "you shall have it, sir" and set to work on packing up.[19]

As with the Sanitary Commission, the Christian Commission tried to anticipate when and where the next engagement was to take place so that it might be able to deliver supplies quickly. In this instance, the Christian Commission, in studying the armies' maneuvers, looked for them to meet near Emmitsburg and set up en route a supply depot at Frederick to draw upon. The battle had just ended when the commission's first load of provisions arrived at the railhead at Westminster. It sat there only long enough for its delegate to find Gen. John Buford in the chaotic scene that existed at the army's primary source of supply. The cavalry leader, who had played so prominent a part in the first day's fight, quickly ordered an army wagon made available to the delegation.

Arriving at the Second Corps field hospital, the relief party was bombarded with calls from the surgeons for lint, bandages, sponges, and other basic supplies. The single load was stretched as broadly as possible. Once the railroad was restored and a distribution site had been secured, however, the commission was able to move into full operation. Delegates, most of them clergymen but some lay women, began to arrive with every train of provisions until up to 300 were on the scene, and were lodging in private homes. Each was given a specific assignment and dispatched to a hospital that then became his or her personal responsibility. Tents were erected at each corps hospital (except the Sixth which had not suffered heavy casualties) and the delegates assigned there had to see to its stocking. Every day, they would come to the diamond with a list of requirements, dictated by the surgeons and the army's quartermasters.

Goods were consigned to the commission for distribution from York, Hanover, Carlisle, Harrisburg, Lancaster, Baltimore, Philadelphia, and, indeed, from almost every direction.

"But a few days before they were in dread of the invading army," one delegate said of the donors. "Now, with grateful hearts and willing hands, they were bringing of what had been saved, and offering it to supply food and clothing for the wounded, who had borne the burden of their defense."[20]

So much was coming in, in fact, that the commission had to secure the use of the upper floors of Apollo Hall, a large building on the opposite side of the square. Of the scene there, a member of the commission's Committee of Maryland related:

> The rooms thus provided were soon filled with goods, which were kept in almost constant motion by receipt and distribution.

Fifteen hands were employed, and were occupied day and night in the labors of the warehouse. Every visitor was drafted for service, and it was a rare sight presented in the mixed corps of laborers, consisting of ladies, clergymen, teachers, lawyers, merchants, mechanics, and colored laborers. The boxes and barrels upon the pavement at times reached more than half way to the second story, and drays and carts were before the door, loading and unloading, during nearly the whole of the day. The clerks and laborers of the warehouse were so completely worn down, that service was imposed upon every one that came in.[21]

Not only were the field hospitals being supplied but requests came from those in town at the college, the seminary, the court house, the public school, the warehouses, the churches, and the private homes. Some, like young Dr. Baruch, drew on both commissions for their needs.

Louis Muller, the agent in charge of the commission's feeding department, reported on July 8, five days after the battle:

We have fed at least two thousand wounded men in this town today, and about the same number of rations have been sent by our delegates to those in the field, besides wagon loads of all kinds of supplies.

No man can estimate the amount of suffering we are relieving. . . . The rebels have swept this country of everything eatable. . . .[22]

"The amount of labor required in the mere receiving, opening, unpacking, distributing and then arranging and sending out, is incredible," another volunteer worker sighed.[23]

What speeded the distribution was the lack of formality practiced; the supplies were made freely available. "We had not learned the red tapeism [sic] which would suffer a patient to starve to death while the goods rotted on hand, waiting for those requisitions to come in the name and on the behalf of men who had no one to attend to them, or speak to them, men who had neither pen, ink, paper or a hand with which to write their need," one official explained of the approach being taken. "Just such an institution as the Commission was a necessity."[24]

Of the system that gave each delegate a specific area of responsibility, another observed:

> It was often amusing to see the delegates that came in from each of these hospitals daily to receive such supplies as were needed. A mother could not have been more anxious for the supply of her children than these men were to procure whatever would make comfortable the wounded in their particular district.[25]

As at the Sanitary Commission down the street, the bulk of the wagons blocking movement in front of the Christian Commission's depot were army wagons loaded with soldiers, who were there to tap a source of supply that had been improvised to compensate for their government's temporary inability to sustain both the Army of the Potomac pursuing Lee and the army of wounded that had been left at Gettysburg.

To one person dispensing the donations, "the whole hospital demands seemed for days to fall on the Commission for every kind of things needed." At least publicly, Reverend Bellows of the Sanitary Commission had to acknowledge "the enterprise, zeal and blessedness of the labors of this sister institution."[26]

So established was the Christian Commission now as a conduit for giving that its local committee felt comfortable in appealing through the Adams County newspapers for specific items that had not been arriving in sufficient quantity to satisfy the volume of requests.

"Help the Wounded Soldiers," read the entreaty that appeared several times in each newspaper.

> There are now in the hospitals in and around Gettysburg several thousands of wounded soldiers, most of whom will remain for months.
>
> For proper nursing and comfort of these men, many articles are necessary in addition to those supplied by the government. Those most needed at present are butter, eggs, chickens, apple butter, dried fruit, dried beef, potatoes, onions, and pickles; also sheets, pillows, cushions, shirts, drawers, socks and slippers. The local committee of the United States Christian Commission earnestly appeals to their benevolent and patriotic fellow

citizens to send in supplies of the above articles, and every other that may be suggested as suitable for hospital purposes, in order that this terrible suffering of our brave soldiers may, as far as possible, be relieved, and that they may be restored to their families and country.

But the Sanitary and Christian commissions were hardly alone in their relief effort. Ten men from the No. 4 Fire Department in Baltimore arrived to offer their skills in assisting the injured.[27] The governors of various states chauvinistically sent in teams to locate the wounded of their own regiments and to see to their exclusive needs. The Rev. Isaac W. Montford was a minister with the Indiana Military Agency, located in Washington. He was charged with looking after the welfare of Hoosier soldiers. He learned of the conditions in Gettysburg from an officer of the 19th Indiana who arrived at Willard's Hotel the day after the battle with a bandaged hand minus two fingers and his cheek grazed by a bullet. Montford's response to what he learned from the casualty was instant; he telegrammed his governor, "I leave with 5 men— with lint & bandages & wine on the 1st train tomorrow."

The Schick store (at right), which became the U.S. Christian Commission's supply depot. *Gettysburg National Military Park.*

The railroad carried the Indiana delegation only as far as Westminster where the provost marshal warned that Rebel cavalry was operating between there and Gettysburg, and cautioned against going any further. The next day, however, the group traveled aboard a wagon train of grain, "each one of our party carrying his sack of lint bandages & wine." Upon arrival, they began seeking out members of the five Indiana regiments that had fought at Gettysburg, though hardly in a very good state themselves. Said Mr. Montfort, "This region is eat out. I arrived yesterday on a cherry pie and a glass of water."[28]

Traveling with Montfort's party from Westminster and reclining on bags of forage, very near the canvas covering of a huge government wagon, was Charlotte Elizabeth Johnson McKay. A widow, she had gone off to nurse the soldiers of the Army of the Potomac from South Reading, Massachusetts, shortly after the death of her only child, "with no tear for my departure, and no smile to welcome my return." There was no escaping her personal trouble, however, for as Mrs. McKay attended the wounded at Chancellorsville, she learned that her brother had been killed in that battle only hours after she had last seen him.[29]

Serving at the Second Corps hospital spread about Rock Creek, she was one of many attendants who sought to obtain supplies for the wounded in her care from various relief agencies, and shopped at their depots on a daily basis. "The programme for a day at Gettysburg was to rise as early as possible in the morning, and send out everything that was available in the way of food to the wounded," she explained of her routine.

> An item for one morning was a barrel of eggs, and as it was impossible to cook them all, they were distributed raw, the men who had the use of their hands making little fires in front of their tents, and boiling them in tin cups, for themselves and their disabled comrades.
>
> Breakfast being over, I would ride to the town, and gather up everything in the way of sanitary supplies that I could get, from the Sanitary and Christian commissions, the large and generously filled storehouse of Adams Express Co. or any quarter where they could be obtained. I would take butter, eggs, and crackers by the barrel, dried fish by the half kettle, and fresh meat in any quantity, and having seen them loaded on an army

wagon, would return in my ambulance, which was well filled with lighter articles, in time to give some attention to dinner. The remainder of the day would be devoted to the distribution of such stimulants as eggnog and milk punch—which would be prepared in large buckets, and served to the patients in little tin cups—or supplying them with clothing, pocket handkerchiefs, cologne, bay rum, anything that could be had to alleviate their sufferings.[30]

If nurses like Mrs. McKay could be regarded as consumers or customers of the relief agencies' offerings (and therefore in position to appreciate how essential they were), groups such as the Patriot Daughters of Lancaster played both parts. That is, they came to distribute directly to the wounded things they had gathered and brought along themselves. When these ladies came to town they thought Providence had had a hand in designating where they could most help. The only rooms they could obtain happened to be directly opposite Christ Lutheran Church, where many of the Union First Corps wounded were. If their temporary quarters were conveniently situated, one woman noted that "the entrance was by no means imposing." The building was in a long, narrow alley in back of a store and embraced three rooms—a storeroom, a dining room, and a kitchen.

As soon as they were settled, they had a board placed over the entrance on which was written in large letters in chalk "Patriot Daughters of Lancaster," and their work commenced. Some had agreed to cook while the others went into the church and nursed. When a surgeon was asked what his patients needed, his reply was simply "everything." What they perceived to be the most pressing service they could render, however, was to make the men more comfortable because scores of amputees were being forced to lie on the bare wooden floor with only a blanket under them and nothing to rest their heads on.

"I went back to the rooms, and we all commenced sorting the pillows, shirts, sheets, etc., sending at the same time to the Commission for some bed-sacks which the man attendants filled with straw," said one of the providers.

When the improvised bedding was delivered, the wounded "looked their gratitude, which was more elegant than words," she recalled. Before the ladies left to make arrangements for their supper, each soldier was given a feminine touch, which, in their miserable surroundings, was much appreciated. Perhaps it served as a reminder of a more civilized, refined society. It was a handkerchief wet with cologne.[31]

The food supply problem became one of the first of the major problems at Gettysburg to be overcome. In addition to the large shipments of fresh meat, vegetables, and fruit the Sanitary Commission was sending in daily on refrigerated cars from distant cities now that rail service was restored, and the food coming from other relief groups, the army finally managed to establish its flow of rations.

On July 9, Captain Rankin informed General Ingalls that 300,000 rations were now on hand at the quartermaster depot and added, "The officers of subsistence have notified their chief to send no more at present."[32] After more than a week of hunger, the military personnel in the area now had more than enough to eat. If the army fare was more basic and less appetizing then the cooled oysters, jellies, and other delicacies the private agencies were offering, it was plentiful. The civilians who were associated with the commissions or who had wounded soldiers in their homes were also able to get enough to eat from one source or another.

The ones who would suffer from empty stomachs now were the thousands of visitors coming in either out of curiosity or in search of relatives. The influx was far too great for the few hotels and inns in town to accommodate. There were no restaurants as such and a new problem of sustenance began to appear as the other was being resolved.

While the food situation for the wounded soldiers had been vastly improved, enhancing their chances of recovery, the other major shortages continued unabated. There were still far too few medical personnel available. Transportation remained woefully inadequate. Better shelter was desperately needed, particularly for the Confederates. And, despite assertions by the army brass to the contrary, medical supplies were still sorely lacking even a week after the battle. Uniformed soldiers from the hospitals not only stood in line to apply for donations from the civilian relief agencies, but the surgeons were forced to go to the counters of the two drugstores in town to fill their needs.

As late as July 9, Medical Inspector Vollum, no man to silently or inactively endure, said "the demand for stationery, disinfectants, iodine, tincture of iron, and some other articles was so great and immediate, that I purchased them in Gettysburg, and sent the bills to the quartermaster there for payment."[33]

The cost of the battle had been astronomical just in terms of ammunition expended and property destroyed; surely the government could afford to bear the cost of repairing the human damage. Of the exasperating wait for the army to organize an adequate stream of supplies to the scene, Cornelia Hancock could only observe, "Uncle Sam is very rich, but very slow."[34]

The volunteering surgeons arriving on the field found themselves with doctors who were at the brink of collapse. On July 6, three days after the fighting ended, Dr. John Shaw Billings, a brilliant young physician who had entered the army as one of those oft-ridiculed contract surgeons, was writing to his wife from the Fifth Corps hospital near Little Round Top: "I am utterly exhausted mentally and physically, having been operating night and day and am still hard at work. I have been left here in charge of 700 wounded with no supplies and have my hands full."[35]

Three days later, he wrote his spouse, there had been no letup. "I am covered with blood and am tired out almost completely, and can only say that I wish I was with you tonight and could lie down and sleep for sixteen hours without stopping. I have been operating all day long and have got the chief part of the butchering done in a satisfactory manner."[36]

Great things lay ahead for Dr. Billings professionally, including establishment of the renowned Johns Hopkins hospital in Baltimore, but at this point in time he was laboring under the most primitive conditions. After several days of crude battlefield surgery, he had to get an orderly to "scrub all the blood out of my hair with Castille soap and bay rum," later complaining, "my scalp feels as if a steam plow had been passed through it."[37]

Dr. Gordon Winslow was all over the field, and said of the pressures on the surgeons available:

> The work is unending, both by day and night, the anxiety is constant, the strain upon both the physical and mental faculties, unceasing. Thus, after this battle, operators had to be held up while performing the operations, and fainted from exhaustion, the operation finished. One completed his labor to be seized with partial paralysis, the penalty of his overexertion.[38]

A Christian Commission delegate put it this way: "To say in such a field that surgeons were busy is needless. . . . There was not more than one for ten that were needed."[39]

Under the circumstances, Dr. Bushrod Washington James, who had come from Philadelphia with a Christian Commission delegation laden with supplies, found his services "gladly accepted." He was placed in charge of a row of tents at a field hospital near Rock Creek, the occupants of which had all undergone amputations at the hip-joint or along the femur, but he also was called upon to perform operations. James had gone to the army after Antietam to assist, but was not braced for what he was encountering on this field.

> Every surgeon in the hospital was kept busy nearly a week amputating limbs, probing for and removing bullets or sewing, bandaging and dressing the wounds of those who were too badly mangled and shattered to be aided in a more hopeful manner.
>
> Over hours the improvised operating tables were full, and many of the poor fellows had to be operated upon while lying upon the damp ground. We could not help it. . . . Worse than that, my heart grew sick when I saw men, some officers among them, feverish or bleeding or weak almost to death because there were not then surgeons enough to operate on the vast multitude in time to save them all ere gangrene set in. . . .
>
> I have worked hard in my profession many a time, but the horror of that scene I can never forget. Nor the arduous labor of those days. It exceeded all I have been called upon to perform before or since that fearful time. We toiled nearly all day and night, snatching a few hours for rest only when we became too much exhausted to continue and began again, as soon as nature would permit us to feel equal to the necessity. . . . We were such a pitiable few among so many wounded!

Finally, James gave out and could work no longer.

> With the deepest regret I was compelled to leave the hospital in the woods and start for home, so weak that I could but crawl to an old hay wagon that was going to the town.

The farmer lifted in my valise, then he helped me up into the springless vehicle, and bolted, bruised and shaken up he conveyed me to the railroad station, and after a tedious railroad trip by way of Baltimore I was enabled to reach home, where I suffered both illness and weariness for weeks.[40]

The work of doctors like James, who came on the field and did as much as they could, helped ease the prejudices of some of the army medical personnel toward the civilian volunteers.

"As far as my observation extends," said Medical Inspector John M. Cuyler, who was a thirty-year Army veteran, "the medical officers of the army, and the citizen surgeons who were employed during the emergency, discharged their arduous duties with fidelity and ability. I never saw men work harder or complain less of the difficulties that surrounded them."[41]

But to others who had long been exposed to the manner of some of the so-called "contract surgeons" serving with the army, doctors who had been recommended by the Sanitary Commission and who came under the commission's control, this prejudice was only reinforced. To their detractors, the private physicians were a spoiled lot with little tolerance for personal discomfort and a distaste for sustained labor in the field. These regulars were tired of listening to the whining and complaining from demanding physicians accustomed to the pace of private practices.

While 30 volunteer surgeons offered their services to Dr. Dwinell at the Second Corps hospitals, he found "only four or five were really of much benefit."

"A number reported for duty and I never saw them afterwards," he said. "I have had them report to me at night stating that they would remain as long as their services were required. They would then stroll about the hospital a couple of hours, get their supper, lodging & Breakfast, and leave immediately after."

"Most of them did not choose to operate," Dwinell said, "Yet they would insist upon expending their time at the operating table. Not a few of them seemed to have a horror of dressing a stump."[42]

As might be expected, the volunteer surgeons didn't always hold a very high opinion of the regular surgeons either. When he heard of the situation at Gettysburg, Dr. Theodore Dimon, who had served in the army earlier in the war, telegraphed Surgeon General Hammond on July 8 to say that, "I would report to any Army medical officer for duty, without expense to the Government, if my services were needed." The very next day, he had a response from Washington telling him to report to Medical Inspector Cuyler as soon as possible. On his return to the field (after journeying from Auburn, New York, with money advanced to him by friends there) Dr. Dimon found "the volunteers to be the most busy and the regulars to have the most leisure as usual, and probably for the reason that very much of their business was attended to for them by others."[43]

Unfortunately, Medical Director Letterman seemed to count himself among the critics of the civilian doctors, asserting frankly that "the fact is so well known in this army that medical officers prefer to do the work rather than have them present." He even quoted Dr. Janes as telling him that the volunteer doctors coming to him "were of little use."[44]

It was a rather aloof attitude for a young man such as Janes, with his two years of military service, to adopt toward his medical associates. And more so for Letterman, whose absence, along with so much of the army's medical staff had, after all, created the desperate demand for whatever professional assistance could be speedily procured. On July 7 he had merely requested that Surgeon General Hammond send twenty more surgeons to Janes. He knew not whether they were ever sent and apparently was totally unaware of how inadequate such a meager reinforcement would have been.

Those caring women who started out for Gettysburg intending to nurse the wounded had to confront an obstacle as formidable as the provost marshal's road guards and the army surgeons' bias against civilian practitioners. That was the strategically positioned presence of Dorothea Lynde Dix. The women who made their way to the Baltimore railroad depot, the major terminus for moving on to Gettysburg, encountered the deceptively unimposing slight figure of Miss Dix, a soft-spoken woman of sixty-one with a chronic respiratory problem.

As superintendent of women nurses, Miss Dix had the power to rule on the acceptability of all applicants for service with the army. Regardless of experience or professional skill, anyone who desired to join the Bureau of Nursing had to pass her muster.

And Miss Dix—although not a nurse herself—had very much her own ideas of what sort of woman was suitable for field hospital duty. In fact, she plainly stated when she assumed her office in July 1861 (at that time, the highest executive position in the Federal government that a woman had ever held) her image of what an efficient army nurse should be, right down to the manner in which she must dress.

First of all, "no woman under 30 need apply to serve in government hospitals." Moreover, "all nurses are required to be plain-looking women" and "their dresses must be brown or black, with no bows, no frills, no jewelry, and no hoop skirts."[45]

Few other civilian officials could have gotten away with the sorts of demands she was arbitrarily imposing, but she was after all, Dorothea Dix, a woman of enormous reputation upon which she was ready to capitalize to the fullest. This was the driven woman who had succeeded in focusing international attention during the 1840s and 1850s on the horrible abuses being inflicted on the insane in asylums. She had, with cyclone force, whisked about the country demanding to inspect facilities for the mentally ill and, by carefully cultivating the press, had exposed conditions of neglect, cruelty, and needless suffering that brought the nation to tears and politicians scrambling to end the barbaric practices. Even Queen Victoria had appointed a Royal Commission to study treatment at asylums in England after Miss Dix visited and issued one of her uncompromising appraisals.

The drive that consumed Dorothea Dix had early become evident. So disgusted had she been with the atmosphere at her home in Hampden, Massachusetts, created by an uncaring mother and a father who was a religious fanatic that, at the age of ten, she insisted upon living with her grandparents in Boston. Only four years later, she began her teaching career at an academy there and, by her own admission, she "never knew childhood." She wrote books as frequently as others wrote letters. Her major social crusade began when she was in her late thirties and continued until the beginning of the Civil War. During one three-year period she calculated that she had traveled more than ten thousand miles inspecting institutions and chronicling the offenses she would bring before Congress and state legislative bodies. Her energy was boundless. What inspired her on her solitary mission? As Miss Dix—a person who it is difficult to imagine ever having been addressed as simply Dorothea—assessed herself: "I have no particular love for my species, but own to an exhaustless fund of compassion."[46]

When war came, she plunged into the conflict with her customary gusto. She rushed to Baltimore to treat the injured members of the 5th Massachusetts Regiment who had been attacked by pro-Secession Marylanders, then went immediately to Washington with her ideas for the creation of a corps of women nurses for the army.

Though the military initially demurred, Miss Dix carried her proposal to the White House, where she got a more receptive ear from the president's aides. In a matter of days, she had a commission from Sec. of War Simon Cameron that she might very well have worded herself, so total was its authority. As Superintendent of Women Nurses, Miss Dix was "to select and assign women nurses to general or permanent military hospitals, they not to be employed in such hospitals without her sanction and approval, except in cases of urgent need."[47]

While the significant words in the order would seem to have been "select and assign women nurses," Miss Dix apparently had no intention of stopping there, and soon began inspecting hospitals with the regularity that she had barged into mental institutions, questioning the staffs and generally becoming meddlesome. As one hospital director observed, "She has the rank, pay, honors, and emoluments of a major general of Volunteers and if you've got her down on you, you might as well have all hell after you."[48]

Probably, George Templeton Strong, the Sanitary Commission treasurer, was best able to identify the essential weakness that Miss Dix revealed in her new capacity when he wrote: "She is energetic, benevolent, unselfish, and a mild case of monomania. Working on her own hook, she does good, but no one can cooperate with her, for she belongs to the class of comets and can be subdued into relations with no system whatever."[49]

Mary Livermore, who was another mainstay of the Sanitary Commission, observed that, "unfortunately, many of the surgeons in the hospitals did not work harmoniously with Miss Dix. They were jealous of her power, impatient of her authority, condemned her nurses, and accused her of being arbitrary, opinionated, severe, and capricious."[50] Arbitrary? Curiously, another legendary figure, Louisa May Alcott, used the same word in describing Miss Dix, calling her "a kind old soul, but very queer and arbitrary."[51]

Sometimes the superintendent made herself look foolish when she ventured into areas that were really not her forte. Her notion that the troops would be made comfortable in the hot sun of the Southern states by wearing havelocks on the back of their caps set thousands of ladies stitching some 20,000 of these attachments to which, in fact, few soldiers would ever grow accustomed. She also designed, out of a woman's ignorance, a pattern for men's underdrawers that proved to be so ill-fitting and uncomfortable that they were rarely donned.

But it was perhaps Miss Dix's notions about what sort of woman could best serve the needs of the soldiers and meet the ugly and brutal demands of field hospital life that most undermined her popularity. "She personally examined the qualifications of every applicant," noted Mary Livermore. "Many of the women whom she rejected because they were too young and too beautiful entered the service under other auspices, and became eminently useful. Many women whom she accepted because they were sufficiently old and ugly proved unfit for the position, and a disgrace to their sex."[52]

One nursing applicant, in fact, had taken the tack of writing to Miss Dix that "I am plain enough to suit you and old enough. I have never had a husband and I am not looking for one. Will you take me?" She did.[53]

Cornelia Hancock was one of those who had encountered the superintendent at the Baltimore station and was rejected on the basis of her appearance but managed to get around her.

"She looked the nurses over and pronounced them all suitable except me," the New Jersey Quaker recalled. "She immediately objected to my going on the score of my youth and rosy cheeks. I was then just 23 years of age. In those days it was considered indecorous for angels of mercy to appear otherwise than gray-haired and spectacled."

Cornelia showed her determination, however, by refusing to give up her seat on the train and, when it finally reached Gettysburg, she found that "the need was so great that there was no further cavil about age."[54]

Another of Miss Dix's rejects was a lively young schoolteacher from Auburn, New York, Sophronia E. Bucklin. Though accepted for service at a hospital in Washington, Sophronia's frequent requests to go to the army were met by the superintendent with a firm, "No, you are too young for field duty." After news of the battle at Gettysburg came, however, Sophronia couldn't contain herself, and when a representative of the Sanitary Commission asked her to accompany him to Gettysburg to help distribute supplies, she immediately agreed. In twenty minutes they were on their way. At Baltimore, however, they encountered Miss Dix and she demanded to know why her orders were being disobeyed. But sensing Sophronia's fervor, the stern supervisor reneged and let her pass and, in fact, gave her a hospital assignment. Countless soldiers would benefit in the coming months from this rare relaxation of Miss Dix's standards.[55]

Dorothea Dix, the often-difficult superintendent of nurses. *Library of Congress.*

A Unitarian, Miss Dix exhibited another prejudice in her selection process: Only nurses who were Protestants were acceptable. At Gettysburg this bias was to cause no little friction, because the Sisters of Charity had established early on such an impressive and almost saintly presence. Quietly, but with great skill they directed countless volunteers from the town in the care of the wounded. They had done it in such an unobtrusive, seemingly subservient manner as to endear themselves to the surgeons in charge of the hospitals, who were becoming ever more annoyed with Miss Dix for not properly acknowledging the physicians' authority.

Thousands of patients and staff members were given glimpses of Miss Dix flying in and out of the Gettysburg hospitals on her inspection tours. They set the town abuzz with remarks such as, "Do you know who that was? Why, that was the celebrated Dorothea Dix!" But no one seemed to know just what exactly she was accomplishing. Her activity seemed to lack purpose and direction. While concentrating on the improvement of the plight of the mentally deranged, the conditions that appalled her were clearly defined; the solutions apparent. Transferring these energies to an administrative role in wartime appeared to be too much for her. The Superintendent of Nurses just didn't seem to know what she was about and sowed more confusion than order, while all the time insisting on proper respect for her governmentally decreed station. "A self-sealing can of horror tied up with red tape," is the way one journalist brutally described her.[56]

In the end, Dorothea Dix would herself become, in terms of public service, another casualty of the battle.

In disaster situations, those eager to help often attempt to do so in accordance with their own personal perception of what is needed, providing what items or services they, in their subjective judgment, have decided would be most appreciated by the victims. It is a natural response but one that invariably results in excesses and misunderstanding.

In this instance, an extraordinary number of clergymen became convinced that the greatest demand that existed at Gettysburg was for spiritual comfort, and they were determined to provide it, welcome or not.

Those associated with the Christian Commission who entered the hospitals with a Bible in one hand and a loaf of bread in the other were usually warmly received. But little patience or attention was extended, however, to the pious men of the cloth who cast their eyes upward to solicit mercy for the suffering soldiers, when, if they had lowered their gazes and regarded their newly chosen flocks more closely, they would have seen that the more immediate need was for something to drink or a retightening of a bandage on a wound that had reopened.

Decimus et Ultimus Barziza had, like many of the Southern wounded, been moved from a Union field hospital down to Pennsylvania College in town, the "Confederate Hospital." There he was particularly struck by a type of minister who came frequently visiting:

> New England preachers, indelibly and unmistakably stamped with the hypocritical sanctity of Puritanism, stalked back and forth, with long faces and sanctimonious pretensions; they would occasionally come into a room and after sighing, and wheezing, and sucking their breath, would condescendingly give a poor rebel a tract and a cracker.[57]

Even the Christian Commission had a few delegates, one civilian noted, who had been "failures in ministerial and other lines of work. Their intentions, doubtless, were all right," he acknowledged. "They lacked brains and plain horse-sense."[58]

The clergyman who indelibly impressed Lt. John Dooley as he lay with other Confederates in a Union Second Corps field hospital was one affiliated with the Sanitary Commission with a voice "ruined by a terrible twang of the nasal organs." The minister would come to their tent morning, midday, and night and each time "dropping on his knees elevates his voice in prayer to the most high clouds and prays alike for friends and enemies for the preservation of the Union and the success of its glorious arms."

One night he came rushing into their tent, half frantic, and cried out, "Glorious news, this evening, boys, glorious tidings of victory! General Lee and his whole army have been intercepted before reaching the Potomac and have been destroyed or taken prisoners." When questioned why he thought his listeners would rejoice at such a development, the preacher suddenly looked mortified and exclaimed, "Excuse me, boys, excuse me! Really I thought you were OUR boys, and rushed in without perceiving how you were dressed."[59]

In the view of Captain Nickerson of the 8th Ohio, the clergymen he observed could be divided into two classes: "those who depended upon prayer and works, and those who relied exclusively on prayer without works." To illustrate the latter, he remembered one portly man who "carried with him a large bible and a hymn book" but, he added, "I do not recall that he ever brought anything else, or even asked a patient to take a glass of water."

The first time he approached Nickerson, the captain recalled, "he asked me how I felt, and if I were prepared to die." Then the preacher began to bombard Nickerson with readings from his Bible, lengthy hymns delivered in a wheezy voice and a long prayer "in which advice to the Creator was the most prominent feature." This ritual was repeated daily at a time when the captain was finding "every breath I drew was like the thrust of a dozen daggers." Finally, the surgeons took notice of what was going on and forbade the minister from entering the tent again.

In striking contrast, Nickerson recalled a minister from Maine who wore neither a round collar nor carried the Bible, but "never came into my tent that he did not do something for my comfort." He remembered particularly how the man had walked some ten miles to procure some potatoes for the captain, the only food he could, in his condition, bring himself to eat.

It was only at the officer's personal request for a prayer that the clergyman laid aside his hat and knelt by his bunk.

> He was still without his coat, his sleeves were rolled up, and his hands were grimy with the ashes from his potato roast. His throat was bare of necktie, the collar thrown wide open, and great beads of perspiration stood on his broad forehead; but what a prayer! Like his works, it was fervid, earnest and apropos. Nothing seemed to have been forgotten, and yet it appeared to be such a short prayer.[60]

In too many instances, the clergymen had to fill the role of the missing surgeon, offering the hope that medicine, in the crude way it was then being practiced in the interest of time and circumstances, could not. But to the observer, it became a question of whose needs were being served—the ministers' or those for whom they were supposedly interceding.

Transportation was the key to bringing the situation at Gettysburg under control. Herman Haupt's construction crew, after having seen its first attempt to replace the burnt railroad bridge at the edge of town literally washed away by the flooding of Rock Creek, finally succeeded in replacing the span on July 10. The next day, for the first time, cars proceeded directly to the Gettysburg railroad depot. It was an ornate structure designed in the style of an Italian villa and built in 1858 only a few hundred feet from the diamond.

By that date, Lieutenant Colonel Vollum, that very active medical inspector managing transportation for the wounded, had been able to move some 4,000 Union soldiers out of the area from the makeshift terminal outside of town. About as many more had boarded trains at Westminster and Littlestown after either being transported to those points by one of the few ambulances available, or by finding their own way. There were still more than 10,000 wounded on the scene. But now, with better access to the trains for unloading and disbursing incoming supplies, and for boarding the wounded, many of whom were on litters, the pace of evacuation began to accelerate.

The day that service from the town center was resumed, the first Confederate wounded were sent off. A band of 76 men headed for Baltimore and, ultimately, Point Lookout, the prisoner of war hospital/stockade situated where the Potomac enters the Chesapeake Bay. A larger bunch, 327 men, was shipped out the next day. About this time the general commanding the Middle Department in which the camp was located was being informed that he might soon have a problem on his hands because there were only 1,400 hospital beds there.[61]

That commander was Maj. Gen. Robert C. Schenck, a political general from Ohio who had been disabled for further field service by an arm wound sustained at Second Manassas. Few harbored the level of personal hostility toward the enemy that this former Congressman nurtured, an anger displayed at every opportunity. His reaction to the advisory that he had received was to notify Washington "that it might be best to send the rebels as far as practicable to hospitals north of this point, unless it is thought that Northern copperheads will sympathize with and pet them too much."

Another reason for dispersing the horde of prisoners being sent his way was "that rebel officers have a bad influence on their men, many of the latter of whom are penitent when they are permitted to be, and they ought therefore to be separated both in prisons and hospitals."[62]

Situated as he was in the center of a region heavily populated with Southern sympathizers, Schenck served notice that he was going to tolerate no subversive activity at the prisoner of war facilities under his authority. He issued an order stating that "no person not thoroughly loyal will be permitted under any circumstances, to visit or have access to any military hospital."

Schenck proclaimed:

> If any person or persons within this department be found harboring, entertaining or concealing any rebel officer or soldier in his or her home, or in his or her premises, or in any place after twenty-four hours from the publication of this order, the person so offending will be at once sent beyond the Union lines into the rebel States, or otherwise punished, at the discretion of the military authority.[63]

The effect of the department commander's attitude toward the Confederate prisoners became evident to Lt. John Dooley of Virginia when he arrived in Baltimore on July 12, his twenty-first birthday. He observed "a rampart of bayonets excluding all assistance which comes not stamped with loyal brand and under loyal approbation."[64]

The wounded Texan Barziza was another one of those moved to Baltimore, though he had hardly recovered enough to make such a rough trip. "We were in a sorry plight," he said of his arrival there.

> Our wounds had not been dressed for forty-eight hours; our clothes had never been changed since the battle—thus, bloody, dirty, ragged, bare-footed, bare-headed, and crippled, we marched through the streets of the monumental city, a spectacle of fiendish delight to some, but one of pity and sympathy to thousands of true subjugated Southerners, who inhabit this city.
>
> If a little girl dared wave her handkerchief at the Confederates, she was arrested or maltreated by the armed minions of despotism. Ladies, with baskets of provisions, followed tremblingly on the side-walks, and would be shaked roughly by the arm and insulted, if they approached us. Sympathy and pity shone upon the features of hundreds; and the sly look and

troubled countenance showed plainly how they had been taught
to fear the arms of their own Government. Baltimore is literally
crushed and broken by high handed tyranny; the petty, ill-bred
plebeians with the shoulder-straps on, actually lord it over those
unfortunate people, with all the mean oppression which characterized men of low estates who have been suddenly elevated to
power.[65]

If Schenck was included in the reference, what had been experienced
thus far was only the beginning of what the Confederates could expect now
that the residue of the battle was surfacing in the testy general's relatively
inactive sector of responsibility.

The very fact that Rebel prisoners were being moved from the hospitals at Gettysburg into Schenck's domain was a reflection of the dramatically improved railroad situation. While enough of a schedule was being
maintained that the newspapers felt confident enough to publish a
timetable of arrivals and departures, the problem of getting the wounded to
the depot lingered.

Surgeon General Hammond paid a brief personal visit to the scene and
had some grasp of what Dr. Janes was confronting. He helped a bit by
dispatching fifty additional ambulances to Gettysburg from Washington
(though they were painfully slow getting there). Considering the fact, however, that the Army of the Potomac had a total of a thousand or more ambulances with it that were currently idle (the Second Corps alone operating
with 120 ambulances), the reinforcement sent to Janes seemed rather
trivial. Still, it represented nearly double the number of conveyances with
which he had been forced to function, as cruelly absurd as was that
demand.

It is noteworthy that whatever the Army of the Potomac had taken with
it, whether or not put to use, was never sent back to Gettysburg to relieve
the situation. That is, neither personnel nor transportation and supplies
were returned. Meade's involvement with Gettysburg had been forever terminated. In his view, whatever needed to be done there would have to be
the responsibility of some other government department.

In addition to the new fleet of ambulances en route from Washington,
some unexpected help came from the Adams Express Company in Baltimore, a firm that maintained a freight office next to the depot in Gettysburg.

William Hammond, surgeon general of the Army. *Library of Congress.*

Its superintendent, S. S. Shoemaker, had wired War Secretary Stanton that "the God of Battles having so far given us the victory, our next care is for the wounded. This company proposes to get up a hospital corps of their own—sending men, food, suitable comforts, etc. to the front, with a number of spring wagons to bring in the wounded . . ."[66]

The proposal was "heartily approved" by the secretary, who told Shoemaker, "I give you herewith a pass through the lines for your agents and employees." When the Baltimore fire company also offered the use of its emergency vehicles, that offer of assistance from an organization thought by some to have Secesh leanings, was also quickly accepted, so great was the army's need for transportation of any sort.[67]

The reopening of service from the rail depot did not alleviate the need for the Sanitary Commission's feeding station; it only changed the location where the facility would be required. There were still thousands of soldiers being forced to wait long hours for the trains that were now supposed to depart at 9 A.M. and 3 P.M. daily. Those who couldn't get aboard the late train and were forced to remain overnight still had to be sheltered. The commission simply struck its tents outside of town, carried them to the depot, and pitched them anew.

Georgy Woolsey and her mother were still an integral part of the relief effort, much to the continued surprise of the other Woolsey girls at home. "Just imagine Mother in a straw hat and heavy Gettysburg boots, standing cooking soup for 200 men at a time, and distributing it in tin cups; or giving clean shirts to ragged rebels; or sitting on a pile of grocer's boxes, under the shadow of a string of codfish, scribbling her notes to us," one of the cultivated woman's daughters observed in wonderment.[68]

Georgy provided a graphic description of the atmosphere and routine they found themselves absorbed in at the new location:

> On the day that the railroad bridge was repaired we moved up to the depot, close by the town, and had things in perfect order; a first-rate camping ground, in a large field directly by the track, with unlimited supply of delicious, cool water. Here we set up two stoves, with four large boilers, always kept full of soup and coffee, watched by four or five black men, who did the cooking under our direction, and sang (not under our direction) at the tops of their voices all day.

Then we had three large hospital tents, holding about 35 each, a large camp-meeting supply tent, where barrels of goods were stored, and our own smaller tent fitted up with tables, where jelly pots and bottles of all kinds of good sirrups, blackberry and black current, stood in rows. Barrels were ranged round the tent walls; shirts, drawers, dressing gowns, socks, and slippers (I wish we had more of the latter), rags and bandages, each in its own place on one side; on the other, boxes of tea, coffee, soft crackers, tamarinds, cherry brandy, etc. Over the kitchen, and over this small supply tent, we woman rather reigned, and filled up our wants by requisitions on the Commission's depot. By this time, there had arrived a 'delegation' of just the right kind from Canandaigua, New York, with surgeon dressers and attendants, bringing a first-rate supply of necessaries and comforts for the wounded, which they handed over to the Commission.

Twice a day the trains left for Baltimore or Harrisburg, and twice a day we fed all the wounded who arrived for them. Things were systemized now, and the men came down in long ambulance trains to the cars. Baggage cars they were, fitted with straw for the wounded to lie on, and broken open at either end to let in the air. A government surgeon was always present to attend to the careful lifting of the soldiers from ambulance to car. Many of the men would get along very nicely, holding one foot up, and taking great jumps on their crutches.

Once the soldiers were on the trains and made as comfortable as possible, Georgy and the other volunteers would go from car to car, with soup made of beefstock or fresh meat, full of potatoes, turnips, cabbage, and rice, with fresh bread and coffee and, "when stimulants were needed, with ale, milk punch, or brandy. . . . All our whiskey and brandy bottles were washed and filled up at the spring, and the boys went off, carefully hugging their extemporized canteens, from which they would wet their wounds, or refresh themselves, till the journey ended."

Georgy particularly recalled one Confederate soldier asking her, "Have you friends in the army, madam?" as she gave him some milk while he was lying on the floor of a car.

"Yes, my brother is on Meade's staff," she responded.

"I thought so, ma'am. You can always tell; when people are good to soldiers they are sure to have friends in the army."[69]

She, too, was rather amazed at her mother's performance in this, her first exposure to war.

> Mother put great spirit into it all, listened to all their stories, petted them, fed them, and distributed clothes, including hand-kerchiefs with cologne, and got herself called 'Mother, this way, mother,' 'Here's the bucket, mother' and 'Isn't she a glorious old woman?' while the most that I ever heard was, 'She knows how; why, it would have taken our steward two hours to get round, but then she's used to it, you see' which, when you consider that I was distributing hot grog and must have been taken for a barmaid, was not so complimentary!"[70]

Not to be outdone, the Christian Commission also set up its feeding station near the depot and, in direct response to a request from Medical Inspector Vollum, opened another at Hanover Junction in order that the wounded aboard the trains might be given some more nourishment while en route to Baltimore or Harrisburg. Said one delegate of the activity at the usually deserted junction, "here many thousands of soldiers were fed, the trains being halted for this purpose; every man received suitable food and drink."[71]

July 11, the day that full train service was restored, by no means marked the end of the crisis at Gettysburg. But, from that date on, the situation no longer seemed quite so hopeless. Residents felt reconnected with the outside world and were no longer alone in their struggle to deal with the effects of the battle. They could actually hear the familiar rumbling and whistles of the trains that reminded them that they were part of a larger civilization. The exhausted medical staff and volunteers striving to assist them could sense that there was now at least a means of getting the exposed, bedless wounded to someplace where they stood a better chance at survival. If only they could hold on a bit longer until their turn for removal finally came.

A Second Invasion

As soon as Gettysburg could be reached by train, another invasion force descended: an assortment of visitors from many states with widely different motives and interests.

There were those who came to help and those coming to search: wives, mothers, and fathers not knowing for certain if their wounded loved one was still alive or where he might be located among the scores of hospitals on the vast field.

There were those who came to profit, including many morticians ready to offer their assistance in exhuming bodies and embalming them for shipment back to the places from which the fallen soldiers had originally come.

Then there were the relic hunters, seeking not just personal mementos but quantities of bullets, bayonets, and other items that could be hawked on city streets as being from the great battle. Also arriving were newspaper correspondents, each usually with several publications to satisfy.

Perhaps most nettlesome to those scurrying frantically to see to the wounded and dispose of the dead, were the merely curious. They came in legions in Sunday finery just to gawk and stare, gasp and exclaim at the ghastly sights afforded by an actual battlefield, but had no inclination to assist in any way.

The townspeople struggled to accommodate the multitude that eventually swelled the population to five times its normal size. Sally Broadhead, whose husband was an engineer on the railroad (no doubt back to work now), recorded that in her small row house on Chambersburg Street, "twenty are with us tonight, filling every bed and covering the floors." She told of one man who came to the door who "had sat on a chair in front of a hotel last night, and was glad to get even such quarters."[1]

Young Leander Warren remembered how, with the five small hotels in town soon filled, "many of the people had to walk the streets all night because they could not find a place to stay."[2]

A *New York Times* correspondent wrote on July 9, even before the major influx began, that "there are no accommodations or food here for visitors and last night many were compelled to roost in the barns, or upon the steps of dwellings."[3]

A reporter for the *Philadelphia Public Ledger* included in his July 15 dispatch a helpful appeal to his readers to stay away from Gettysburg because the town could not handle any more curious visitors.

> Let no one come to this place for the simple purpose of seeing. To come here, merely to look at the wounded and dying, exhibits a most vitiated and disgusting taste. Besides, every such visitor is a consumer, and adds to the misery of the sick, by subtracting from the means that should be given exclusively to them. Let all that come, come with stores for the sick, and ready to work for them, but let all mere sightseers stay at home.[4]

It was one of the few dispatches sent from the scene that the townspeople could regard as in any way sympathetic of their plight or beneficial to their situation.

Those disembarking from the trains who did somehow manage to find places to stay (no matter with how many others they had to share their rooms) generally discovered that, unlike the attitude displayed by the avaricious farmers in the region, the women in town were stubbornly unwilling to accept from them any payment whatsoever for either the use of their beds and sofas or for the food and drink they provided.

Georgy Woolsey and her mother vividly recalled how "the Gettysburg women were kind and faithful to the wounded and their friends, and the town was full to overflowing of both." They themselves had, she said, "literally begged our bread from door to door" when they first arrived in town and when they offered to pay the first lady who was able to give them something to eat, the response was, "No ma'am, I shouldn't wish to have that sin on my soul when the war is over." The same woman gave up her own bed to a stranger and spent the night on the floor because, as she simply explained, the caller was "an old lady, you know, and I couldn't let an old lady sleep on the floor."[5]

Fannie Buehler, with six children of her own to care for and her postmaster husband David away, took several wounded into her home, including Col. John C. Callis, an officer with a bullet in the lung, though it meant exposing her children to the frightful sight of his frequent hemorrhaging. After awhile Mrs. Callis came from Wisconsin to help nurse the colonel. "We gave his wife the freedom of the house, and did all we could to make her and her husband comfortable, free of all expense," said Mrs. Buehler. "Indeed, we charged no one for anything they ate or drank, or for any service rendered during this fearful summer."[6]

One advantage she did have was that all persons who had wounded men in their homes could procure an order from the Sanitary Commission for as much fresh meat as they required, paying for it if they were able to do so. "This was perfectly right, and we had all that we needed," Mrs. Buehler said.[7]

Just finding something to eat in the strained community was, for many of the civilians who arrived, as difficult as locating a place to sleep. Said Dr. Dimon, the volunteer surgeon from distant Auburn, New York, after a futile search, "nothing to eat was purchasable in the town."[8]

The group of Patriot Daughters of Lancaster, trying to set up their aid station and awaiting the arrival of their own supplies, discovered "even a cup of tea and a few boiled eggs are unattainable, with no fire or stove on which to cook them."[9]

While all too willing to extend themselves for the wounded and their kin, the townspeople had little patience for the idle visitors. Of the prevailing attitude, Mrs. Mary Horner, the wife of a local physician, said:

> If there has been complaint of lack of hospitality on our part, surely no soldier clad in gray or blue can ever say he suffered and we succored him not. If such a complaint has been made by the curiosity-seekers who flocked here after the battle, we must confess we did nothing for their comfort because we could not.[10]

Despite his painful wounds, Col. Robert M. Powell of the 5th Texas Infantry, lying in an open tent at a Union field hospital not far from Little Round Top, took a rather bemused attitude toward the "vast concourse of sightseers, whole families with the baby" he could observe traipsing about.

"The big show was gone, but they seemed content to look over the ground where it had been. A torn and bloody garment would attract a crowd, which would disperse only to concentrate again to look at a hat perforated by bullets. . . . The habiliments of the men and variegated plumage of the women made an interesting scene." But what most struck the Rebel prisoner was that all seemed "animated only by idle curiosity, seeming without thought or care for the hundreds of suffering men lying so near them without notice or sympathy."[11]

For those under the stress and anxiety of having dear ones among the wounded, arriving at the site was traumatic and in no way reassuring. Their first exposure to the terrible odor that hung over the place, a condition to which the residents were adapting somewhat, was in itself overwhelming.

"Possibly they came here wearied from travel and exposure to heat and were the more susceptible to the poison that lurked in every breath of air," said Mrs. Horner, but the newly arrived seemed to be sickened more by the awful smells of decay.[12]

Then there was the task of negotiating the noisy, jostling confusion of the depot where hundreds of wounded scrambled to come aboard the trains that the newly-arrived had just vacated. Scores of supply wagons and nervous teams congested the area. Nearby was the strange sight of a great mound of rusting muskets that had been accumulated—weapons that might have been used by or against those the relatives sought.

Once clear of the bedlam, the visitors began the frustrating search for some place to stay, to just set down their carpetbags for a time and recover from their journey. Still confronting them was the difficulty of ascertaining from some authority where the wounded of a particular unit might be gathered. Even when that was determined, they had still to find the way to that location through the complex road network that radiated from the square. They traveled alone and on foot, for they quickly learned there was no hope of finding army or other transportation.

In such a state of physical and emotional exhaustion did the visitors usually arrive at the dreadful field hospitals that Cornelia Hancock, by now feeling much aged and thoroughly disheveled—her clothes but a clinging mass of stained, rent fabric—found dealing with them one of the more heart-wrenching aspects of her work at the Second Corps hospitals. "The most painful task we have to perform here is entertaining the friends who come from home and see their friends all mangled up," the Quaker volunteer wrote home. "I do hate to see them. Soldiers take everything as it comes, but citizens are not inured." Immediately after having said that, however, Cornelia became conscious of the impression she was leaving on her family in New Jersey, and added "You will think it is a short time for me to get used to things, but it seems to me as if all my past life was a myth, and as if I had been away from home seventeen years."[13]

The civilian population's response to the situation at Gettysburg, if notable for its volume and range, was still not unlike the sort of reaction that occurs in most communities when news comes of a flood or a hurricane that has left large numbers of people in need.

What made the convergence on Gettysburg singular was that never before had Northern women left their homes in such numbers to go to a battlefield to personally seek out and attend to their wounded men.

Until then, almost all the battles in the east had been fought in distant Virginia and the kin of those who fell there, if still alive, were forced to wait until they were brought back to one of the vast army hospitals at places like Washington and Philadelphia before they could even visit them.

But Pennsylvania was Union soil and the battlesite was relatively accessible. If the reports were true that the wounded there were far too numerous for the government to tend, many wives and mothers who had learned their husbands and sons were among the casualties were simply unwilling to let them be neglected.

So many came that every ward was dotted with the forms of anxious exhausted ladies in travel-worn clothes who never left the bedsides of their men, save to steal away for a few hours late at night, make their way into town in the darkness, and try to get a few hours sleep in one of the residences crowded with visitors like themselves.

It was they who bathed their bedridden men, fanned away the tormenting flies, cut their matted hair and tried to rid them of lice, prepared favorite dishes for them, changed their bandages as gently as they could and provided "those peculiar attentions which none but a wife, mother or sister could with propriety give," and, at the same time, endured the cries and groans of the other patients in their tents.

All too often, the women were there holding firmly yet tenderly their loved one's hands as surgeons probed for shrapnel or resutured a wound that had opened. As the men healed, it was their womenfolk who gave them strength as the soldiers attempted to get back on their feet and the women who helped them adapt to the crutches that would be with them for the rest of their lives. If the soldier succumbed to his wounds, it was the wife or mother who served as the lonely escort who brought the body home for burial.

For the nurses, dealing with the relatives of the patients was one of the most distressing aspects of their work. None touched Sophronia Bucklin more deeply than the wife who, "clasping to her bosom a little child of eighteen months, sat for hours with bowed head, leaning over the prostrate form of her husband, whose frightful wound (he was gut shot) made it necessary to keep him stupefied with morphine, so that his unearthly groans should not keep the whole tent in undue excitement."

She continued:

> He lay in this unconscious stupor, and the stricken wife waited in vain for some signs of recognition. A human heart lay in the bosom of our surgeon, and he allowed the drug to exhaust itself, and the consciousness to return, that he might recognize his wife and child before he died.
>
> Slowly it passed away, and his mangled body was racked with intensest suffering. He lay on his face, with his eyes turned toward her, that when his senses revived, she might be the first to meet his gaze. After a while he looked up—the wild glare of pain in his eyes—and said as he saw whose face bent toward him, 'Oh! Mary, are you here?' His groans were terrible to hear, and in mercy he was again given the opiate, and slept his life out. . . .
>
> How our hearts were pained for that wife, sitting motionless beside the body, holding in her lap the little boy who was so soon to be fatherless, tearless in her great agony, stricken as by the withering stroke of palsy—yet breathing and living.[14]

As grateful as the men might have been to see their women arrive at their sides (or disconcerted that they were being exposed to sights they fervently wished they might be spared), few had ever expected to see them appear at a place so strange to both. So much of the dread of falling wounded on any field was the sense of desertion that accompanied the occurrence, the feeling of being left totally alone by the unit to which one felt so much a part and being deposited among indifferent strangers. But this time things were different. Not the way it was to have been struck down at Fair Oaks, Chancellorsville, or some other place deep in Rebel country. It was different as well for the families for whom, as distressing as it was to see their menfolk suffering under such horrible conditions, there was a sense that they could at least do something to make the soldiers more comfortable and were not being left behind idle and useless.

Until now, the war, for the North, had seemed far away, so geographically remote. This dreadful battle had brought it home and Northern women, for the first time (except for the campaign in divided Maryland the year before), had an opportunity to provide the kind of care and attention only someone close to the injured could.

Whether it was simply a natural desire to have their dear ones interred close to home or a revulsion to leaving their bodies under the crudely marked mounds erupting haphazardly all about the field, many of the visitors were determined to take their dead away from this horrible battleground—at any cost.

In many cases, the soldier had died in a hospital while the relative was at hand to make immediate arrangements for his removal by train. However, when the family already knew that someone had been killed and was coming simply to retrieve the body, the remains had to be located and exhumed. Some of the graves were carefully identified, but so many of the fallen were so badly disfigured that no positive identification could be made by the burial parties. In those instances, numerous graves in the vicinity of where a particular unit was known to have fought were opened in search of some physical clue a family member might be able to provide about the person being sought.

After an extensive search, the wife of Cpl. William Strong of the 2nd Delaware took out an advertisement in the *Compiler* on July 27, stating that she had been hunting his body for the past week and asked that anyone who might know of its location please contact her. Another couple brought home what they thought was the body of their son for reburial only to discover that he had not been killed after all and the remains deposited in the local cemetery were those of someone else, once more unidentified.

The smell of the battlefield that was so obnoxious to the uninitiated became the scent of commercial opportunity to scores of undertakers, who packed their embalming instruments and fluids and followed it to the scene. They set up for business near the field hospitals, where they could be readily noticed by relatives as soon as their services might be required. Often, a plank resting on a pair of barrels in back of a tent was the only identification of the establishment. Other practitioners, however, put on more professional airs. One paid for an advertisement in a local newspaper to tell potential customers about "metallic coffins for transportation of bodies to any part of the country." The boxes were "warranted air-tight" and "can be placed in the Parlor without fear of any odor escaping therefrom."[15]

Young Albertus McCreary remembered "a man came to the town with patent coffins, and many a poor fellow took his last journey in one of them. The lid had a box in which ice was placed, thus making it possible to take bodies any distance."[16]

"Since the battle, Gettysburg has been an extensive coffin mart & embalmer's harvest field," Pvt. Justus M. Silliman of the 17th Connecticut observed. "The coffins were stacked on the streets blockading the side walks. These coffin speculators made an enormous profit."[17]

Henry Garlock was a Gettysburg carpenter who made coffins in a shop on Baltimore Street, and watching him at work was no doubt a disconcerting sight for the wounded soldiers placed in his house. "As can be readily imagined," one officer observed, Garlock had "all the business that he could attend to."[18]

How many coffins were being sold? The *Adams Sentinel* reported on July 21:

> We learn from one of our undertakers in town, that the number of coffins manufactured here for the transportation of the dead soldiers home by their friends amounts probably to 600 or 700 already and we presume this mournful business will be kept up for some time yet. The town is full of inquiring relatives for those near and dear to them.[19]

As rapidly as they were being produced, William C. Way of the 24th Michigan noted woefully: "Many are dying, and it is almost impossible to get a coffin for their remains, so great is the demand for them."[20]

Sanitary Commission Secretary Olmsted observed on his visit that "a great business is being done in disinterring bodies for embalming and shipment North. There are half a dozen fit embalmers competing for it. The Governor of Pennsylvania I believe pays for the removal of all Pennsylvania dead to their friends."[21]

To Daniel A. Skelly, "the scenes on the streets near the improvised hospitals where the relatives were having their loved ones prepared for shipment by the large number of undertakers who had come into Gettysburg for the purpose were indeed distressing."[22]

Over at the Globe Hotel, John C. Wills could see that "a number of our citizens made quite a good thing out of this gruesome business of taking up the dead for those people and assisting them in preparing them for shipment to their homes." The hotel got its share of the income because, said Wills, "men who were engaged in this work bought whiskies in large quantities . . ."[23]

After a few weeks, however, this booming business was suddenly deflated by an order from the provost marshal to cease the opening of graves until colder weather arrived. Conditions were unpleasant enough during the summer heat without adding to it through mass exhumations. Those embalmers who decided to stay on in the town would simply have to content themselves with the volume of bodies being provided by the hospitals on a daily basis, which was enough to keep a good many busy.

Dr. Janes, in making one of his regular accountings to his superior, Jonathan Letterman, reported on July 14—eleven days after the battle—that 5,800 Union and 1,500 Confederate wounded had been sent away from Gettysburg by rail, and about 4,000 more had departed from the depots at Littlestown and Westminster. "I think about 3,000 Union and 6,000 Confederates remain," he said, adding: "Probably 3,000 cannot be moved."[24]

Acknowledging that the Rebel cases were generally the more serious, the number still indicated that there was a point at which the equal treatment of friend and foe terminated at Gettysburg, and that was in order of evacuation.

Only one in five of the Confederate wounded had thus far been fortunate enough to reach a regular hospital for treatment, whereas only a small fraction of the Union casualties remained at the makeshift field hospitals.

Regardless of the mix, Letterman might well have been impressed with the rate at which Janes and his limited staff were managing to dispose of the great multitude of wounded on their hands.

As for help from Washington, Janes could cite little, even at this late date. Inspector Cuyler had appealed to his own Surgeon General's office for more ambulances and on July 13 was assured that a number had been sent. "I will try to ascertain where they are delayed," one of Hammond's aides promised him.[25]

As late as July 15, the reinforcement of twenty surgeons Letterman had asked for apparently still had not arrived, because on that date, the superintendent of hospitals in Philadelphia was being told bluntly by acting surgeon General Smith: "You will inform this office whether you have sent the twenty Medical Officers to Gettysburg as directed by telegram."[26]

How like the army, some might grouse, that some fifty surgeons not immediately required could have been rushed to Letterman in less than forty-eight hours while Janes, working his staff to the point of collapse, was still waiting for a contingent less than half as large.

Secretary of War Stanton was sufficiently concerned about the state of the Medical Department that he took the extraordinary step of directing Surgeon General Hammond to make a personal inspection and report back to him. Hammond—not Stanton's choice for the position he held—spent five days in the field and then advised the secretary that "at Gettysburg there was considerable suffering which under the circumstances was unavoidable." Just as had Letterman, Hammond blamed the trouble mainly on the medical supply trains being held back by Meade.

"Consequently, for several days after the battle the wounded had no medical supplies other than the comparatively small quantities contained in the Hospital knapsacks and ambulances."

He also reported (grossly inaccurately) "the rebel wounded which fell into our hands to the number of about 11,000 were left by the rebel commanders with scarcely any supplies and with an insufficient number of Surgeons."

Bringing up the old grievance about the cutback of medical transportation his department had sustained, Hammond reminded Stanton that "previous to leaving Falmouth the General Commander of the Army of the Potomac [Hooker] in opposition to the wishes of the Medical Department reduced the medical transportation of each regiment one half," adding

"I cannot but attribute a considerable amount of the suffering at Gettysburg to this cause."

Admitting to his own department's woeful inadequacy, Hammond took pains to point out to Stanton that "the Sanitary and Christian Commissions, the Adams Express Co. and numerous benevolent individuals rendered incalculable service in transporting supplies to the battlefield and in giving their personal aid to the Medical Director."

Hammond did leave Stanton somewhat relieved by asserting that "medical men and supplies to a large extent were pushed forward as soon as the [rail] road was open and the wounded were and are now being transferred to comfortable hospitals at the rate of 1,000 per day." It is noteworthy that in referring to "medical men," the surgeon general made no distinction between army and civilian doctors.[27]

While the situation now appeared under control, Hammond's dispatch could only have confirmed for Stanton the truth of all he had heard about conditions at Gettysburg, and he could only speculate on the degree to which, with better management, the dreadful experience could have been averted.

Captain Henry B. Blood of the Quartermaster Department in Washington, and Captain William W. Smith of General in Chief Henry Halleck's staff arrived in Gettysburg July 7 in response to an order from General Meigs "to collect all property left by both armies in the vicinity." They soon found they had a two-fold task on their hands.[28]

The officers had to arrange to gather up the debris that remained scattered about, and send to the Army of the Potomac all the equipment, horses, wagons, and other property that was still serviceable. They had also to locate and recover the enormous amount of property that had already been taken away by local residents and prevent any further looting by the throngs of arriving visitors.

The energetic pair attacked these responsibilities with a vengeance. Captain Smith, a relative of General Halleck, also had to see to the burial of the last of the Confederate dead. Though Provost Marshal Patrick had, before leaving, contracted out that responsibility, it was apparent that if the job was going to get done, additional government help would have to be provided to ensure the necessary manpower and transportation. Just as the medical department was in the embarrassing position of having to go to local pharmacies to purchase medicine to treat the wounded, the quarter-master branch had to advertise in the newspapers for basic transportation and laborers.

To some degree Captain Smith addressed his manpower problem by putting to work on burial details anyone discovered taking a gun or any other piece of government property from the battlefield. At times, Confederate prisoners doing the work were allowed to hand over their shovels to the civilian pilferers and observe their penance. Watching one squad of purloiners being marched out to bury dead horses, a Union officer noticed that it included "a loquacious gentleman, of portly presence, who had been caught with a U.S. musket, as a battle trophy, in his hands. Deep was his wrath and eloquent his protest and fierce his threats at sending him, 'a gentleman and a member of the legislature of this state,' to do such disgusting work," said the amused witness. "He promised to have all concerned in issuing the orders dismissed, but he had to make the march all the same and at least go through the formality of 'burying dead horses.'"[29]

Captain Blood offered an alternative to grave-digging to some looters he caught: "If they had a team, we made them haul a load of arms to town," he said.[30]

His first night in town, Captain Smith had gotten an idea of what he was up against when he encountered seventy-six wagons leaving the battle area. When he examined thirty of them he discovered every one contained government property.

By his estimate, "three to five thousand persons visited the battlefield daily, most of them carrying away trophies." With the 100 cavalrymen assigned to him, as the post commander, Smith felt he "could not disarm and unload one-tenth the persons carrying off arms."[31] The captain used the newspapers again to warn citizens against making off with government property, and demanded the return of any already in their possession. One farmer was sufficiently alarmed by the notice that he gave up a cache that included ten muskets, a sabre, two cartridge boxes, fifteen blankets, fifteen tent sections, twenty-five knapsacks, some clothing, and a horse.

By July 16, public appeals were exhausted, and Smith was ready to launch a systematic search of the area with the aid of two companies of the newly-formed 21st Pennsylvania Cavalry. The men were instructed to "examine thoroughly all houses and barns in the county always asking one member of the family to accompany [you] . . . through the house and in no instance shall more than two men enter the same house, no private property to be unnecessarily disturbed."[32]

The canvass produced bountiful results, with blankets and weapons being uncovered by the wagonload over a fifteen-mile radius. A six-pound gun was found lowered into a well. One day, accompanied by only two cavalrymen, Smith went on a tour of farms in the area, stopping at twelve, and in every one found hidden government property ranging from saddles to shovels. At each stop, he ordered the farmer to harness a team and load it up with the stolen property that had been uncovered and follow Smith on his rounds. By the time the day was over, Smith observed as he started back to town that he was at the head of a wagon train.

Not unexpectedly, those people whose treasures were being confiscated took a sour view of the soldiers who came calling, and Smith's cavalry "had become so unpopular with the countryside folks that they were being universally designated the Forty Thieves," wrote one resident. A local politician would claim of the confiscation activities of Smith and the men with him that they "have become a perfect terror to our quiet farmers and are more dreaded than the Rebels. Our people have been outraged to such an extent by them that the cause of the Government has greatly suffered."[33]

Sometimes Smith's men encountered "parties who positively refuse to give up the property." In two instances, he said, "persons have drawn revolvers to frighten us away. In both instances, we got a wagon load of property. I am not very careful how I treat such parties."[34]

Captain Blood was also active in the recovery operation and was labeled by Nathaniel Lightner, a carpenter-farmer, as "the meanest man in the world" for arresting him when he discovered that Lightner had sold "two or three dollars worth of things." Some children had gathered on the battlefield "bullets, buckles, canteens and the like," which Lightner sold to a man from New York who had come specifically to buy relics of the battle.[35]

Leander H. Warren, just fifteen at the time, would remember that "there was a man named Captain Blood who came around and collected all blankets and tents. The women washed them, expecting to use them, but he took them to New York and sold them."[36] Though no doubt utterly false, that such accusations were even being made was an indication of the level of disdain in which Blood and Smith were regarded.

A big step in putting a stop to the grand-scale looting came with the cavalry's routing of the Spring Forge band of scavengers. A squad of horsemen caught up with a caravan of the looters as it was headed back to York and "the dose the rag gatherers received was an ample sufficiency to give them the shivers from all future life at the barest glimpse of a blue uniform," one resident in the area noted.

> Their plunder was confiscated, their teams and they themselves put to work. The work they did was hard work; it was menial and repulsive work; but there were glittering bayonets to enforce activity and diligence in their tasks. It was a long time before the trio ever saw Spring Forge. When they did they were sadder men; likewise, wiser. They had lost all desire for battle-field plunder.[37]

Such a crackdown was bound to produce instances of overzealousness, and one of the victims of this pettiness was Tillie Pierce. The young girl was heartbroken when a musket that had been given to her by a soldier who had been attending wounded at her house was confiscated. She told the two provost-marshal guards who came to her (after "I suppose I had been bragging too much about my relic") that "if they are mean enough to take the gun that they can have it; but it is my gun. They seemed sorry to as they rode away with my highly prized treasure, and I have no reason to doubt their sincerity."[38]

For his part, when Captain Smith began to feel some official heat over his methods, he explained to his superiors:

> On my arrival here I found that at the rate property was being carried away, three or four days would clear the field, and the Government would find its property, scattered hundreds of miles. . . . With the immense amount of labor to be performed and the imperitive necessity of immediate action, I could not stop to hear every gentlemen's explanation of what he was doing with government property.

There was one individual, however, to whom Smith made no apology— a farmer from whom an army overcoat had been seized after the possessor admitted to purchasing it from a hungry Union soldier for just a loaf of bread. Rather than demand the return of the coat, Smith told the farmer in disgust that "he ought to be ashamed to rob a soldier who had come here to fight for him."[39]

The result of Smith's summary judgments was that on some days as many as seventy-five private citizens would be stripped of their souvenirs and pressed into work gangs as the provost marshal sought to deal with his labor shortage while discouraging the thievery that was his consuming concern.

Aside from the value of the items being taken from the field there were some genuine safety concerns about the public, particularly children, handling loaded weapons and live ammunition.

Albertus McCreary and his young chums got themselves involved in one precarious enterprise after the battle.

> Lead was very scarce, and we could get 13 cents a pound for it, so all the boys hunted lead bullets. We would go along Culp's Hill, pick among the leaves, and sometimes find what we called pockets, a lot of bullets in a pile—eight or 10 pounds. As it took only eight of a certain kind to make a pound, I gathered many pounds myself in this way. The large shells were full of bullets and we found many of them that had not exploded; we would unscrew the cap and, if we were careful, fill the shell with water before we undertook to extract the bullets.

But, he acknowledged, "sometimes boys became careless." He remembered how a schoolmate had found a shell on Cemetery Hill and, "the contents not coming out fast enough for him, he struck it upon a rock upon which he was sitting and made a spark which exploded the shell. We carried him to his home, and the surgeons did what they could for him, but he never regained consciousness and died in about an hour."[40]

Despite such mishaps, the young boys living about Gettysburg were having the time of their lives; the sights and experiences for them were thrilling. A favorite "trick," Albertus recalled, "was to go to the woods, place five or six large Wentworth shells among dry leaves and sticks, set fire to the pile, and run off to a safe distance and wait for the explosion. It made a racket that put Fourth of July in the shade."

It can be imagined how such antics played on the battle-frayed nerves of the townspeople. In their own way, the schoolboys continued to add to the defacement of their surroundings. When the visitors came, they all wanted relics, said Albertus. "We were always on the lookout for bullets and pieces of shell, in fact, anything that could be easily handled, to sell to them. We found that a piece of tree with a bullet embedded in it was a great prize and a good seller."

Consequently, he continued, "every boy went out with a hatchet to chop pieces from the trees in which bullets had lodged." Their notches remained on the trunks for posterity in the same way as initials carved in a heart.[41]

When all was tallied, the government property collected by the Army of the Potomac infantry units before leaving Gettysburg, and what was picked up or recovered by Captain Smith and Captain Blood, as well as the 36th Pennsylvania Emergency Regiment, amounted to a staggering inventory for the Washington Arsenal (the depository) to sort and reissue.

The great pile of weaponry and materiel that had been built up over weeks at the depot in town and then loaded on trains (with the help of Confederate prisoners) to Washington included 24,976 muskets and carbines, 10,591 bayonets, 14,000 rounds of ammunition, 1,834 cartridge boxes, and 366 sabers. For one reason or another, only five revolvers were included in the mass of firearms, Union and Confederate.[42]

Col. Henry Clay Alleman, commander of the 36th Pennsylvania, made his own accounting of what had been collected and while in substantial agreement with the quartermasters on the number of muskets and bayonets picked up, Colonel Alleman's inventory went further. He reported turning over a huge amount of blankets and clothing to the War Department for reuse. In addition to 702 blankets, the colonel noted forty wagonloads of clothing and six wagonloads of knapsacks and haversacks were delivered. The regiment also sent off 510 horses and mules left on the battleground. Also considered part of the debris of battle were 1,637 stragglers from both armies who had been picked up, men who during or after the battle had for whatever reason left their units. The hundreds of Rebels roaming about town long after the battle, "some of which walked the streets discussing Southern rights," was a particular peeve of Captain Smith, and no doubt he had most to do with their round up and delivery to prison camps, where they belonged.[43]

In processing the vast store of arms turned in for possible reissue, the staff of the Washington Arsenal accumulated some telling statistics of its own. Of the 27,574 muskets that eventually came into the arsenal from Gettysburg, 24,000 were found to be loaded. About half this number, however, contained two charges. A quarter held from three to ten charges. One piece was found to contain twenty-three charges inserted by some terrified infantryman who had repeatedly gone through the motions of biting cartridges and ramming home powder and ball without any idea that the weapon he thought he was firing wasn't even discharging.[44]

What must it have been like for a man to have behaved so irrationally? The behind-the-lines ordnance clerk examining the unfired musket could only wonder.

Baltimore, fifty miles away, emerged as a private source of relief for the wounded Confederate prisoners at Gettysburg. Southern sympathizers—most of them refined women from leading Maryland families—arrived in pairs or small groups daily to supply and nurse the much-ignored Rebels. Many people in town suspected their ministrations weren't limited to nursing but extended to helping the soldiers with clothing, money, and other means to escape when they became fit enough to make the attempt. Most were open about their sentiments; others covert. Several of the Christian Commission delegates, for example, were found to be using that organization's access "to seek out friends among the Rebel wounded," one official acknowledged. "Some brought clothes, and others had them sent to them."[45]

The four Baltimore women who stayed at Liberty Hollinger's house were "very delightful ladies and were well supplied with money," the Gettysburg girl found. But, the daughter of the house explained, their stay was brief.

> They spent the whole day out on the field and in the hospitals where the Confederate wounded were. We did not suspect their intentions at first, but when they tried to buy up men's civilian clothes, and even women's clothing, we began to understand what they were about. As soon as my father learned what their real mission was, he insisted that mother must send them away.[46]

Perhaps it was the same group Mrs. Edmund Souder had in mind when the nurse related how "some ladies from Baltimore made themselves a name and a fame, a few days since, by furnishing citizens' clothes for some rebels to flee in. They stole several horses, and made their escape but most of them were retaken." In fact, "there are many Southern sympathizers here who devote themselves exclusively to this class," she observed.[47]

When a physician from Maryland—the border state that probably contained the most ardent Confederate supporters—was reportedly arrested "with three or four cuts of clothing on his person, conveying them to the College Hospital," it was assumed that the garments were intended as a disguise, not merely as a replacement for torn and bloodied uniforms that were no longer serviceable.

What Mrs. Mary Horner, who related that incident, mainly resented about the Marylanders, however, was that they "were permitted to bring in carloads of luxuries to their friends, and that there was no disposition to give a share to Uncle Sam's boys."[48]

Colonel Alleman of the 36th Pennsylvania was equally annoyed at the degree of attention focused on the Rebel prisoners, and decided to bring it under stricter control. On behalf of the Military Department of the Susquehanna, he issued an order that was published in the *Adams Sentinel* on August 11 that stipulated "No citizen will be permitted to visit any of the Confederate hospitals without first establishing their loyalty, and having their passes approved at these Hdqs."

Further, he required that "any luxuries sent to the hospitals for the wounded Confederates by their sympathizing friends, must be handed over to the surgeons in charge, and under his direction will be distributed equally among the Union and Confederate wounded.

"Under no circumstances whatever will citizens' clothing be permitted to be carried into any of the hospitals," the angry colonel ordered.

But assistance continued to come to the Rebel captives in myriad and unexpected ways. One destitute Virginian at a Twelfth Corps hospital managed to get a letter off to an old friend in Baltimore asking for a loan and was more than a bit surprised when, a short time later, two Sisters of Charity came to his tent, inquiring for him by name.

> One of them took me aside and, unobserved, placed in my hand
> a package of money, saying it was from a friend, and requested

no name be mentioned. They declined to give me any information. I never knew who they were. There was a mystery about them. They could not have come for my sake alone. But this I know; they were angels of mercy.[49]

If Mother Superior had been aware of such clandestine activity on the part of some of the sisters, it is doubtful that she would have shared the Southerner's saintly image of them, attempting as the order was to maintain the strictest neutrality in its activities. Treating the wounds of prisoners was one thing; smuggling currency to them was another matter entirely.

Confederate surgeon Simon Baruch, laboring with the wounded of McLaw's division about Black Horse Tavern, recalled "two young women belonging to a historic Maryland family came to the hospital, under the chaperonage of an elderly English nurse, and remained with us, occupying garret rooms, until the hospital closed." The ladies administered to the wounded, prepared the food and dressings, "and read the burial service over those who succumbed," said the young doctor, calling their assistance "inestimable."[50]

But, in a material way, what was most rewarding for him was the visit of a physician from Baltimore who, after observing the brilliant young doctor performing an operation, complimented him on his technique and, the following day, brought him a splendid Tiemann field operating case with his name engraved on its cover.[51]

At the College Hospital, Decimus et Ultimus Barziza was also the recipient of a memorable gift. While "many ladies from Baltimore came to visit us, and spoke words of good cheer and encouragement," Barziza said he would "ever remember a gentleman from Baltimore who came into the room where I was and left me a bottle of fine brandy; it was a glorious treat and right heartily was it enjoyed."[52]

In some instances, the visitors came empty handed but were of enormous support to the soldiers left behind by their army and feeling much abandoned in a strange, distant place. Three proud Christian women from Baltimore came out to the field hospital where the badly wounded of Hood's Division had been gathered and erected a tent just outside the area where the casualties of that unit, the shock troops of Lee's army, lay.

"Refined, cultivated, elegant women . . . they knelt by the pallet of straw on which the dying soldier lay and gave him such consolation as the word of God read by them could afford to the dying," recalled a private of the 4th Alabama. "There was no minister of the gospel in that land of the enemy who sought us out and offered comfort."[53]

To one of the Confederates among the nearly eight hundred at the College Hospital, "the ladies of Baltimore were preeminently the persons to whom we were indebted for everything that made our situation bearable."

> For weeks, they had been preparing for the entry of Lee into Maryland, into Baltimore, and comforts, clothing, delicacies of every description, they had hoarded up, hoping soon to be able to distribute them, with their own fair hands, among the men, who were fighting for the cause they loved.
>
> When the dreadful news of our repulse reached them, their first thought was to visit our hospitals and supply our wants. What if passports to leave the city on the railroad were denied to all except those who take 'the oath;' did they not take their carriages and ride through the country? What if the bridges were guarded, did they not ford or ferry the stream? And when the hotel keepers in Gettysburg were ordered not to receive them in their houses, did they not go to the houses of private citizens, stay in barns, and outhouses, or remain with us day and night in this hospital, reclining in a chair or resting on the floor, in a room of the building we vacated for them, when sleep would overcome them?[54]

Of all those belles who came, none would be remembered with the same fondness and respect as Miss Euphemia Goldsborough—Miss Effie. From a long established Maryland family, twenty-seven years old and rather tiny, she made up in spirit what physical strength she lacked, and all of that energy was concentrated on the achievement of Southern independence.

She had gone to Frederick after Antietam to nurse the Confederate wounded there the year before, and carried things to Point Lookout for the prisoners. At the Pennsylvania College hospital, no exertion was too great for her, no task for the filthy bedraggled soldiers too distasteful. In one instance, she offered her ninety-seven-pound frame as a prop for a Virginia colonel who was shot in the lungs. To breathe at all he had to remain seated upright. For hours the woman sat on the floor behind him, back to back, absolutely motionless lest the officer's wound be disturbed and he hemorrhage again.

Her tenderness is seen in the letters she wrote to the families of those she attended. To the bereaved mother of a member of the 5th Texas Regiment, she wrote feelingly of a lost son:

> It was my privilege to nurse him six weeks, during which time I looked to his comfort as I would my own only brother and learned to love him just the same. He died in my arms . . . his precious brown eyes fixed in mine, without a struggle, and his last fleeting breath I caught upon his lips. . . . I hope that we may meet after this unhappy war is ended and that I may be able to give you back your darling son's dying kiss.

In a postscript, Miss Effie apologized for what she regarded as "a faulty letter," explaining "I have no control over my feelings while writing or thinking of the subject." Eventually, the cost of the depth of her feelings in regard to the Confederate cause and those fighting for it would be her very freedom.[55]

It was not only Maryland women whose feelings went out to the Rebels confined to Gettysburg by their wounds and facing a dreary prison camp as soon as they healed sufficiently. As in any war, the young were drawn to one another by forces far stronger than the ideological and cultural differences that may have existed between them. Wounded Southern boys who began as unwelcome and helpless guests in the homes of Gettysburg girls became, after close prolonged association, first their companions and, in time, often their beaux and sometimes their husbands. Some Confederates taken to farms would, after their wounds had healed, help with the harvest and other chores. Provided with work clothes and concealed from inquiry, a few stayed in the area throughout the war and beyond.

Most instances of fraternization, however, involved simply acts of kindness toward those with no one to care for them and a desire to cheer, in a feminine way, young men who had ample reason to be despondent. Private W. C. Ward of the 4th Alabama never forgot the visits of some of the local girls to the Confederate hospital where he was taken after being wounded at Little Round Top:

One sad, terrible day as we lay under the tent fly, the shadow of a woman fell over us, and looking up, we saw a handsome young woman, whose kind and intelligent face expressed gentleness and sympathy. She called to a sister, who was not far off and who rapidly came to where we lay. We soon knew them as Misses Mary and Sally Witherrow, whose home was in Gettysburg.

The soldier learned that the two sisters had ventured in his direction after having heard "that out in the fields, behind the line of battle, a large number of Confederate wounded were laying."

Mary Witherrow returned at various times with different young women from the town, sometimes bringing little delicacies. On one occasion her gift was a bottle of Madeira. She probably never knew that the grateful Ward had given most of it to a weakened comrade to help restore some color to a face that was showing "the pale marble emblem of death."[56]

Many of the women who approached the stranded Rebels did so merely out of curiosity and daring, or even with the intention of being mean or scolding to the enemy prisoners. When "some ladies of intensely loyal inclinations" decided to pay Confederate Gen. James Kemper a visit at the Lutheran Theological Seminary, where he was being treated for very severe wounds suffered while leading his brigade in Pickett's Charge they were not prepared to be so charmed by the Virginia politician turned soldier.

A companion of Kemper's said he was "advised by a wicked glance of his eye that he intended to make a conquest of these zealous dames." The general spoke eloquently to them not of war but of womankind and of what a comfort they could be to men in need. Before long, "the ladies, forgetting their mission, moved their seats nearer and, while one used her grateful fan to cool his fevered brow, the other bathed his parched and burning hands." As they left the crippled soldier, unaware of how their feelings were being toyed with, "handkerchiefs were in requisition to stay the evidence of sympathy."[57]

Maj. Henry Kyd Douglas, a young Marylander close to home, was another of those being treated at the seminary hospital. In writing of his experience there with the fair sex, the staff officer related that "nearby lived two young ladies who were great favorites in the Hospital because their generous hearts did not, apparently, distinguish the color of uniforms— loyal as they were."

Some nights, Douglas said, "I would stroll with them to make visits in the town, the marks on the sleeve of my uninjured arm being artfully concealed by some little female headgear which I was directed to carry just that way, and marching between the sisters . . . we generally landed at Duncan's and made an evening of it."

"It never seemed to occur to them that they were harboring a Rebel, and nothing occurred to me except their graciousness and attractiveness," he confided.[58]

James E. Crocker, a Virginia lawyer who had graduated from Pennsylvania College as valedictorian of the class of 1850, returned to the school as one of the casualties of Pickett's Charge. When he had recovered sufficiently from his wound, Crocker obtained a pass to circulate about town. For the many Union soldiers on the streets, Crocker thought it must have been "a queer, incongruous sight to see a rebel lieutenant in gray mingling in the crowd, and apparently at home. They could see, however, many of the principal citizens of the town cordially accosting, and warmly shaking by the hand, the rebel."[59]

There was altogether too much of this sort of fraternization going on in the town to suit some Federal officials. Ultimately, Dr. Janes, the man who supposedly held custody of all the wounded, received an admonition from one of the generals functioning in that vicinity, Orris S. Ferry.

"It is reported that Rebel officers have been seen in town as late as 11 o'clock p.m. in company with females," the medical director was informed, as if he didn't have enough to deal with already. "It is not deemed conducive to the best interests of the service to permit such passes."[60]

Janes also found himself under mounting pressure to move out the wounded, particularly the officers, to prison camps as soon as possible. This civil war was becoming obviously too civil at Gettysburg, as far as some of the Union authorities were concerned.

None of the prisoners was as much a source of concern to the Union authorities as Isaac Ridgway Trimble. He was sixty-one years old, and had just had a leg amputated after being shot while fearlessly riding on horseback during Pickett's Charge. The Confederate major general would hardly seem to be a threatening figure any longer, but only if the strength of Trimble's personality and influence were overlooked.

Trimble was a West Pointer who had served as an artillery officer in the regular army for a decade before resigning in 1832 to use his engineering skills in the booming railroad industry. An active secessionist in Maryland, Trimble had a hand in the burning of the bridges around Baltimore when the war erupted that hampered the movement of Union troops to Washington. The mischief old Trimble had caused in his adopted state—a state that Federal officials were trying desperately to retain in the union—wasn't forgotten when he finally fell into their hands.

Provost Marshal Patrick, as hostile as he often demonstrated himself to be toward the enemy, apparently regarded Trimble with somewhat less animosity than others. Perhaps it was due to the West Point tie. At any rate, when the Marylander appealed to General Meade (who was, according to Patrick, under some personal obligation to him) to be moved into town from the house in the country where he had been left to recover, it was Patrick who rode out some three or four miles to see him. He had, as he put it, "a pleasant interview" with the prisoner and then made the arrangements himself to have Trimble, his staff officer, and a wounded lieutenant put up at the Chambersburg Street home of Robert McCurdy. McCurdy was president of the Gettysburg Railroad and therefore something of a kindred spirit, at least professionally, as far as Trimble was concerned.[61]

There the hypercritical Trimble had to admit that he was "well treated with the most tender kindness." So pleased was the general, in fact, that his hosts, in turn, came to regard him as a "delightful and appreciative guest."[62]

When a report began circulating, however, that General Patrick had directed that Trimble be sent to Baltimore and there paroled to recuperate with his family, the reaction in Washington by officials at the highest levels of government was quick and furious.

The response started on July 11 when Simon Cameron, a former Cabinet member and a staunch supporter of Abraham Lincoln, felt compelled to wire the president from Gettysburg about Patrick's order.

Cameron asserted of Trimble:

> From his knowledge of the railroads in Pennsylvania, Maryland and Delaware, he is a dangerous man. He burned the bridges between Philadelphia and Baltimore in the beginning of the rebellion. Within the last ten days he directed and superintended the burning of the bridges between Baltimore and Columbia and York and Harrisburg. He resided in Baltimore for 25 years and is in close connection with all the rebel sympathizers in that city.

Maj. Gen. Isaac Trimble, a troublesome Confederate prisoner. *Library of Congress.*

He is now living in comfort at the house of a rebel sympathizer in this town, while some of our wounded soldiers are still unattended. While he should and would receive from loyal men, all care a wounded man requires, he ought not to be allowed communication with persons who would transmit from him information helpful to the enemy. I therefore respectfully recommend that he be removed to be confined in Harrisburg or Pittsburgh, as a prisoner of war.[63]

Probably at the behest of President Lincoln, no less a personage than Edwin M. Stanton, Secretary of War, now became involved in the matter. That same day, Stanton wired the department commander in Baltimore, General Schenck, about Patrick's action and (using Cameron's very description) advised him:

That Trimble is a dangerous man, raised in Maryland, has resided in Baltimore, was engaged in destroying the bridges when the war broke out, and ought not to be permitted to go at large or be visited. If he comes to Baltimore you will see that he not be allowed to be paroled nor to hold communication with any one until he is exchanged.[64]

Stanton was dealing with the right man. He need have no fear that the aggressive Schenck would not follow his instructions to the fullest. "I will look out for the rebel General Trimble, as you direct," Schenck reassured Stanton. "He is notorious here as a bridge burner and 19th of April leader. He has not appeared yet himself, but two days ago his assistant adjutant general, Major Hall, came here on parole from Gettysburg to prepare accommodations for his chief. I revoked the parole and put the major in Fort McHenry. . . ."[65]

Not only was parole now out of the question for Trimble, but it was decided that he was altogether too comfortable at the McCurdys. Neighbors were complaining and, after two weeks he was, despite vehement protestations, moved to the Lutheran Theological Seminary where other high-ranking prisoners were being kept under close watch. The officers were confined to three rooms. Two guards were posted at the door to each and, according to one of the inmates, "the utmost vigilance enjoined and all the formalities observed in mounting and relieving guard."[66]

At one point, Mrs. Edmund Souder, during a break in her nursing routine, thought she might have a look at the notorious and supposedly "fierce looking" prisoner. While admitting to having "some curiosity to see him," when she found that he was "under guard and not to be seen without a special permit," she abandoned the idea. She did mention, however, "I understand he receives a splendid dinner daily from the bounty of some sympathizer."[67] Whether the dishes actually reached Trimble, however, is questionable because the guards were said to hold back any food sent to him and he himself groused that the lieutenant in charge of the detail, "a Penna. blackguard, takes every occasion to vex us & circumscribe our privileges. May the chances of war put him some day in our power," Trimble fervently prayed. Actually, old Trimble was behaving so obnoxiously with his captors that it is a wonder he got anything to eat at all.[68]

"For men like General Trimble, I have no sympathy," said one nurse who was aware of the crusty officer's conduct.

> Theirs was the infamy of inaugurating this wrecked rebellion, and they should be the sufferers. Had any of our poor officers in their Southern dungeons dared to show half the audacity of this man, he would have been immediately shot.
>
> General Trimble would order the best of everything cooked and if it did not please him, send it back to the kitchen. I was there one day when his dinner was returned; it consisted of nice fried ham and eggs, with mashed potatoes and onions, but it did not please him. Norris, who was the cook, asked me what he should do. I suggested letting him wait until his appetite improved, which was done. No other dinner was supplied.[69]

Sixteen-year-old Liberty Hollinger and her sister Julia went out to the seminary to see the general one day. "I do not know how we came to do this, but I remember that we gave him a bouquet of flowers, and that he and his orderly were very polite and kind to us."[70]

Apparently Liberty encountered a different guard than the one who confronted Mrs. Souder when she tried to gain admittance to the celebrated prisoner—and a different Isaac Trimble.

Trimble would be there only a few weeks before his wound was deemed sufficiently healed for him to be moved to Baltimore, and a subsequent long imprisonment at Johnson's Island.

The confused inconsistent treatment of Trimble and so many of the other prisoners of war only pointed to the uncertainty even the most passionate unionists felt about how they should regard their subdued foes. And, of course, his attitude didn't help the dilemma.

The conditions that had produced a traumatic change in the daily lives of the inhabitants of Gettysburg had, in a matter of weeks, become so familiar it was difficult to recall the slow, humdrum routine that preceded the battle.

A new social atmosphere developed, one marked by sights and sounds now so common as to no longer cause a stir or prompt a second glance. That few of the women seen coming and going from the hospitals wore hoopskirts because they were too encumbering for the work to be done was hardly noticed. With the churches still filled with wounded, the habit of attending Sunday services had been broken and, for the families with whom soldiers had been left, there simply was no day of rest. The constant congestion at the diamond generated by the Sanitary and Christian commission depots gave the community the chaotic look of a boomtown to the newly-arrived. Downtown was now much ignored by the locals who knew back-alley routes to their destinations.

The once-familiar sight of supplies and shipments being loaded on wagons by farmers and merchants and freight handlers had been replaced by glimpses of people carrying burdens of another sort about the busy streets.

"A perpetual procession of coffins is constantly passing to and fro, and so it has been ever since we have been here," said one volunteer nurse, a parade generated by "strangers looking for their dead on every farm and under every tree."[71]

It now required something extraordinary to attract any degree of attention, with all that had taken place there. One was afforded by the passing on the street of Dr. Mary E. Walker, the only female surgeon in the army, though her gender wasn't always apparent because of the way she dressed. Her ensemble generally included "a low silk hat, with bloomers, and a man's coat and collar."[72]

But having the famous Dorothea Dix popping in and out of hospital tents seeing to whatever it was she supposed she was looking after was hardly noticed, no more than the activity of Mathew Brady, young Timothy

O'Sullivan, and the other photographers from Washington making wet-plate images for sale, quickly processed in their canvas-covered wagons.

Children still played noisily in the streets, but the games had been changed by the events that had taken place and one passerby was struck by how "mere scraps of boys amused themselves with percussion caps and hammers," and denigrated their playmates by calling them the worst thing they could imagine, "you Rebel you." And, at the college, playful students made bowling alleys of the corridors, using cannon balls to knock down the pins.

Lads who once offered to do odd jobs had found new ways to earn spending money, and not always by peddling souvenirs to visitors. Less commendably, they were selling tobacco to wounded soldiers, purchased in bulk at warehouses in town for far less than they were asking the suffering men in need of a soothing smoke.

When neighbors met along the red brick sidewalks, they now inquired about how well the soldiers being cared for in one another's homes were healing as casually as they had once inquired about the state of health of family and friends.

So smooth-running had the Sanitary Commission feeding lodge at the railroad depot become that Georgy Woolsey could expand her attentions to the houses in town being used as hospitals. These were identified by the little red flags hung from the upper windows and had been much over-looked by the doctors and staffs of the larger field hospitals because they were out of the way and contained relatively few patients.

As much as the residents were willing to share their provisions with those staying with them, Georgy found that "nice little puddings and jellies, or an occasional chicken, were a great treat to men condemned by their wounds to stay in Gettysburg and obliged to live on what the empty town could provide."[73]

Dr. O'Neal continued to make his rounds with his old nag but was now stopping frequently to make notations in his physician's log. He had taken to recording the names lettered on the graves of the Confederate soldiers scattered all over the area and, as random and unscientific as his survey was, the hundreds of entries in his little book became the only directory available as to the whereabouts of the Rebel dead.

As her service at the Second Corps field hospital wore on, Cornelia Hancock—living in a tent and without access to either her bath or her wardrobe—became "black as an Indian and dirty as a pig." She said the rough work of cooking in great kettles for hundreds of men and attending their various needs had "torn almost all my clothes off of me and Uncle Sam has given me a new suit. . . ."[74]

Though her labors were arduous, she was extremely fulfilled by what she was doing and perfectly content. Cornelia admitted that she had reached the point where "I could stand by and see a man's head taken off I believe." But despite all the suffering she was exposed to, she was able to tell her family that she found the doctors and nurses and attendants with whom she worked "very jolly" and said "sometimes we have a good time."[75]

Cornelia didn't doubt that "most people think I came into the army to get a husband. It is a capital place for them, as there are very many nice men here, and all men are required to give great respect to women. There are many good-looking women here who galavant around in the evening and have a good time. I do not trouble myself much with the common herd."[76]

It is unknown exactly who Cornelia had in mind when she spoke about the carousing, but someone remembered three women in particular with "foxy faces, weasel-like eyes and a heart-hiding smile that chilled like

Field hospitals similar to this Union Second Corps facility dotted the battlefield. *Gettysburg National Military Park.*

dagger points" who showed up and were provided with a wall tent by one of the barns used as a hospital. The "ladies," supplied with an ambulance and a uniformed hospital attendant, proceeded to canvass the countryside, making fervent pleas for provisions for the wounded. But each night when they returned with their contributions a party erupted in their tent. "High jinks were celebrated till well into the wee hours" with the affairs attended by the hospital staff who arrived with bottles of fine wines and brandy from their stores. "Each night the revel grew louder and louder and finally it grew too loud—as proprieties were flung to the winds in the wall tent."

Before long, the provost marshal was notified of the carousing and the women were told to pack up, as their services were no longer required. In addition, several hospital attendants, having demonstrated how ablebodied they were at the soirees, were quickly returned to combat duty with the Army of the Potomac.[77]

With all these goings on, long-time residents of Gettysburg couldn't be faulted for seriously wondering if their town would ever return to the way it was.

"It is scarcely necessary for us to make an apology to our readers for failing to issue our paper during the past week," the *Gettysburg Compiler* editorial stated when it resumed publication.

"Part of the time the Rebels had possession of the town, and of course it was then impossible to do anything in the office. We hope, however, to be able to do better in the future, and we feel certain that our subscribers will see at once that our apparent neglect of them was unavoidable."[78]

Such apologetic language, under the circumstances, might be regarded as betraying a serious lack of confidence in reader loyalty. But the townspeople of Democratic leanings were as happy to have the *Compiler* back as the Republican followers of the *Sentinel* and the *Star and Banner.*

All three newspapers, of course, were markedly changed in content. The weeklies, with a sudden abundance of local news to present, chronicled the accidents that occurred in connection with unexploded ammunition on the field and discarded firearms as routinely as they had, in the days before the battle, related petty thefts and farming mishaps. They recorded the arrivals and departures of different military units and the transfer of wounded soldiers from the depot to distant hospitals as matter of factly as they had reported the arrival of shipments of goods and the opening of new businesses. With the community bursting with visitors, circulation of all the papers was undoubtedly robust.

In its columns, the staunchly pro-administration *Sentinel* appeared to gloat over the legal problems the editor of the rival *Compiler* was having with the government and found the anti-administration weekly's editorial minimizing the Union victory so amusing it reprinted portions. One choice excerpt claimed "Lee's army was not driven away. It was not routed. It voluntarily fell back at a time when nobody was fighting it."[79]

For his part, *Compiler* editor H. J. Stahle had to shuttle between Gettysburg and Baltimore while the proceedings against him dragged on for allegedly giving away the place of concealment of Union soldiers to the enemy.

Probably as a sense of business obligation, the *Sentinel* felt compelled to report that the "Bank of Gettysburg has resumed its operation and is transacting business as before the Rebel invasion. This excellent institution has suffered no pecuniary loss, beyond the inconvenience occasioned by the hasty removal of its valuables to a place of safety. . . ."[80]

Among the advertisements it carried was one from Dr. Robert Horner stating that "having retired from the active practice of my profession, I take pleasure in announcing . . . I have opened a new drug store."[81] Left unsaid was whether the demands placed on doctors there in recent weeks hadn't hastened the decision to transfer his knowledge to a less stressful practice.

The *Sentinel* also served as a vehicle for a joint appeal from the presidents of the related Lutheran Theological Seminary and Pennsylvania College for contributions to help repair the battle damage done to their buildings and for "purification and painting" after having been occupied as hospitals.

> Will it not finally be a pleasing reflection, that the institution whose soil was plowed up by the cannon balls, whose halls were stained with blood in defense of the Union, and around which are buried some of the martyrs who died in a holy cause, were not permanently injured, but by the liberality of christians and patriots, their latter days were more prosperous than the first?[82]

The college later reported that it realized $1,864.51 from the fund-raising effort.

The papers dutifully ran the Christian and Sanitary commissions' acknowledgements for all the contributions that arrived at the depots, right down to John M. Bucher's chickens and Mrs. S. J. Cooper's apple butter, acknowledgments that couldn't help but encourage further giving, whether out of simple generosity and compassion or a demonstration of one's level of patriotism.

One reason Gettysburg residents were pleased to have their own newspapers available once more was their disgust with how their town was being depicted in the out-of-town press. Originally, the locals had turned to the papers from New York, Philadelphia, and Baltimore for an overview of the colossal battle that occurred in their midst. In fact, these papers were their only semi-authoritative sources of news of the war in which they had been so unexpectedly drawn. "If you could mail me a newspaper, it would be a great satisfaction as we do not get the news here and the soldiers are so anxious to hear," Cornelia Hancock appealed to a cousin on behalf of some of the men who had fought the battle.[83]

Of his desperation for news, surgeon Robert Hubbard wrote his wife Nellie as late as July 9:

I have never been so completely shut out from all communication with the world in general as at present. Altho I can send a letter occasionally yet I can get no news whatever. I have seen only one newspaper since I came here & the Army has left & I know nothing about where it is or what it is about.[84]

The residents voraciously consumed the accounts in the newspapers that reached town, but were sickened by the characterizations that began to appear. One after another, following the same line, correspondents began to ridicule the avaricious behavior of the citizenry toward the wounded soldiers and the visitors flocking to the town. Antipathy soon developed against these nasty scribes, who were indiscriminately slandering the whole community for the behavior of a few. Most deeply offended were the housewives who had emptied their larders for the army and worked themselves to exhaustion caring for the injured without thought of compensation of any kind.

They received a testimonial from a David Blair of Huntington, Pennsylvania, in the *Sentinel* in which he stated (after having been accommodated in a small house where eleven wounded soldiers were being sheltered along with as many of their relatives), "It may have been that mere curiosity-seekers and self-important newspaper correspondents did not receive all the attention which they considered due to them but I venture the assertion that the first word of complaint by a single wounded or sick man by their friends against the citizens of Gettysburg has yet to be uttered."[85]

None of the reports was more brutal than that of L.C. Crounse of the *New York Times,* who alluded to the "cravenhearted meanness" of the people in Gettysburg and vicinity. "I do not speak hastily," the journalist asserted. "I but write the unanimous sentiments of the whole army—an army which now feels that the doors from which they drive a host of robbers, thieves and cut-throats were not worthy of being defended." He went on to list the exorbitant prices for lodging, food, etc., including "20 cents for a bandage for a wounded soldier."[86]

Many other reporters then picked up on the theme. Under a subhead bringing attention to the "Shameless Conduct of Citizens of Adams County," a soldier/correspondent for the *Lancaster Daily Express* wrote for the July 13 issue about the atmosphere at Gettysburg:

> Here is a farmer who has twelve stray cows, all of which he has milked daily, in addition to his own, whose farm and crops have been protected from the hands of the despoiler, by the blood of the slain, and whose barn is filled with 200 bleeding, dying patriots. Does he give them milk when they ask and plead for it? Yes. At five cents a pint! Does he give them one loaf of bread when they have saved for him 10,000? Yes. At forty cents a loaf. Here is another who has been driven from his home by the invading hosts, who bought tobacco at eight cents a plug and sells it to the wounded at 15. Bought letter paper at a cent per sheet and taking advantage of their misfortune, sells it to the disabled at five—all because they have unfortunately fell defending his home. They seem to be proud of the opportunity, and laugh at their cunning in counting their gains—it is not cunning, it is something less than duplicity.
>
> This is sufficient to dampen the patriotism of any soldier, and woe, woe I say unto the soldier who falls among his friends, if these are our friends.

Irrefutable was the fact that benevolence, if more common in the town than on the surrounding farms, was, as a Christian Commission delegation would report, "not universal among the inhabitants of Gettysburg and its surroundings. There were some," it was found, "that refused the contribution of their means and services in the afflictive emergency. Others reluctantly engaged in the labor of relief, impelled by feelings of human sympathy they could not resist."[87]

What particularly incensed professor Michael Jacobs of the college was "the gratuitous slander put forth by some reckless newspaper scribblers and extensively published abroad that the male inhabitants ran off like a set of cowards and permitted women and children to do the best they could. . . . No one," he insisted, "so far as we know, had forsaken his home and family through fear or cowardice."[88]

Such sweeping judgments based on scanty and questionable information were being made in some of the accounts—written by people who knew they were just passing through and would not ever have to confront the wrath of those they so brazenly offended—may have been characteristic of much of the journalism of the day. But to people who had never been exposed to such treatment before and were the guiltless targets of the allegations, it was not only hurtful but appeared to reflect little appreciation for the ordeal they had been through.

Consolidating the wounded had long been on the minds of Dr. Janes and, apparently, his absent superior, Dr. Letterman. Having the casualties scattered at nearly a hundred locations made supplying and servicing the various facilities more difficult, particularly the Confederate wounded in the outlying camps. The dispersion demanded a great deal more transportation equipment and, most of all, medical personnel.

Janes, with the help of Medical Inspectors Johnson and Vollum, had found an ideal location for a general hospital just off the York Road and by the railroad about a mile outside of town. But not until an eagerly awaited shipment of tents arrived from Washington on July 15 could Janes begin to set up and organize the central hospital that, however patronizing it might sound, had been designated Camp Letterman.

Janes's eagerness to get the general hospital established actually led to two nasty incidents involving one of his most devoted volunteer nurses, Charlotte McKay—encounters in which he was made to appear rather heartless and unfeeling.

Mrs. McKay had been cooking at the Jacob Schwartz farm for the wounded of the Second Corps. She was using kettles suspended over an open fire by poles and desperately needed a proper stove. There were stoves in town to be purchased, but when she put in a request, it was disapproved by Dr. Janes. When she personally visited the chief medical officer to urge him to reconsider, Mrs. McKay found, "I might as well have appealed to a rock." He was going to receive some stoves from Baltimore for a general hospital soon and she could have one then, Janes told the nurse. She would have to wait.[89]

On another occasion, she was turned down by Janes when she asked to be issued some sheets for the men who, she said, were being tortured by flies. Coarse army blankets were their only defense, she explained, "and those were terrible on their wounds in the hot weather. . . . I have seen men, with both hands disabled, crying in helpless agony from the tortures of these merciless little insects," she recounted.

Again she was put off by Janes "with the excuse that he would need them all for the new hospital." All she was able to obtain were "a few I begged from the Sanitary and Christian Commission," related the sympathetic frustrated nurse.[90]

But no sooner was Janes able to get his camp hospital opened on July 22 than pressures began to build for him to expedite the removal of the wounded from the public buildings in town. On August 4, the local school board wrote to solicit the medical director to move the wounded out of the school house on Baltimore Street so that classes could be resumed.

> There is no building in the town whose use for this purpose could work as much public inconvenience. By its occupying, not only are all our teachers (most of whom are in dependent circumstances) thrown out of employment, but all the children of the borough, numbering four hundred, are thrown upon the streets and deprived of school privileges.[91]

The administrators of the Lutheran Theological Seminary were just as impatient to have the soldiers occupying its premises removed. Their concern was to have their buildings and grounds restored to normal for the opening of the fall term, and when they got wind that Janes intended to delay the closing of that facility, they appealed to the Surgeon General in

Washington to consider their situation. As a consequence, Janes was directed to have the campus cleared by August 30.

Only a few days before that deadline—which Janes could not meet because of the condition of some of the wounded there—the harassed physician received another wire from the brass in Washington. "It is reported that there is much sickness in Seminary Hospital at Gettysburg owing to the proximity of bodies imperfectly buried. You will please report the facts of the case at once and take such action as may be most proper to remedy the evil, reporting your action also."[92]

"Imperfectly buried?" My God, Janes may well have exclaimed, this whole place is a cemetery filled with imperfectly buried bodies. What was he to do about it with the resources at hand?

The Sanitary Commission, too, was a target of the town's desire to return to normal, an attitudinal change that seemed to class the disabled soldiers as public nuisances.

Fahnestock Brothers, with its merchandise sitting in its car at the railroad depot, was impatient to reopen for business and called upon the relief agency to vacate its store on Baltimore Street. Under the circumstances, the commission declined.

Finally, Lt. Col. Edward G. Fahnestock, a member of the firm who came home with the 165th Pennsylvania after being mustered out with that ninety-day regiment, used his influence to compel the commission to vacate. Fortunately, the commission was able to move its considerable inventory to a building at the diamond, opposite its competitor in giving, the Christian Commission, which only added to the congestion already there.

Still another source of pressure on Janes to close the field hospitals stemmed from the strong desire of his own medical personnel to rejoin their units. The medical director could now count about 250 physicians under his jurisdiction: the Army of the Potomac surgeons left behind, the civilians of varying degrees of competence and willingness who had offered their services, and those Confederate doctors who remained with their wounded.

Both armies were as eager to have the doctors back with them as they were to return. All had had more than enough of field hospital duty and the primitive form of medicine it entailed. They had done their share.

"All Were Gone"

The rows of white tents at Camp Letterman presented all the symmetry and precision of an elite military unit at attention and awaiting inspection. Nestled between two groves of oaks on a gently sloping stretch of the George Wolf farm a mile east of town, the general hospital was only about 150 yards from the railroad track. This meant that the wounded, when they improved enough to travel, could be easily carried by stretcher to the trains and transported out of the area. Arriving relatives and other visitors would no longer be exposed to the ordeal of trying to find the soldier they sought at scores of widely scattered facilities; he could be located speedily on a camp directory.

To one nurse, whose thoughts were more poetic than martial, the identical canvas tents arranged in double rows seemed "like great fluttering pairs of white wings, brooding peacefully over these wounded men." There were six such rows made up of some 400 tents in all; each had 12 beds (the men were no longer having to sprawl on the bare ground, but were being placed on bedsteads with straw-filled mattresses). Each tent was numbered and then grouped into lettered wards. Busy walkways in between the uniform rows created a town-like effect of streets and avenues.[1]

In addition to tents for patients, each equipped with a Sibley stove, there were others for staff, for the Sanitary and Christian commissions transferring their lodges, for surgery, for cooking, and for laundering. There was a cool spring nearby and a number of wells had been sunk that insured an abundant supply of fresh water. So self-sufficient did this

Camp Letterman as a model of organization and order. *Gettysburg National Military Park.*

carefully planned community appear that it would have fulfilled the societal dream of a Brigham Young.

The hospital opened officially on July 22 and as Sophronia Bucklin trekked to her new nursing station she had no difficulty finding her way for "a line of stretchers a mile and a half in length . . . told us where lay our work."[2]

So enthusiastic were the authorities to consolidate the wounded at the new facility that they were rushed over as soon as the last tents had been raised. Such a backup was created in situating the patients that, as Sophronia had observed, the procession of litters and ambulances leading to the site extended all the way into town.

Though it appeared every hospital in the area was being emptied, several were not included in the migration of invalids. Much to the disappointment of town officials, the public schoolhouse continued to be used as a hospital, as did the theological seminary and two warehouses.

The Confederate wounded remaining at Gettysburg were all severe cases, men too badly hurt to be taken back to Virginia, so it was expected that a disproportionate number of the patients being transferred to Camp Letterman were Rebels. In fact, about half of the 4,000 wounded being carried there were Southerners.

As the wounded were admitted, officers were segregated from the enlisted men, but the Union and Confederate wounded—no doubt at Janes's insistence—were otherwise closely integrated at Camp Letterman. This was the case right up to the point of burial at the hospital cemetery, conveniently set up just beyond the tents, next to an embalming station and the temporary "dead house" where the deceased were processed. And, of course, the mortality rate was high because, as a Sanitary Commission agent rather callously put it, the patients there were "in truth the very dregs of battle from two armies."[3]

At the cemetery, too, all was in perfect order. The mounds were uniformly spaced with each accurately and legibly identified, but with the incongruity of a soldier from Virginia resting next to one from New York and a corporal from Alabama lying beside a sergeant from Indiana.

Adaptation to the new surroundings came smoothly and swiftly. Of the routine set up by the Christian Commission to service the tent city, one delegate recorded:

> With our haversacks loaded, with soldiers books, letter paper, pencils, envelopes, etc., each delegate takes a tour of one row of tents, ascertaining what is needed, supplying it either from our haversacks or writing an order on our tent agent, which the tent nurse presents at our counter and is filled.[4]

As transient as were the kinds of services the relief agencies offered, the Sanitary Commission had no more difficulty than the Christian Commission in transferring its activities; all it basically needed was a tent and it had a base of operations.

Naturally, Sarah Broadhead had somewhat mixed feelings when the soldiers she had taken into her modest home on the Chambersburg Pike were so abruptly removed from her custody and taken to Camp Letterman. They weren't ready yet to be disturbed; they needed more time, by her maternal reasoning. "We had but short notice of the intention, and though we pleaded hard to have them remain, it was of no use," the schoolteacher fretted. She wrote of her suddenly silent surroundings no longer set apart by a fluttering red flag:

> A weight of care which we took upon us for duty's sake and which we had learned to like and would have gladly borne until relieved by the complete recovery of our men, has been lifted off of our shoulders, and again we have our house to ourselves.[5]

Cornelia Hancock had similar feelings of personal loss when her Second Corps hospital was broken up and the wounded carried away, though she was to be one of the more than forty nurses joining the Camp Letterman staff. "It is a great deal nicer there," Cornelia had to admit of her new situation, "except that I have but fourteen of my old boys which is very trying—it is just like parting with part of one's family. I go to see the boys and some of them cry that I cannot stay."[6]

She did have one precious object, however, to forever remind her that the work she had done as one of the first volunteers on the field was sincerely appreciated. It was a silver medallion that a group of soldiers had somehow arranged to have struck. On one side was inscribed, "Miss Cornelia Hancock, presented by the wounded soldiers 3rd Division, 2nd Army Corps" and on the other, "Testimonial of regard for ministrations of mercy to the wounded soldiers at Gettysburg, Pa. - July 1863." The medal had cost the men $20 but to the sensitive Cornelia it was priceless.[7]

For many of the volunteers who had come to the field, the opening of Letterman spelled the end of their usefulness. A much smaller staff would be required at such a compact installation. Only about forty surgeons were to remain, nine of them Confederates; the rest were packing up to either return to the army or to go home to their private practices.

Among those leaving Gettysburg after three weeks of exhausting labor were Georgy Woolsey and her mother. There was no longer a need at the depot for the Sanitary Commission's feeding station and lodge, which had fulfilled such a vital function when the wounded were being forced to wait for hours, or even overnight, for rail transportation out. By Georgy's estimate, 16,000 good meals had been served and more than 1,200 men sheltered at the lodge when they failed to get aboard departing trains.

The staff had maintained a policy throughout of equal treatment toward the soldiers of both armies and Georgy acknowledged, "the cloth-ing we reserved for our own men, except now and then when a shivering rebel needed it. But in feeding them we could make no distinctions."

Georgy was struck by the change in attitude that came over many of the volunteers. "It was curious to see among our workers at the lodge, the disgust and horror felt for rebels giving place to the kindest feeling for wounded men."[8]

The last soldier they had sent off before striking their tents was a Union lieutenant from Oregon who had lost a foot. He was dispatched on his long journey home with a cup of hot soup and the last handkerchief in their stores, one sprinkled with cologne. Then Georgy and her mother arranged to board a train themselves to return to their comfortable New York home, and the large loving family they had left what seemed like so long ago.

As they waited for the train to pull out, the Woolseys, too, found that their efforts were not unappreciated. To their delight, two military brass bands marched to their car and played a farewell salute to the misty-eyed ladies that was worthy of a commanding general's send-off.

With the opening of Camp Letterman, the services of another group also became to a large extent superfluous—the Confederate medical per-sonnel. As their own particular hospitals were vacated, the surgeons and attendants were ordered to assemble at Pennsylvania College. Getting together their belongings, they fully expected that they were to be deliv-ered within their own lines.

A year before, the U.S. Adjutant General's office in Washington had issued an order stating that, "the principle being recognized that medical officers should not be held as prisoners of war, it is hereby directed that all medical officers so held by the United States shall be immediately and unconditionally discharged."[9] Only weeks afterward, the Confederacy's bureaucratic equivalent released a similar order.

The doctors were so wedded to the idea that those aiding the wounded should not be looked upon as combatants that every one of the Confederate surgeons left at Gettysburg had agreed to sign a petition to General Lee calling for the release of the Sanitary Commission agents seized and being held in Libby Prison, citing as grounds that the agents were succoring the needy of both sides.

Against this backdrop, there was no particular concern when the surgeons congregated at the college, now emptied of patients and in the process of being prepared for a new semester. Young Simon Baruch was among the late arrivals. Once the wounded of Kershaw's South Carolina brigade had been disposed of, he and his associates were ordered to report to the provost marshal. Baruch thought that offer "of a type which I had not before encountered. He was an impudent, pompous chap, probably under the influence of liquor." That Baruch was in for some trouble was indicated when he told the officer, whom he did not identify by name, that he was ready to be sent home and got as a reply: "I guess you are. Just come here tonight at seven. I have a lot of other Rebels and you may go along with them."[10]

Perhaps more alert than Baruch to what might be in store were the Baltimore ladies who had been serving at his hospital. They insisted he take some money from a roll of greenbacks they had brought along for just such an exigency. At first, Baruch declined, but though he was still confident he was to be sent back as he had been the year before Antietam, he finally accepted five dollars from the cash reserve.

Among those Baruch may have joined at the college was Dr. L. P. Warren, the surgeon of Pettigrew's North Carolina brigade. He was in the position of having to part with a younger brother, John C. Warren of Edenton, North Carolina, who, by sheer chance, he had come upon at a field hospital two weeks after the battle. The eighteen-year-old lieutenant was riddled with five bullet holes and was lying on some blankets on the hard ground in a tent. He had been given up as a hopeless case by the Federal surgeons who were doing nothing for him but administering morphine. Dr. Warren was allowed to remain several days with him, washing him and replacing his brother's blood-stained garments with his own. Through his constant attention, the youth gradually recovered his strength and, even with one bullet lodged in his shoulder blade after passing through his lung, became fit enough to be removed to Point Lookout while the doctor headed in another direction.[11]

The motley band of professional men marched in irregular fashion to the railroad depot from the nearby college where the surgeons were herded with wounded prisoners onto a train that Baruch said was "loaded to its utmost capacity, my own position being in a cattle car." When the train arrived at Baltimore in the morning, a file of soldiers was waiting and a sergeant bellowed, "All you men what is surgeons in the Rebel army fall in here."

The command signaled to Baruch that the medical people were being segregated in order to send them to Virginia while the others were to go off to prison camps. Instead, the doctors were marched under guard to Barnum's Hotel on Monument Square and locked up. That afternoon, the physicians, accustomed to being mounted on horseback, were forced to tramp through the hot, dusty streets of Baltimore to Fort McHenry. As he walked along with his coat thrown over his shoulder, Baruch could only think of the last time he had been in the city, the previous October, and had been driven about the streets in the comfort of a fashionable open carriage.[12] Though he was then technically a prisoner, he had been free to circulate and had even found himself being entertained at a dance arranged at the home of a wealthy Baltimore family. Obviously, this time he was to be in for a different experience.

The *Sentinel* had noted the departure of the Southern medical personnel by stating simply that "a considerable number of Rebel Surgeons and nurses left yesterday for Baltimore. Some of them are rather pleasant in intercourse; but, as a general matter, they are very bitter in feeling. We feel great regret at their delusion."[13]

Perhaps the most sullen physicians had, unlike Baruch, an inkling of what was ahead for them and the reason for it. Doubtless, few had until then ever heard of a Dr. William P. Rucker, a pro-Union resident of Covington, Virginia, who had been accused of committing a murder by the Commonwealth of Virginia. Rucker had been arrested on the charge by a Confederate cavalry on July 25, 1862, at a time when he was serving as a surgeon in the Union army in West Virginia. Despite the agreement between the belligerents governing the treatment of medical personnel, the Confederate authorities refused to accede to Union demands for Rucker's release. With so many Confederate doctors now in their hands as a result of Gettysburg's slaughter, the Federal leaders felt they had sufficient leverage to force Rucker's release.

Still, the Richmond government would not budge. It was not until October that the impasse was broken by Dr. Rucker's escape from imprisonment. With no further need to hold the Confederate surgeons as hostages, they were released en masse. But, with every day the standoff continued, both sides deprived themselves of the life-saving skills of the

company of trained physicians made to sit idle at Fort McHenry and doing
no one any good.[14]

On July 20, two days before Camp Letterman opened, Medical Inspector John M. Cuyler—following one of the numerous and peculiar chains
of command that were being observed by the medical, quartermaster,
infantry, and other army personnel serving at Gettysburg after the battle—
brought his direct superior in Washington, Surgeon General Hammond, up
to date on the number of wounded still at Gettysburg.

By then, according to the inspector's tally, 12,552 Union soldiers had
been sent off and 2,151 remained, while 2,922 Confederates had been
transferred out, with about the same number remaining. Of that combined
total, Cuyler related, "3,072 will have to remain here for the present. So
says the medical director."[15]

The last reference was, of course, to Dr. Janes, who, as the man in
charge of all the wounded, was cooperating closely with the various
inspectors sent from Washington to help him. In the rather confused structure of things, Jonathan Letterman, though still acting as medical director
of the Army of the Potomac, had his involvement with Gettysburg officially terminated on July 18 "when the hospitals were taken from under my
control."[16]

Surgeon General Hammond had decided that it made more organizational sense to place the wounded at Gettysburg and environs under Surgeon W. S. King, medical director of the Department of the Susquehanna
within whose geographic borders the battlefield was situated. It was King
who became Janes' new superior.

As part of his new responsibilities, King, who was headquartered at
Chambersburg, Pennsylvania, was told to "make contracts with such doctors as you may be able at $112.83 per month and to thus relieve with all
practicable dispatch the Medical officers of the Army of the Potomac who
will be sent to their regiments when so relieved." How attitudes had
changed toward the civilian physicians! "You will understand," King was
directed, "that it is desirable as soon as possible to close the hospitals at
Gettysburg."[17]

As the personnel turnover accelerated, King was notified a few days
later by the Surgeon General's office that "a number of contract Physicians
have been employed by this office and ordered to report to you for duty,

and others will be engaged as the proper material presents itself. Should any of those Surgeons prove incompetent, you will please annul their contracts at once and report the fact to this office."[18]

Janes, who held the rank of major, remained the man responsible for all the hospitals at Gettysburg, while Cuyler and Vollum concentrated on the evacuation phase of the operation. Both were lieutenant colonels with Vollum, under orders to report to Cuyler.

The inspectors' presence at Gettysburg, as well as the appearances of Inspector Johnson and the specimen collector, Brinton, reflected the personal interest Surgeon General Hammond was taking in affairs there. As active as he had become, Hammond recognized that all the support he was able to provide was inadequate to the demands. On August 1, the *Christian Advocate* published a letter he wrote to the U.S. Christian Commission in which Hammond acknowledged that "owing to the military necessities of the occasion, the suffering would have been much greater than it was but for the aid afforded the medical officers by the benevolent individuals who came to their assistance."[19]

Such a position, of course, distanced Hammond somewhat from his close friend, Jonathan Letterman, on the need for outside help. It was not in the nature of the six-foot-four, 260-pound giant whom the Sanitary Commission had campaigned so vigorously to place in the Surgeon General's office to remain passive in such a situation as existed at Gettysburg, once he became aware of what was going on.

The thirty-four-year-old son of an Annapolis, Maryland, physician, Hammond had entered the army a year after earning his medical degree at the University of the City of New York in 1848. In the next decade, he served at various frontier posts, much as had Letterman. He utilized the idle time between campaigns against hostile Indians to pursue his interests in physiology and botany, and won a prestigious prize from the American Medical Association for a lengthy essay he wrote on the nutritional value of albumen, starch, and gum. Hammond also completed a tour of duty at West Point. In 1859, he resigned from the army to teach at the University of Maryland. While a member of that faculty, he had occasion to treat some of the wounded of the 6th Massachusetts after that unit was attacked by a Baltimore mob.

He re-entered the army as an assistant surgeon at the outbreak of the war. He was serving as an inspector of camps and hospitals under General

Rosecrans in West Virginia when his work attracted the attention of the Sanitary Commission, which was, at the time, much dissatisfied with the manner in which the surgeon general's office was being administered. In the spring of 1862 Hammond, then only a lieutenant, was appointed to the post with the rank of brigadier general.[20]

Hammond had a big booming voice to match his stature, and he soon became a dominating figure in Washington, actually attracting too much attention for his own political good. Secretary of War Stanton particularly disliked Hammond and thought his ideas for reforming the medical service (which he advanced in close cooperation with Letterman) as too costly and extreme.

While he made at least one appearance on the field at Gettysburg, Hammond's main contact was through the inspectors that he had functioning there.

Regardless of who was reporting to whom, there was ample work for all and Janes appeared to be working civilly if not cordially with the inspectors from Washington. Actually, it was much to Janes' advantage to have with him these men from headquarters. They had the clout to communicate directly with Hammond and obtain what was needed at the hospitals which were now completely bypassed by the line of supply to the Army of the Potomac that ran from Washington to Virginia via Frederick, Maryland.

On September 2, Janes got a brief message from the Surgeon General asking: "Are you in need of any supplies? Has there been any deficiency of food for the patients?"[21]

Janes may well have reflected on the contrast with the early days after the battle, before Washington became aware of what he was up against.

From a medical standpoint, the dire cases remaining at Camp Letterman provided some valuable evidence of what surgical techniques might be most effective for unusually severe injuries. Careful records were maintained, to the point of sending body parts to the surgeon general's laboratories for post-mortem analysis.

"The most fastidious surgeon could not mangle . . . flesh or bones more splendidly for scientific purposes than this continuous battle has done," observed a Sanitary Commission agent. "Every class and character of contusion and fracture and penetrating wound from shot and shell of the worst description is to be found under the 300 tents which constitute Camp

Letterman Hospital." Among those cases were 345 gunshot fractures of the femur. In 158 of these wounds, amputation was performed and, it was recorded that 101 had resulted in death, an indication of the mortality rate involved in particular surgical procedures.[22]

Those patients considered untransportable were those who had sustained penetrating wounds of the head, chest, abdomen, and pelvis, or compound fractures of the limbs. Because the cases at Letterman were the most grievously hurt in the battle, the level of suffering to which the staff was exposed, despite the much improved conditions there, was the most intense and concentrated they were to see. All their strength and dedication was required to endure the sights and sounds they had to confront day after day. "It is heart-rending to pass through streets and hear the cries of agony that burden the air," wrote F. W. Stoke, one of the soldiers on guard there. "I have heard them when I was away from the hospital a half mile."

A steward told him that up to seventeen men were dying each day.[23] Indeed, at one point when there were 1,600 patients at the hospital, surgeons there predicted to a Christian Commission delegate that "at least one-third would become occupants of the secluded spot they had apportioned to the dead."[24]

"Oh, mercy, the suffering!" Cornelia Hancock poured out in one letter home. "All the worst are dying rapidly. I saw one of my best men die yesterday. He wore away to skin and bone, was anxious to recover but prayed he might find it for the best for him to be taken from his suffering. He was the one who said if there was a heaven I would go to it. I hope he will get there before I do."

With all she had seen, Cornelia could only conclude: "I think war is a hellish way of settling a dispute."[25]

More than half of the wounded men in nurse Sophronia Bucklin's ward were Confederates, who she described as "grim, gaunt, ragged men—long-haired, hollow-eyed and sallow-cheeked." But it was a ratio that did not exist for long because of the higher mortality rate of the Rebels. Of the disparity, the "vacationing" teacher chauvinistically observed:

> With the same care from attendants, and the same surgical skill, many more of the rebels died than of our own men—whether from the nature of the wounds, which seemed generally more frightful, or because they lacked the courage to bear up under

Sophronia Bucklin, a volunteer who served until the last of the wounded were evacuated. *Our Army Nurses.*

> them or whether the wild irregular lives which they had been leading had rendered the system less able to resist pain. [Why] will always remain a mystery to me.[26]

Though the cause eluded her analysis, she said, "of 22 rebels who were brought into my ward at one time, 13 died, after receiving the same care that was given to our men." In fact, so many were dying in her ward that, in what passed for a bit of hospital humor, someone suggested that Sophronia deserved a government pension for having killed off more Confederates than probably any soldier in the ranks of the Union army.[27] But the weighted mortality rate was hospital-wide. By Sophronia's estimate, more than two-thirds of the 1,200 graves in the hospital cemetery at one point were Confederate.

While maintaining so many men in a single hospital may have had its administrative advantages, it also presented logistical problems, mainly related to feeding. A large, wooden cookhouse had been constructed for the massive task of providing meals for the huge camp. The building had no walls, but a roof did provide cover for the kitchen staff. With such a multitude to feed, "you may know that they have to have the pots middling in size," Cornelia Hancock informed her niece about the operation. "If you ever saw anything done on a large scale, it is done so here."[28]

Rebel hospital attendants stood on the same lines with everyone else to draw rations for the wards under their supervision and one nurse observed:

> A sharp contest often arose when the attendants meet at the cook house to draw food for their respective patients. Our men were often knocked down in the struggle and the triumphant rebels appropriated all and everything upon which they could lay their hands.[29]

It seemed the longer the members of the two opposing armies cohabitated at the hospital, the more they forgot their relative positions. "It was not until they were sent to Baltimore," it was observed of some of the Confederate personnel at Camp Letterman, "that they began to realize themselves as prisoners of war . . . They had become sleek and fat and the change from plenty to scarcity was a blow to their ravenous stomachs which they felt keenly."[30]

While being confined in such close proximity led to some hostile exchanges between the Union and Confederate wounded, to a far greater extent the discourse it afforded served to break down the differences between them. For the time being, regardless of where they had come from, they were simply men trying to endure and survive the same types of painful, disfiguring, impersonally inflicted injuries. Disarmed and out of uniform, they were no longer Rebs and Yanks. They were all just wounded soldiers and the staff and the volunteers who came into the camp almost universally regarded them as simply that.

Provisions for the camp were, to a large degree, purchased locally, and the orders that Dr. Janes certified showed that he was not being overly frugal. One included such huge quantities as 1,532 pounds of butter, 1,232 dozen eggs and 825 chickens for $900.79, and another covered 101 gallons of oysters (undoubtedly from Chesapeake Bay) costing $111 "for the use of the sick in Hospital under my charge."[31]

The formidable Anna Morris Holstein, the thirty-seven-year-old Pennsylvania woman who, with her husband, had been nursing at general hospitals at Antietam and Frederick, commanded the special diet kitchen at Camp Letterman and, as the matron in charge, she exercised her authority to the fullest.

With Mrs. Holstein in control, the other nurses found they were "forbidden this privilege of preparing extra food ourselves, and were not even allowed to go inside of the kitchen," noted one with annoyance. As proprietary as most women felt about access to their culinary domain, Mrs. Holstein went so far as "to keep a guard, with fixed bayonet, at the entrance."[32]

She took it upon herself to decide just what would be good for the patients and "often she refused to fill the orders from our surgeon," said one nurse. So angered was the doctor at her apparent insolence, "he often went to the kitchen himself and, with his own hands, cooked the food, saying that what was the rightful property of the patients, that they should have."[33]

But in defense of Mrs. Holstein's nutritional knowledge, one soldier, Capt. John Hilton of the 145th Pennsylvania, did attest that, "having been one of the doubtful cases, I know had it not been for such care as I received from Mrs. Holstein, I never could have recovered."

The captain noted:

> All we know is that Mrs. Holstein had full charge of the diet kitchen and all of the many delicacies we received were from her hands, and in addition to this she constantly visited the wounded to ascertain what would be good for them and to encourage them, and give them a motherly care.[34]

Dorothea Dix was still frequently about, but she found that her role was diminishing and her screening authority much ignored. Said Cornelia Hancock a bit dismissively, "Miss Dix was in camp today and stuck her head in the tents, but she does not work at all, and her nurses are being superseded very fast."[35]

Aside from the frictions that developed over purview and authority, a serious problem in administering the vast sprawling facility was simple traffic control. So many of the visitors coming to Gettysburg were

The formidable Anna Holstein (in striped dress) with her husband William (left), the Rev. Gordon Winslow (right), and other volunteers in front of the Holsteins' tent. *MOLLUS–MHI.*

descending on the hospital and lingering about that it was disrupting operations. Many of the civilians drifting in were Marylanders sympathetic to the Confederacy and there was genuine concern that they might aid in escape attempts. Several men, obviously in better physical shape than was thought, had, with their help, skipped away at night and were shepherded South. As a result, the authorities had to impose a 4 P.M. curfew. Enforcing the restriction, however, was in the hands of a guard of fifty-six men commanded by a captain; a unit that was pronounced by one medical inspector as being "very inefficient."[36]

On July 5 when General Meade was about to leave Gettysburg, he said that he could not "delay to pick up the debris of the battlefield," and requested "that all these arrangements may be made by the departments." Now Dr. Janes seemed to be hearing from all these jurisdictions and from officers whose names he didn't even recognize who were taking an interest in affairs at Gettysburg. The latest harassment came from a Colonel Hoffman in the "Office of Commissary General of Prisoners" telling the medical director:

> I have to request that you will forward to the Depot on Johnson Island near Sandusky, O., all rebel officers among the sick and wounded prisoners in your charge, as fast as they are sufficiently recovered to bear the fatigue of the journey. None must be permitted to escape by being detained there beyond the proper time for their removal.[37]

Obviously, Henry Janes' role was expanding. He had been operating strictly as a medical officer; now he was being asked to think of himself as a jailer as well. He had to view his patients not only in terms of how well they were healing but he also had to be concerned that none of them had become so healthy that they posed an escape threat. If the doctor shook his head as he read this latest dispatch from an obscure source, no one could blame him.

Many of the wounded Rebs were in need of clothing, for either the prison life that awaited them or for an attempt to escape and travel across country. Fervent Effie Goldsborough had now moved from Pennsylvania College to Camp Letterman, and was one of those determined to help the Southerners in any way she could.

Miss Goldsborough was assigned to a ward where fifty-five Federal and fifty-five Confederate soldiers were being treated. The rules specifically prohibited giving the men boots, but that didn't deter the spirited young woman. She secured a permit to go to town and an army ambulance. In town she bought a pair of boots at one of the stores for a soldier she had in mind, and then cleverly figured out how she could get them to him. She tied them to her waist underneath her hoopskirt and was able to smuggle them back into camp without their being seen or heard (though she did face a crisis trying to get on and off her conveyance without disclosing her hidden cargo).[38]

Despite his enormous administrative responsibilities at Gettysburg, Dr. Henry Janes somehow found time to carry on his practice of treating some casualties himself after each battle.

The young doctor selected cases that challenged him and then recorded the patient's progress in a large felt-covered journal he faithfully maintained throughout the war. Frequently, he had photographs made of the men exhibiting their wounds so that he gradually assembled, in the interest of medicine, a rather ghastly gallery of some of the more distressing injuries he had encountered.

As the man in charge of all the hospitals there, he insisted that the Union and Confederate wounded be provided the same treatment, and at Camp Letterman he had the wards closely integrated. In addition, his finely written journal entries are replete with case histories of Southern soldiers he personally treated. More important to Janes than to which army a wounded soldier belonged, was the nature of the case and the effectiveness of the treatment prescribed, treatment that was often the product of his own imagination. He frequently took on nearly hopeless situations and he dutifully recorded in his journal his failures as well as his successes.

Janes' entries for the Camp Letterman period not only reveal the dreadful physical condition of so many of the Rebels at the time they were wounded, but also the limitations of the surgeons, given the state of medical knowledge and technology at that juncture, in dealing with the types of injuries they were seeing.

Of the death of a Virginian named D. S. Edwards, who had suffered only an upper arm wound on July 3, Janes noted in his meticulous handwriting:

> He was very much emaciated and completely exhausted by long continued diarrhea. He has no control over his bowels and no appetite. On the back is a large bedsore which is sloughing and extending rapidly. Suppuration is profuse and exceedingly fetid. . . . Sept. 11 died from exhaustion.

J. F. Adams, a thirty-four-year-old Georgian wounded on the second day of the battle, Janes not only managed to keep alive but on October 1 was able to record optimistically, "general health improved." The very next day's entry, however, he faithfully reported, "Oct. 2 appeared better early in the morning but at 9 a.m. complained of severe pain in both back of head and neck. About 3 p.m. had symptoms of tetanus, succeeded by death."

The extent of the medical profession's ability to handle head wounds was rather pathetically shown in Dr. Janes' case history of a thirty-nine-year-old Pennsylvanian named Jacob Morfrid who was, according to the journal, "wounded July 3 by minie ball causing a fracture of the frontal bone, through which the pulsations of the brain were visible."

Morfrid was able to hang on and even show signs of improvement until Aug. 15 when Janes noted the patient "is comatose, pupils dilated." The next day, he wrote, "Aug. 16 died: Treatment applications of cold water and ice to head."[39]

Though Janes had some 21,000 wounded to be concerned about, the fact that he was personally treating some of them perhaps gave him a sense of active, hands-on participation in the recovery process that a more detached director may have lacked. Janes maintained a keener sense of the levels of suffering that continued not just weeks, but months after the battle was over.

On August 18, the editor of the *Adams Sentinel* decided that he might give his readers a glimpse of Camp Letterman, which was somewhat remote from the flow of traffic in town and a place those not involved in the care or supply of the wounded had little occasion to see. The paper reported:

> This receptacle of the wounded soldiers, has been arranged in the very best manner, and everything connected with it is in the most perfect order and cleanliness—exciting the admiration of all who have been its visitors. Everything is being done to relieve and soothe the sufferers, that attention and kind, humane hands can do.
>
> Deaths do daily occur, but from the severity of many wounds, this cannot be prevented—all that skill and careful nursing can do, however, is being done. There are over 1,600 wounded there, making a population in camp, including surgeons, nurses, other attendants, and guards, of over 2,000 persons. The hospitals in the country around the town have been broken up; and there are none now, we believe, independent of the General Hospital except those in town, at the Public School house, the Seminary, and Sheads' and Buehler's Hall. The wounded there are getting along very well—as are also those in private homes.

On September 23, the sort of relationship that had developed between the blue and gray at Gettysburg was confirmed by a remarkable event.

At a time when the Army of the Potomac and the Army of Northern Virginia were confronting one another a hundred miles away, the Christian Commission and a group of Gettysburg ladies arranged a banquet for *all* the wounded soldiers at Camp Letterman, with Dr. Janes' full approval. It was an affair to be savored, not for the dishes that were being prepared, but for the coming together of supposed enemies whose empty sleeves and bandage-swathed heads placed them in fraternity.

While the camp officials thought the party would be good for the morale of patients and staff, most of whom had been confined to the hospital scene at Gettysburg for over two months, such an affair would have no doubt riled the rabid Abolitionists and fire-eating Secessionists had they been aware such a gathering was being contemplated. But to the guests of honor, it was a welcome respite from the dreary monotony of their painful existence.

The day selected turned out to be bright and balmy and, said nurse Anna Holstein, "tempted many who had not yet ventured outside their tents into the open air, hoping they might be able to participate in the promised enjoyments." According to Mrs. Holstein, for the occasion, the streets and tents of the hospital had been decorated with evergreens "and everything on this gala day had a corresponding cheerful look."[40]

And what a repast it was for men so long accustomed to hardtack and coffee! The Christian Commission had solicited many of the contributions from its supporters in Philadelphia and the local women had scoured the area for offerings. Between the two efforts, the *Sentinel* reported, some 500 chickens had been found as well as thirty hams. Also on the tables were such rare treats as oysters, pies, and ice cream.[41]

"When the hour came for the good dinner," Mrs. Holstein said, "hundreds moved upon crutches with feeble, tottering steps to the table, looking with unmistakable delight upon the display of luxuries."[42]

Although she did not mention it, Mrs. Holstein was no doubt aware that this was actually the second attempt at such a banquet, the first having been marred by some rough Confederate hospital attendants rushing the refreshment tables, elbowing aside the wounded and, according to one angry and disappointed soldier at the scene, "gobbled up most of the delicious food."[43]

The kitchen at Camp Letterman. *MOLLUS–MHI.*

Learning of the failed effort from the Christian Commission, members of three churches in Philadelphia took up a special collection and raised $1,100 to stage another picnic. Sophronia Bucklin said of the second effort:

> This time the rebels were kept under guard until the Union soldiers had been served, and bountifully loaded trays carried into the wards, and the contents distributed amongst those who were allowed to eat of them.
> In due time all received an ample supply of the choicest food their condition would admit of.[44]

A band had come from York to play for the event, and at night there were various races staged, a greased-pole climbing contest organized, and a minstrel show, with the performers all patients from the hospital. The latter, Mrs. Holstein thought "the crowning pleasure of the day."

The nurse then recounted, "At an early hour, the large crowd who had enjoyed it all with the patients, quietly dispersed."[45]

To those who attended, the get-together had been looked upon as a form of social recreation for the long-suffering soldiers. Probably no one was conscious of the fact that it represented one of the first acts of reconciliation that would take place in the nation. And it was one that probably would not have occurred if the battle had not, by the magnitude of its destruction, taken away so much of the ardor for war of those fortunate enough to have survived.

Gov. Andrew G. Curtin of Pennsylvania had come to Gettysburg the week after the battle and was appalled—not only at the level of carnage but by the manner in which the remains of those who had died on the field were being hastily interred. The shallow graves were haphazardly scattered about, often with body parts already protruding. And Curtin's tour was conducted before outsiders began to arrive and instituted a wholesale exhuming of graves in search of their loved ones. Each successful hunt left a cavity, for few of the diggers bothered to refill the graves they emptied. If the wrong body was disturbed, the unsatisfactory corpse was then recovered even more imperfectly than when it was initially buried.

Something had to be done and, understandably enough, the governor's particular concern was for the more than 535 Pennsylvania soldiers who had been killed in the fighting. From a political standpoint, Curtin had to be uneasy; he was up for reelection that November and had to be sensitive to the scandal that might erupt if his opponents revealed the mistreatment of the heroic dead at Gettysburg.

The governor's first action was to announce that, upon a family's request, the state would defray the cost of removing any Pennsylvanian killed at Gettysburg to anywhere in the state for reburial. He also made himself familiar about the field hospitals, seeing to the treatment being given soldiers of the Keystone State.

Curtin appointed a successful, local young attorney, David Wills, to serve as the state's agent at Gettysburg. He could not possibly have anticipated how broadly Wills would view his assignment. The thirty-year-old lawyer, whose large brick home and office was a conspicuous structure at the town square, began to meet with representatives of other states similarly distressed over the condition of the soldiers' graves on the field. From a conference late in July emerged a novel suggestion, one that would deal with the concerns of all the states that had lost men in the battle. The proposal was that a soldiers' national cemetery be established at Gettysburg. If the ambitious project was not Wills' own idea, the proposal was at least conveyed to Governor Curtin by his representative on the scene.

A capital idea, the governor responded. It would, after all, be the first such military cemetery in the country. Fully anticipating legislative concurrence, Curtin authorized Wills to begin making arrangements for the acquisition of land for the burial ground and to arrange for its design and development, including the transfer of the dead soldiers.

For $2,475.87 Wills managed to acquire as a site a seventeen-acre cornfield atop Cemetery Hill, adjoining Evergreen Cemetery, with its imposing arched gatehouse. The location had been a key artillery position during the battle and the strong stone breastworks the 11th Corps had created around the open grounds served as a natural border.

A fiscal arrangement was worked out under which Pennsylvania would make lots in the cemetery available without cost to each of the seventeen states with dead upon the field. Each state, however, was to be assessed (in proportion to its population) for the expense of removing bodies and preparing the cemetery, including the construction of a suitable central monument. To design the facility, Wills secured the services of William Saunders, a landscape gardener for the U.S. Department of Agriculture in Washington.

The contract for removing the dead was let out to bid and no fewer than 34 proposals were presented. The high bid was $8 per body and the lowest offer of $1.59 was presented by a local resident, F. W. Biesecker. A second contract for reburying the dead in the coffins provided by the Quartermaster General (to this point, the Federal government's only material contribution) was also granted to Biesecker for the same amount.

But if Mr. Biesecker was anticipating a quick profit from his labors, he was not figuring on having a man like Samuel Weaver looking over his shoulder as agent Wills' superintendent of exhumations. Weaver, who did hauling in town, approached his responsibility like a detective examining a crime scene, determined that every effort be made to identify every body uncovered. By his insistence, "there was not a grave permitted to be opened or a body searched unless I was present."

Weaver said of his painstaking process, "Where the grave was not marked, I examined all the clothing and everything about the body to find the name."[46]

Clues to identification came from a variety of objects: letters, a Bible inscription, express receipts, or names placed on pieces of clothing or equipment. As he sifted through the personal effects that escaped the battlefield scavengers, Weaver created little packages of belongings, 287 in all, that might, if they wished, be claimed by relatives. Included were such items as money, diaries, combs, daguerreotypes, knives, and, in one instance, the actual bullet that had killed the soldier and fallen free of the skeleton.

The work of exhuming began on Oct. 27 but it would be March before Weaver proclaimed the last Union soldier had been located and removed. Of the 3,512 bodies taken up, Weaver, despite his exhaustive efforts, would be unable to identify 979. In succeeding to the extent that he had, however, he eased the anxiety of scores of families that had never learned officially what had become of a loved one and, even if reconciled to the presumed loss, had no idea where the remains might be found.

To attorney Wills, "the grateful relief that this work has brought to many a sorrowing household" was immeasurable.[47]

Of his efforts, the meticulous Weaver would assert with consummate pride, "I firmly believe that there has not been a single mistake made in the removal of the soldiers to the Cemetery by taking the body of a rebel for a Union soldier."[48]

For the most part, the exhumers were satisfied to leave the Confederates in the great trenches in which they had been deposited en masse, with no attempt made at individual identification. Those in charge of seeing to the belated veneration of the Union dead adopted a procedure under which no more than 100 bodies would be brought up in a single day so that the reburials in the soldiers' cemetery could keep pace. But with the winter freeze approaching, it was clear that the bulk of the work would have to await the following spring.

William Saunders was a Scotsman who had, since his arrival in this country, involved himself in the design of private estates and cemeteries, and his concept for the national cemetery was quite impressive. It called for the coffins to be placed in trenches arranged in a vast semicircle and grouped in sections by state with the center reserved for a monument.

"The prevailing expression of the Cemetery should be that of simple grandeur," the forty-one-year-old designer had decided. It was an effect that could be achieved by arranging the graves "in easy harmony, avoiding abrupt contrasts and unexpected features."[49]

It would take years for the effect that Saunders was seeking to be achieved, years before a monument could be carved and put in place and the thousands of small, low gravestones symmetrically arranged, years for the grounds to be cultivated in the precise manner he desired. But the cemetery was at least sufficiently advanced by late October that a suitable dedication ceremony could now be arranged.

A certain snobbery surrounded the sophisticated and refined founders and officers of the U.S. Sanitary Commission. The remarkable organization they had created was doing an extraordinary job at Gettysburg. What would have become of the wounded there without the commission's timely and massive assistance was almost too dreadful to contemplate. But there seemed to be a need among these prideful men—Henry Bellows, George Templeton Strong, and Frederick Law Olmsted—that everyone be fully aware of what the commission was doing.

Olmsted was the efficient energetic administrator with a capacity for dealing with an infinite number of details at one time. He became particularly annoyed over what he perceived to be an effort by the upstart Christian Commission to claim undue credit for its work at Gettysburg.

The indefatigable general secretary alerted his associates that the Sanitary Commission's role should not be diminished, and that they must counterattack vigorously to protect its standing in the public's eye, using advertising as its primary tactic.

He wrote to the executive committee of the commission from Frederick on July 9, and, in almost a derisive tone, stated:

> I observe in the newspapers of Philadelphia and Boston a great many excited, sensational appeals from the Christian Commission and various one horse societies, founded on their alleged grand operations at Gettysburg.
>
> I am informed that fathers of the Christian Commission have stated that they were at Gettysburg before us and that their operations were much larger than ours.

Though no evidence was apparent that such things were actually going on, Olmsted felt compelled to act. He continued:

It is sometime since we have advertised much, for reasons, and I have had many enquiries. I send draft of advertisement which I request may now be published a few times, largely and prominently, heavily leaded throughout, in the prominent papers of New York, Boston and Philadelphia. It should be so leaded as to occupy a column, with no display lines or other trick except large type and leads.

He acknowledged to the group that "this might possibly cost $1000" but added, "I think it might be worth $100,000. It is striking for steady cooperation, when the iron is hot and small fry frantic."[50]

In specifying the precise typography to be used in his advertisement, Olmsted revealed one of his few faults as an administrator which was his insistence that everything be done exactly as he wished. Even Dr. Bellows, who thought he alone truly appreciated Olmsted's administrative ability, once wrote of his methods:

Mr. Frederick Law Olmsted is of all the men I know the most comprehensive, thorough, and minutely particular organizer. He is equally wonderful in the management of principles and . . . details. His mind is patient in meditation, careful and acute, his will inflexible, his devotion to his principles and methods confident and unflinching. He looks far ahead and his plans and methods are sometimes mysterious.

Bellows regarded Olmsted as a man who "loves power and is fit to hold it."[51]

If Olmsted felt a need to buy space in the popular press to remind the public of the Sanitary Commission's works and to appeal for continued support, there was no shortage of data to make the case, for no charitable organization kept more careful accounts. The exact number of donations that had been sent to the field and—often to the penny—the value of each was recorded so that when the time came to let the nation know of its service the commission was fully armed.

Frederick L. Olmsted, manager of the Sanitary Commission's relief effort. *Library of Congress.*

By the commission's calculations, it had distributed articles of clothing and sustenance with a value of $74,838 and, let's see, 52 cents.

The breakdown (with each category costed out) included 5,310 pairs of woolen drawers, 2,114 pillows, 2,659 handkerchiefs, 3,560 pairs of woolen socks and 2,258 pairs of cotton ones, 1,500 combs, 250 pounds of Castile soap, 7,000 tins basins and cups, 140 barrels of bandages, 3,500 fans, 11 barrels of chloride of lime, 180 lanterns, 350 pounds of candles, 648 pieces of mosquito netting, and 1,000 pipes.

In the way of sustenance, 11,000 pounds of poultry and mutton had been given to the soldiers at Gettysburg along with 6,130 pounds of butter, 8,500 dozen eggs, 850 pounds of coffee, 72 cans of oysters, and 303 jars of brandied peaches. In addition, 20,000 pounds of ice had been shipped by the commission to Gettysburg for preservation purposes.

In some quarters, what was probably most appreciated of the Sanitary Commission's gifts to the soldiers were the 1,168 bottles of whisky and the 600 gallons of ale that were distributed.[52]

The commission's detailed inventory was revealing in two regards. The accounting not only demonstrated the degree of the agency's effectiveness as a conduit for generating and distributing aid to the army from the private sector; it underscored the full extent and nature of the need that was left unfilled when the army left the scene. If adequate provision had been made for the Gettysburg army of wounded, then there would not have been such volume of demands made on the relief agencies.

That such basic items as soap, socks, candles, and basins were being supplied by the commission in such huge quantities showed how much those left behind were being victimized by the relocation of the army's supply line from Washington as it advanced south. That supply route now passed nowhere near Gettysburg. The wounded—having already been abandoned by most of the medical personnel—came to realize they were no longer considered part of the army and would have to be supplied separately and directly in some other manner. They could not draw on the army's lifeline.

The Sanitary Commission hierarchy welcomed the challenge such a situation provided, seeing it as an opportunity to fulfill the grand purpose they envisioned for their organization. But it was not a work to be undertaken in anonymous fashion. So satisfied was President Bellows with the commission's performance that soon after the battle he asserted with all the humility he could possibly muster, "I believe thousands of lives were literally saved by our succor on that occasion alone."[53]

But the effectiveness of not only the Sanitary Commission's activity, and of all the other relief efforts at Gettysburg, was something that really could not be calculated. Who can say which of the soldiers owed his survival directly to the ministrations of the civilian volunteers on the field or the donations of those at home? Or how many of the wounded were beyond help of any sort? The value of each bit of assistance couldn't be isolated.

All one could do was look at the sum of all that was done by those who came to the scene and at all that was sent there, then try to imagine what conditions would have been like if the sick and wounded had had to depend solely on the government to look after them.

In that light, Dr. Bellows' estimate of how many were saved by his organization alone isn't at all difficult to accept. Given the Sanitary Commission's enormous contribution, who would have challenged it?

The 1,500 combs that the Sanitary Commission distributed were among the most appreciated gifts offered though they had little to do with improving the soldiers' personal appearance. Their primary use was to comb out lice, since both armies were thoroughly infested with them.

There was a large barn on the property of young Albertus McCreary's farm in which some 400 Rebel prisoners had been kept for days, subsisting on their own hardtack and water from the McCreary's pump. When they were moved away to prison "they did not take the graybacks with them," the boy said. "The barn was so alive with them that no one dared go into it until it had been thoroughly whitewashed inside and out."[54]

Few managed to escape the clinging, crab-like pests that the unwashed soldiers carried about in such abundance on their bodies and in their uniforms, regardless of how conscious an individual was of personal hygiene. One Sister of Charity admitted that when they returned to Emmitsburg after having been around so many soldiers of both armies, they "took back with them a plentiful supply of vermin in their clothes."[55]

There is no evidence that Cornelia Hancock and Euphemia Goldsborough ever met at Gettysburg but they were, in many ways, as close in character and emotional makeup as any two sisters might have been.

Only a few years apart in age but both beyond the time when young women were usually married, they had come early to the battlefield from vastly different environments—geographically, socially, and politically. Cornelia, who was of New Jersey Quaker stock, was as fully absorbed in the progress of the war as the fervent gentrified Marylander. Both responded instinctively when word reached them of the terrible suffering taking place at this remote town in Pennsylvania and felt they had to help in some fashion.

At first they labored in different settings: Cornelia at the Union Second Corps field hospital and Euphemia at the college. When they transferred to the more integrated wards at Camp Letterman it is difficult to imagine that they did not become at least casually acquainted.

Neither sought to be conspicuous. A Christian Commission delegate observed that Cornelia "commanded respect for she was lady-like and well educated," yet she was "so quiet and undemonstrative that her presence was hardly noticed, except by the smiling faces of the wounded she passed."[56]

In the end, both would leave the scene at about the same time, thoroughly spent but under dissimilar circumstances. For Cornelia, it was a matter of no longer feeling needed.

She explained to her mother, "The hospital got so full of women that one had to sit down while the others turned round, so I thought the most patriotic one was she who took her board off of Uncle Sam until there was greater need of services."[57]

At the same time, she alerted her parents as she headed home that "as soon as there is another battle, I shall go again," though probably with somewhat more trepidation. "It will be awful to see the next battle, for there are so many men that I know now, some of which will fall in the next fight," she said.[58]

Cornelia was more than a bit uneasy about returning home after more than two months with the army. She had some indications that she was being regarded there as something of a heroine for having gone off to Gettysburg to nurse the wounded.

"If people take an interest in me because I am a heroine, it is a great mistake for I feel like anything but a heroine," she wrote to her niece, Sallie. "I look at it in this way," she explained. "I feel I am doing all a woman can do to help the war along, and, therefore, I feel no responsibility" for not having done her full share.[59]

Even when she got back to her familiar and tranquil surroundings, Cornelia could not fully detach herself emotionally from the wounded in her ward at Camp Letterman, and prepared boxes to send them. The letters she received in return gave her, as much as any presidential citation might have, a sense of how much she was appreciated.

One grateful soldier wrote in a letter to her:

> I received your very affectionate letter addressed to the Boys generally, and if you could have been here and seen the attention they paid while reading your letter to them you would be very proud of them for they will never forget their ministering angel.
>
> The men speak volumes of the nobleness of your generous Heart in sending them such excellent butter and cake and other things too numerous to mention. . . . I am a very poor communicant at best, so adieu God bless you, you generous soul—is the prayers of us all.[60]

Euphemia left Gettysburg right after the death of Samuel Watson, the young member of the 5th Texas whose passing among the hundreds she had witnessed particularly affected her. To her, Watson was "my poor lost darling." It was as if this one tragedy had drained the last measure of emotion and physical energy from her and she had to go home to Baltimore, unable to give anymore of herself.

"At first we scarcely knew her, so worn and changed, so utterly exhausted with the sights of the battlefield and death bed scenes in the hospitals," her sister lamented. "In truth, she was never the same joyous girl again."[61]

Like Cornelia, Euphemia was sustained by the letters of appreciation she had received from soldiers she had helped. A captain of the 22nd Georgia related to the tiny volunteer:

> After being so long with us and being thy majestic self in meekness to meet the wants of the wounded while at the College and here [Camp Letterman], I could not write my autograph without an appreciation of your kindness and benevolence.
>
> Such a being is too lovely for earth, and Heaven's reward can only repay thee.[62]

If Cornelia had her medallion as a remembrance, Euphemia also had her keepsake—a wooden ring delicately carved by a bedridden Confederate soldier with the name "Effie" ornately lettered on its face.

So impassioned was she about the Southern cause that Euphemia could not limit herself to merely aiding the Rebel wounded, and word reached her while she was recuperating at home that Federal authorities were investigating the full extent of her activities at Gettysburg.

She wrote to a Confederate officer of her precarious situation:

> I fear I am implicated most seriously in the attempted escape of a prisoner, a letter directive was found on his person and probably I shall got to 'sweet Dixie' sooner than you—however I am not one bit afraid to defy the whole Yankee nation.[63]

The letter never reached him. Before it could be posted, it was confiscated by a Union provost marshal's detail that had appeared at her Cortland Street house on November 23, with instructions to search the residence for papers and to take her into custody for treason.

For her activities, Euphemia was sentenced to banishment until the end of the war, and conveyed to Virginia on a truce steamer. When she arrived in Richmond, alone but by now well known, President Jefferson Davis himself saw to it that she was given a position in the Treasury Department. The family of Col. W. T. Patton of the 7th Virginia, the officer whom she had nursed so tirelessly at the Pennsylvania College hospital, invited her to reside with his family to show their gratitude. On one occasion, the Maryland Line, that famous unit recognizable by its blue and orange uniforms, invited her to dinner at its camp. It soon became apparent, however, that clerical work was not in itself enough for Miss Effie and she began to divide her time between the Treasury Department and serving at the Richmond hospitals, a routine she maintained until the war ended and she was permitted to return home.

Predictably, Cornelia was back with the Army of the Potomac for the Wilderness campaign and remained with it through the dreary siege of Petersburg. To make her a bit more comfortable during the long winter of 1864–65, some admiring Second Corps soldiers built a small house for her near the hospital where she worked. She returned to her New Jersey home after Appomattox and only after letting her family know that "if I look as if I was ninety when I get home you need not be surprised, for all that has happened to almost all I ever knew."[64]

The two young women were of altogether different backgrounds and had no special skills to offer. But both were too sensitive and compassionate to remain idle as long as there was some way, no matter how menial, to relieve war's suffering. The cries for help that had come from Gettysburg simply were not ignored by either.

The President was coming to Gettysburg!

Even the committee headed by David Wills that was arranging the dedication of the national soldiers' cemetery hardly expected Mr. Lincoln to leave Washington and make an eighty-mile trip to Pennsylvania to attend such an event. In fact, the invitation sent to the White House was the same as those extended simply as a matter of courtesy to hundreds of state and federal officials. The committee actually was far more concerned about the presence of the man who was slated to deliver the oration at the ceremonies—the renowned Edward Everett.

The date for the dedication had even been set back from Oct. 23 to Nov. 19 because Mr. Everett, probably the foremost public speaker of the day, didn't think he would have ample time to research and compose one of his customary two-hour addresses. The sixty-nine-year-old speaker's lecture on George Washington had been delivered to no less than 122 audiences around the country over a three-year period and had added $58,000 to a fund for the preservation of Mt. Vernon as a permanent shrine. But such talks (even though he invariably delivered them without reference to notes) had to be of some factual substance to hold attention and he insisted on devoting adequate time to the task of preparation. The ceremony would have to wait if his eloquence was a desired element.

Having satisfied Mr. Everett, the committee's planning was turned into turmoil anew when the President let it be known that he was eager to participate in the program (and also to fulfill a long-held wish to tour the important battlefield while he was there). On Nov. 2, Wills wrote a personal letter to Mr. Lincoln in which he asserted, "it is the desire that after the oration, you, as Chief Executive of the nation, formally set apart these grounds to their sacred use by a few appropriate remarks."[65]

To be sure, a number of prominent officials who had been invited found excuses not to attend the somber event that promised to remind the country of the heavy cost of the prolonged struggle for the union. From a political perspective, some could see no possible gain in joining the President at Gettysburg. Rep. Thaddeus Stevens, the Abolitionist who was chairman of the powerful House Ways and Means Committee, had no intention of going to Gettysburg, even though he had once practiced law there and was well known in the area (his iron works there had been destroyed by the invading rebels). With thoughts of Mr. Lincoln's influence nearing an end, the congressman coldly characterized the President's mission as a case of "the dead going to eulogize the dead."[66]

General Meade also declined an invitation to attend, with the excuse that his responsibilities with the Army of the Potomac would not permit him to get away, thereby avoiding what might have been an awkward personal meeting with the President, who was bitterly disappointed that Meade had not been able to reap the full benefit of his costly victory there.

The chief executive decided to journey to Gettysburg and to involve himself in the ceremony because he perceived what had been achieved there at such sacrifice afforded an opportunity to shore up the nation's resolve.

If he couched it well, he sensed he could use the Union soldiers' struggle there to encourage his countrymen to see the conflict through to a successful conclusion—if only as a matter of obligation to all those who had fallen there. His remarks would be brief but must be carefully considered. To make certain of the ambience in which he would speak, he even summoned the cemetery's designer, William Saunders, to the executive mansion to describe the setting to him in detail.

The week that the cemetery was to be dedicated was, as it happened, to be the last of Camp Letterman's existence. Only a few patients remained in the huge tent community and the staff had begun the process of dismantling. "The hospital was at last to be broken up," nurse Sophronia Bucklin noted. "No more need seemed to exist of supporting such a giant camp, away from the field of active operations."[67]

The closing of the camp hospital was having a deep emotional effect on the young New York teacher, far deeper than she imagined. "All were gone," she observed. "My occupation was gone; the strain of months was suddenly let go, and I found how much the strength of my hands depended on keeping them steadily employed."[68]

As Miss Bucklin was reflecting on the bare and hard-packed spaces where the hospital tents had stood, and thought of all the suffering that had transpired on each of the uniformly spaced spots, the town prepared itself for a rapid onslaught that was greater than in the weeks after the battle. Trainload upon trainload of ordinary citizens and high elected officials arrived for the dedication on a scale that the organizers never anticipated. It would appear that as many as 20,000 people might attend.

Those using the railroad depot were greeted by the grim sight of hundreds of pine caskets stacked up and awaiting use for the reburial of the Union dead, a process only a third completed at the time. Just as with the influx that immediately followed the battle, only a fraction of the visitors could be accommodated at the hotels and in the private homes in town. Once more people were sleeping in church pews and on their satchels on the parlor floors of the hotels. Some were occupying the vacated tents at Camp Letterman but most spent the night before the ceremony roaming about in a fruitless search for shelter.

The President arrived the night before and was the guest of David Wills at his impressive residence at the square, as was Mr. Everett. In the morning, Lincoln took his brief tour of the field and studied the various sectors with which he had become familiar from dispatches. In the afternoon, wearing his high black silk hat, a black frock coat and white gauntlets, he swung his long legs over a black bay and joined more than 100 other horsemen at the square to ride in a procession up Baltimore Street to the cemetery grounds a mile away.

Store clerk Daniel Skelly, observing Mr. Lincoln, thought him "the most peculiar-looking figure on horseback I had ever seen . . . it seemed to me that his feet almost touched the ground, but he was perfectly at ease, indicating he was at home on horseback."[69]

Nurse Bucklin, suddenly with an abundance of time on her hands, joined the throng gathering for the ceremony, after having "sewed at the garments which were to make us presentable to the superintendent—the long months having told considerably upon our wearing apparel." She would recall that "it was a clear autumn day, and the last leaves of summer were fluttering down under the newly broken soil and over the dense crowd of thousands, who seemed packed like fishes in a barrel."[70]

At the fringe of the cemetery site, the relic vendors at makeshift counters were doing a lively business selling bullets, buttons, and other items gathered from the field to the visitors.

Dr. Janes found that his position as the officer in charge of the hospitals entitled him to a place on the crowded speakers' platform. Those of his staff who wished to attend the event, however, had to mingle in the crowd, their intimate connection with the battle and its victims unknown to those surrounding them. "We stood, almost suffocated, for an hour and three-quarters, listening to the masterly oration of the lamented Everett," Sophronia recalled.[71]

The response to what Mr. Lincoln had to say when his brief moment came varied in intensity with the kind of association the listener had with the battle. To each, the words had different significance and brought to mind different images. To all, the remarks gave a perspective to what they had experienced, some meaning to it all that had been painfully lacking for all the weeks since the battle ended.

Capt. A. H. Nickerson of the 8th Ohio had been convalescing in Washington when he heard of the dedication ceremony that was to take place and decided to pay a return visit to Gettysburg.

When the President stated, "We are met on a great battlefield of that war," Nickerson said:

> My own emotions may perhaps be imagined when it is remembered that he was facing the spot where only a short time before we had had our death-grapple with Pickett's men, and he stood almost immediately over the place where I had lain and seen my comrades torn in fragments by the enemy's cannon-balls.[72]

When he asserted that "the brave men, living and dead, who struggled here have consecrated it far above our poor power to add or detract," the townspeople who had seen the suffering of the masses of wounded in the churches and schools and in their own homes had a vivid understanding of the words.

When he talked of the soldiers having given "the last full measure of devotion," the doctors, nurses, and Sanitary Commission agents in the audience were reminded of many men with whom they had remained until the very end.

When he spoke of creating "a final resting place for those who here gave their lives that that nation might live," thoughts went to the horrid interim locations where the men had been heaped and it was satisfying to see that those who had been so coarsely treated were at last being given their due respect.

Regardless of the scenes that came to mind as the towering figure with the sad anguished face delivered his call for a national rededication to preserving the union, it was an audience that was in too gloomy a state to respond with animation or enthusiasm. Daniel Skelly understood quite well the mood of the gathering:

> The war had been going on for two years and quite a number of the battles had been fought with terrible losses in killed and wounded, and at that time there seemed no prospect that there would be any let-up in the fighting until one side had been decisively victorious. There were present fathers and mothers who had lost sons in the war, brothers and sisters who had lost relatives, and sweethearts whose lovers had been killed or maimed since the war began. Could there be much applause from such an audience?"[73]

The program ended with the Rev. H. L. Baugher, who had lost his son at Shiloh, delivering the benediction. The people began to drift away and Sophronia Bucklin sensed the event was to be, in effect, her farewell to Gettysburg and all she had experienced there. Taking a final look about as she strolled back down to the hospital, she reflected, "Those hills had become familiar to our eyes, and as they receded from our view many parting tears were shed in memory of the dead who died upon them."[74]

Anna Holstein also attended the ceremonies, thinking herself fortunate to have had a place within a few feet of Mr. Lincoln and to have "heard distinctly every word he uttered of that memorable speech." Afterward, sensing "there was now . . . nothing more to be done at Gettysburg," she said "we gladly turned our faces homeward."[75]

The day after the President's visit, the last of the wounded left Camp Letterman and the work of caring for the battle's casualties was finally completed—four-and-a-half months after the armies had left.

The Uncounted Casualties

Despite so much evidence to the contrary, Medical Director Jonathan Letterman would steadfastly maintain that ample medical personnel had been left at Gettysburg and that medical supplies, except for tents and other accessories, were abundant. His superior, army commander George G. Meade, would argue more dispassionately that, acceptable or not, the medical situation there was unavoidable.

Letterman had a supporter of sorts in Medical Inspector John M. Cuyler, who remained at Gettysburg until July 25 and witnessed much of the suffering. In a report to Surgeon General Hammond, the old regular army surgeon argued unconvincingly that "the number of medical officers detailed by Medical Director Letterman to remain with the wounded was thought to be sufficient, and probably might have been had not thousands of the enemy's wounded been thrown unexpectedly on our hands."[1]

Why, one can only wonder, should the discovery of Confederate wounded on the field in large numbers have come as a surprise and not have been anticipated? After every battle, the side that retained possession of the field inevitably inherited the most serious of the enemy's wounded. After Antietam, Lee had left thousands of wounded behind as he withdrew from Maryland and recrossed the Potomac. Surely, a battle of Gettysburg's dimensions must have been expected to deposit an appreciable number of wounded prisoners requiring intensive medical attention from their captors.

Whether expected or not, the large number of Rebel wounded was hardly a factor in a Union soldier having to wait days for surgical attention.

Enemy casualties were to a large extent ignored by the Federal surgeons until they had taken care of their own. Given the number of doctors available, their wait for treatment would have been as long if there were no Reb prisoners on the surgeons' hands.

For his part, General Meade seemed to believe that what occurred at Gettysburg was quite normal, an inescapable if cruel aspect of warfare.

"Although the Government is most liberal and generous in all its provisions for the sick and wounded, yet it is impossible to keep constantly on hand either the personnel or supplies required in an emergency of this kind," the general wrote to a Sanitary Commission official on April 8, 1865, in recognition of the service of that organization.

He explained that the situation at Gettysburg was compounded by the fact that he "was compelled to pursue the retreating foe, and, as I expected, in a few days, to have another battle at some distant point, it was absolutely necessary that I should carry away the greater portion of my Surgeons and medical supplies. . . ."

That he was aware of or became aware of the situation he was leaving behind was revealed by his own explanation:

> At the battle of Gettysburgh [sic] the number of wounded of our own Army alone amounted, by official reports, to 13,713; those of the enemy left on the field, were estimated by our medical officers, as amounting to eight thousand. This would make in all, nearly 22,000 suffering beings, requiring immediate care and attention to save life.[2]

Yet, in the face of such a demand, the general entrusted that great mass to others to tend without knowing when or from where that attention might come.

The people thronging to Gettysburg after the battle were shocked to find the hospitals so woefully understaffed and ill supplied. In response to the furor developing, Medical Inspector Johnson filed a special report with the surgeon general in which he faulted Medical Director Letterman's work, stating that requests should have been made for more surgeons, attendants, and supplies before the army left. He was particularly concerned that the Second Corps hospital, with 3,400 wounded to treat, was left with only thirteen medical officers.[3]

When word of the criticism reached him in Virginia, Letterman responded by sending one of his doctors back to Gettysburg on July 29 (a week after the general hospital opened) to examine the state of affairs there. What his inspector determined, Letterman said, was that as far as supplies were concerned "at no time had there been any deficiency, but, on the contrary, that the supply furnished by the medical purveyor had been and still continued to be abundant." He did acknowledge, however, the shortage of medical accessories, most notably the tents, and for that he blamed Meade's orders.[4]

Despite Letterman's insistence, every box of medicines and bandages the Sanitary and Christian commissions provided and every one of the purchases the army made at the drugstores in town only confirmed the shortages.

Inspector Vollum, who arrived the night of July 8, related how he himself "endeavored to make up the deficiencies in medical supplies at Gettysburg by telegraphing to Surgeon [Josiah] Simpson, U.S. Army, at Baltimore. In reply, he ordered liberal supplies of alcohol, solution chloride of soda, tincture of iron, creosote, nitric acid, permangante of potassa, buckets, tin cups, stretchers, bedsacks and stationery of all kinds for 10,000 men in field hospitals."[5]

However, a high Sanitary Commission official, in his assessment of the situation, asserted:

> Here was a battlefield from which the combatants on both sides disappeared within two days after the conflict ceased, leaving behind them more than 22,000 men, whose condition required not only immediate, constant, and skillful care, but a large quantity of hospital supplies. The Army organization which, in theory, was to provide for all these wants, accompanied the forward march leaving but a very imperfect representation of its various departments to look after those who had fallen.[6]

As far as the personnel situation was concerned, Letterman remained convinced that the lion's share of the surgery had been done before he departed and that the detail he left behind was sufficient for the unfinished work at hand. They were only being cautious in taking so many doctors away from Gettysburg, Meade and Letterman could safely argue about their dispositions. What if the army had been engaged in hostile Virginia, where no local assistance could be expected, and had masses of wounded to care for without its full complement of physicians available?

Yes, there was that possibility, though Meade's timid movements hardly made such an encounter appear imminent. Against that possibility, there was the reality of Gettysburg and the desperate need known to exist there. One can only speculate about how many lives might have been saved, how many amputations might have been avoided, and how many hours of torture might have been averted if only a hundred more doctors had been left behind; a hundred more ambulances from the army's great fleet had been made available to move men to the railroad for evacuation; and a hundred more tents had been provided for shelter. The question remains: Why did the stripping of the field by the vacating army have to be quite so extreme?

During their ordeal, the townspeople of Gettysburg manifested all the classic behavior of people caught up in a disaster. They went through all the predictable emotional stages.

Just as victims of hurricanes or tornadoes do, they emerged from the calamity that had befallen them dazed, stunned, and, at first, apathetic and passive. In those first few hours after the fighting ceased, they wandered about aimlessly, unaware of the dangers that persisted about them.

Predictably, they soon began to seek out friends and neighbors, forming small groups to discuss what was happening and ask for information. The loss of communication resulting from the railroad, telegraph, and newspapers all being out of service only fed their feelings of isolation and uncertainty. The arrival of relief organizations from distant places had the effect of not only material assistance but also recognition and a measure of understanding for what they had been through.

The anger exhibited by so many of the local farmers for having been so randomly chosen by the fortunes of war to have their property destroyed or taken was not uncommon. It was a bitterness fueled by the unanswerable question, "Why me?"

However irrational or misplaced may have been their response, it was a feeling intensified by the fact that so many around them were emerging virtually untouched by the battle. In turning their anger on the Federal soldiers and exhibiting such meanness toward them, they were merely striking out at those they felt were somehow responsible for their losses.

Though they were victims themselves, many of the Gettysburg residents were forced to assume the roles of helpers and became so swept up in their responsibilities that they defied fatigue by their excitement and overwhelming sense of being needed.

As the wounded soldiers were taken from their care and moved from the private homes and churches to the general hospital, they experienced emotions ranging from relief to rejection and ingratitude.[7]

Perhaps what was most peculiar about the aftermath of Gettysburg as a study in disaster relief was how undirected yet ultimately effective the activity was.

Who was telling the Sanitary Commission where to set up their stations or what items to bring in for the wounded soldiers?

What had Dr. Henry Janes to do with the problems of transportation? He had his hands full seeing to it that the wounded were housed and treated.

How did those clusters of ladies coming from Maryland know that there was such a need among the Confederate prisoners for their help?

Who in authority informed the Sisters of Charity how to most effectively deploy themselves?

Who ever suggested to the Adams Express Company that its wagons and other resources could be of such value?

There simply was no one in overall charge and no bureaucracy in place to regulate and inhibit activity. The titular "post commander" at Gettysburg was primarily concerned with the protection and retrieval of government property at the scene and burials. The relief operation went as well as it did because individuals and groups knew their own capabilities and did as much as they could in their own way, trusting that someone else would address the other wants.

The manner in which each element was performed generated such a sense of appreciation among their coworkers, as well as those being helped, that virtually all left the scene far more admired and understood than when they arrived.

The tender ministrations of the Sisters of Charity did much to dispel among soldiers from many states the anti-Catholic feelings that were so prevalent in many areas of the country.

One day an elderly gentleman who had come to town in search of his son and who was staying at McClellan's Hotel where the sisters were housed, noticed a group of nuns leaving their quarters with bundles of

The Humiston children—youngsters whose picture touched a nation's heart.
Tipton Collection, Adams County Historical Society.

clothing to take to the wounded. He exclaimed to the hotel proprietor, "Good God, can those Sisters be the persons whose religion we always run down!"

"Yes," he was told, "they are often run down by those who know nothing of their charity."

When one of the nuns (undisturbed by the incongruity of her habit in a Protestant setting) applied at an army commissary for some supplies to take to the Confederate prisoners she was treating at the Lutheran Theological Seminary she was told by a clerk:

> Yes, Sister, you shall have what you want for the prisoners as well as for our own. You ladies come with honest faces and you shall always get whatever you need for the suffering men whether Rebels or our own. . . . I sincerely hope we shall all worship at the same altar one day.[8]

The Sanitary Commission gained countless supporters for the work it performed at the scene, particularly softening the attitude of the Southern wounded toward the Northerners. An indication of the inroads the commission made in the Confederate ranks by its equal treatment of Rebel and Yank in the distribution of its supplies was evidenced by the fact that every single Southern doctor on the field joined in a petition to the Confederate government in Richmond for the release of Dr. Alexander McDonald, the arrested Sanitary Commission agent languishing in Libby Prison. Their petition attested to the evenhandedness of the commission toward soldiers of both armies and the inappropriateness of making someone like Dr. McDonald a prisoner. In September, he was freed.

The manner in which army surgeon and civilian physician were forced together by the shortage of medical personnel created a new level of respect, if not for one another's skills, at least for the other's dedication to his profession and his medical oath.

And, of course, the numbers in which caring, concerned young women had made their way to the battleground, forgetting all personal modesty and fastidiousness to wash, feed, and comfort bedraggled, helpless boys as young as themselves, forever removed much of the pretense and reserve from the ever-so-formal relationships practiced between the genders at home.

That these new levels of tolerance developed; that the townspeople found within themselves such an infinite capacity to deal with the crisis that descended upon them underscored the transforming effect of disaster (and an unexpected major battle as erupted at Gettysburg certainly can be regarded as such) on not only its victims, but also on those who came to their aid.

In their bloody aprons, bone-saws in hand, and amputated limbs accumulating around them, Union surgeon John Shaw Billings and Confederate Dr. Simon Baruch could not have impressed those who observed them at Gettysburg as men of extraordinary medical talent and promise. Billings himself had referred to the sort of work he was required to do at the Fifth Corps field hospital as sheer butchery. But both were destined to make their mark in their profession.

When sent off to Fort McHenry, Dr. Baruch somehow arranged to have the case of fine surgical instruments he had been given by a Baltimore surgeon shipped to his home in Camden, South Carolina, for safekeeping. Ironically, the case was stolen from his home by some of Sherman's looting troops as they marched to the sea. Baruch accepted his loss philosophically. "Such are the vicissitudes of war," he shrugged.[9]

Baruch did not waste his time during his confinement. A paper he wrote while a prisoner on the treatment of bayonet wounds of the chest would be consulted by army doctors through World War I.

After Appomattox, Baruch returned home to resume his practice and raise a family. He and his wife, Isabel Wolfe Baruch, named the second of their four sons Bernard Mannes Baruch. The middle name was that of a Camden merchant, Mannes Baum, who had sent Simon Baruch, the immigrant from East Prussia, to medical school. Though Bernard exhibited little interest in the medical profession, he appeared to have an extraordinary talent for finance, an ability he developed after Dr. Baruch relocated his family to New York City in 1881 to provide his children with more opportunity. While still in his thirties, Bernard Baruch made a fortune on Wall Street and millions more by providing venture capital for industrial development projects. In time, he became an invaluable advisor to presidents on economic issues.

One of Bernard Baruch's most vivid recollections of his father was the time when, as a young man of twenty, he visited Gettysburg with the doctor and listened to his lively account of his experiences there. (Demonstrating how history can become distorted from generation to generation even within a family, Bernard thought he was being treated at one point to a description of Maj. Gen. George E. Pickett's movement against the Peach Orchard when his father was no doubt relating the advance of his own division, McLaws', in that sector the day before Pickett's Charge against Cemetery Ridge.)

For his part, Dr. Baruch became renowned in his profession for two unrelated contributions—one was the surgical treatment of appendicitis and the other was the use of hydrotherapy. Considered a pioneer in the field of hydrotherapy, Dr. Baruch wrote two books on the subject and was honored for his services to medicine by being appointed professor of hydrotherapy at the College of Physicians and Surgeons at Columbia University.

A few years before his death in 1921, the physician who so early in life had served the Rebel cause, wrote of the attachment he had developed for the United States:

> If I did not stand ready to consecrate heart and soul and all that
> I possessed to the defense of my adopted country, I would despise myself as an ingrate to the Government that has, for sixty years, enhanced and protected my life, honor and happiness.[10]

Dr. Billings transferred to the Surgeon General's Office in December 1864 where he founded the Surgeon General's Library and created the *Index Catalogue* and the *Index Medicus* to comprehensively acquaint medical students and practitioners with the current state of medical knowledge throughout the world.

In addition to his contributions as a medical bibliographer and biostatistician, Billings became a much-sought hospital consultant and, in 1875, while still serving in the army, he developed the plans for the construction of the Johns Hopkins Hospital and supervised the building and development of that Baltimore institution. In his design, he exhibited the interest he developed during the Civil War in controlling the spread of infection by providing for a series of isolated pavilions, which he also applied to plans for other new hospitals.

Dr. Billings, upon leaving the army in 1895, also set out to organize and plan the construction of the New York Public Library. When it was completed, he served as its director.[11]

To such men of achievement as Simon Baruch and John Shaw Billings, their experience at Gettysburg was but an episode in long distinguished careers. But who knows to what degree the scale of death and disablement they witnessed there stimulated them to wring all they possibly could out of life and to take advantage of every ounce of energy they could muster?

Clues to the identification of the dead, as Samuel Weaver demonstrated, took myriad forms.

In the instance of Sgt. Amos Humiston, the only indicator was an ambrotype of three very serious looking little children dressed in their Sunday best that was clutched in his hand when his body was found on Stratton Street. He was one of the soldiers killed as the army was retreating through the town on July 1.

Who did these lovely children—two boys and a girl—belong to? How were they faring with their father gone?

Dr. J. Francis Bournes, a Philadelphia physician serving at the battlefield, was so touched by the photograph that he had thousands of copies made and circulated about the country. In November 1863, a print reached Cattaraugus County, New York, and was recognized as a photo of the Humiston children, whose father was a member of the 154th New York Regiment, a unit of the 11th Corps.

So many people became involved in the search by purchasing a print of the photo and showing it about, that the proceeds of the campaign were sufficient to establish a Soldiers' Orphans' Home at Gettysburg a year after the war ended. Sergeant Humiston's youngsters were the first to be housed there and his widow remained with them as the first matron of the facility.

Gov. Andrew G. Curtin may or may not have been conscious of the ramifications of the battle of Gettysburg on his political career. However, the November election results showed that it had been worthwhile for the Pennsylvania governor to devote so much time and attention to the treatment of the soldiers of his state. While a majority of Adams County voters supported the Democratic slate of candidates, as was customary, the state as a whole backed the Republican governor for reelection, mainly for the concern he had shown for the wounded and the decent interment of the dead at Gettysburg. Curtin became popularly known as "the soldier's friend" and his efforts on their behalf were not forgotten at the polling places.

Bucking the Democratic trend in Adams County, the residents of Gettysburg also gave their support to Curtin, much to the chagrin, of H. J. Stahle, the antisecession editor of the *Compiler.* Stahle once more had his critical pen in hand after having been acquitted of the charge of giving away the hiding place of a Union officer. The matter was settled when the colonel, for whom he had been seeking medical attention from the Rebels, came forward to testify in his behalf.

But Curtin's frequent and compassionate presence on the scene had overcome whatever influence the anti-administration *Compiler* was able to muster with the voters, and the governor could count himself one of the few beneficiaries of the costly battle.

Not in a century would all the debris of the battle of Gettysburg be collected. Every time a rotted or lightning-struck tree fell, the trunk was likely to reveal some gray minie balls that had penetrated it years before. Every spring, plowing was interrupted by having to dispose of fragments of shells and solid shot unearthed by tillers. For as long as a house remained standing, a mantelpiece might display a stray bullet that had come through a window next to a family daguerreotype. Cannon balls remained lodged in stone walls.

But for the early years after the battle, the most constant reminder of the battle were the graves of the Confederate dead, some 4,000 of them, scattered about promiscuously, their neglected appearance accentuated by the contrast they presented with the dignified respectful manner in which the Union fallen were arranged at the national cemetery on Cemetery Hill.

The thought of so many bodies unceremoniously piled into ditches was particularly distressing for both the families of the Southern dead and for many local residents. An eeriness developed about the places where the dead Rebels had been so rudely and insultingly deposited, particularly the sites on Oak Hill where Brig. Gen. Alfred Iverson's North Carolina brigade had been slaughtered during the first day of fighting. Those who had fallen were heaped in several large holes that became known locally as "Iverson's pits," and were skirted by those passing through the area.

In fact, the manner in which the Confederate bodies had been treated was disturbing to many Northerners at the time the interments were taking place. On July 18, two-and-a-half weeks after the battle ended, Robert P. Nevin, a Christian Commission official, related in Pittsburgh's *Evening Chronicle* what he had observed was going on:

> The rebels in the town are well provided with shelter. In the country they lie upon the bare ground without any cover what-ever. Day and night, rain or shine, cold or hot, there they lie. Hour by hour they die off, are carried to the trenches, a foot or two deep, in which they are to lie. They are laid side by side conveniently to these trenches and remain there in continually increasing groups until the parties whose duty it is come around to tend to their interment.
>
> It is awful, it is terrible, it is horrible beyond expression.

As early as Feb. 2, 1864, the *Star* and *Sentinel,* now merged, had become concerned enough about the irreverent way in which the Southern dead had been concealed on local farms like so much garbage. The paper risked having its patriotic sentiments questioned by proposing that the Rebels, too, be collected and placed in their own cemetery. "Common humanity would dictate a removal to some spot," the newspaper's editor opined, "where Southern friends may, when the rebellion is crushed . . . make their pilgrimage there."[12]

There was no rush to pick up on the suggestion and about the only people trying to maintain some record of where the Rebel dead lay were Virginia-born Dr. J. W. C. O'Neal and later, Samuel Weaver. Weaver accumulated a good bit of information on Confederate burials while overseeing the exhuming of Federal corpses for removal to the soldiers' cemetery and the two began to pool their data.

As queries started to arrive from bereaved families in the South and black-clad widows began to make the arduous journey to Gettysburg from distant South Carolina and Georgia, they were referred to either Dr. O'Neal or Samuel Weaver and the two passed on what information they could, though they had accumulated the names and units of little more than a quarter of all the Confederates buried on the field.

The value to survivors of the work they were doing was touchingly revealed in a letter from Mrs. I. A. Mercer, the mother of twenty-one-year-old Oliver F. Mercer, a captain in a North Carolina regiment who was killed on the first day of fighting.

Our Wilmington papers bring the welcome intelligence to many bereaved Southern hearts that you have cared for the graves of many of our Confederate dead at Gettysburg, replaced head-boards and prepared a list of names.

May the Lord bless you is the prayer of many Southern hearts. Oh! We have lost so much. There are but few families that do not mourn the loss of one or more loved ones, and only a mother who has lost a son in that awful battle can and does appreciate fully such goodness as you have shown. I, too, lost a son at Gettysburg, a brave, noble boy in the full bloom of youth, and my heart yearns to have his remains, if they can be found, brought home to rest in the soil of the land he loved so well. I need your assistance and I am confident you will aid me. No sorrow-stricken mother could ask and be refused by a heart such as yours.[13]

When Samuel Weaver died unexpectedly in 1871, ladies' memorial associations in several Southern cities appealed to his thirty-year-old son, Dr. Rufus Benjamin Weaver of Philadelphia, to use his medical skill and knowledge of the field to continue his father's work and arrange for the return of the remains of soldiers from their states. Even if the bodies could not be individually identified, it was hoped that they could at least be grouped by units so that South Carolinians might be returned to their far away roots, and Georgians restored to the red clay soil from which they had come.

Dr. Weaver had assisted his father in his exhumations and inherited all his carefully maintained records. In addition, he was teaching his specialty, anatomy, at the Hahnemann Medical College in Philadelphia, and brought a measure of expertise to the sorting of the scrambled remains in the great Rebel burial trenches. It was an advantage that his father, a drayman, had not had in pursuing his work as carefully and intelligently as his son did.

Though he was far too busy to take on such a mammoth task, Dr. Weaver, another graduate of the Pennsylvania College in Gettysburg, agreed after much entreaty and negotiation to do the work as time permitted. He began in the spring of 1871 and, working through the summer, managed to locate, disinter, and ship the remains of 137 Confederates to Raleigh, North Carolina, 74 to Charleston, South Carolina, and 101 to Savannah, Georgia. He also sent 73 bodies individually to particular families in the South.[14]

Rufus Weaver, an anatomist who saw to
the return of numerous Confederate dead.
Special Collections, Gettysburg College.

Virginia also longed to involve itself in the transference of its dead. The General Assembly appropriated a modest $1,000 toward the cost and the Hollywood Memorial Association of Richmond's historic Hollywood Cemetery began taking collections to defray the cost of moving the Gettysburg dead to its Soldiers' Section.

Late in 1871, the association decided boldly and over-ambitiously to negotiate with Dr. Weaver not only for the removal of all the Virginia dead from the field but every single Confederate soldier left there. They were now talking about thousands of bodies and Weaver alerted the ladies that the cost would be $3.25 to exhume, package, and ship each body to Virginia. What did the association wish to do? Weaver was willing to take on the massive task but he needed a quick decision. He knew the local farmers wouldn't stand for people digging up their land after it had been plowed and sown in the spring.

The group dispatched Capt. Charles Dimmock to Pennsylvania to assess the project. After examining the condition of the graves, the engineer estimated that there were about 500 Southern soldiers who could be identified and another 2,000 who could not. As disconcerting to Dimmock as the difficulty of identification was the ugly way in which the remains were being treated by the local farmers. On the ground of Pickett's charge, he came upon "skeletons which had been ploughed up and now lay strewn about the surface" eight years after the battle.[15]

On the basis of the favorable impression of Dr. Weaver that Captain Dimmock had formed on his visit, the cemetery association determined to have Weaver go ahead with the project. Somehow the funds would be found to compensate him.

Weaver began the job in April 1972, and worked virtually around the clock, with but a few hours sleep. He used the daylight hours for the exhumations and the night for sorting and packaging the bones in his office.

His first shipment arrived by steamship in Richmond on June 15, 1872, and included the remains of 708 Confederate soldiers, seventy of them from Virginia. Five days later, the bodies were carried up to Hollywood Cemetery in a mass funeral procession of wagons draped with Confederate flags and covered with flowers. Flags were being flown at half-staff. Some 325 of the dead (including perhaps Brig. Gen. Richard B. Garnett) were taken from the Codori farm at Gettysburg over which Gen. George E. Pickett's division had charged and the shattered general was part of the escort that accompanied the procession to the cemetery, reminded anew of that terrible day when his once proud brigades had been all but destroyed.

Meantime, Weaver persevered with his work. The insistence of some of the money-grubbing farmers in the area that they actually be paid for the privilege of allowing the doctor and his laborers to dig up their fields to remove the Rebel dead compounded the doctor's difficulties. Their rates ranged from $5 to $50 per body. Others with more heart, however, eagerly assisted Weaver with the task and cared not that their crops were being disturbed by the intrusion.

With his final shipment to Richmond on Oct. 11, 1873, Weaver had sent a total of 2,935 Confederates to Hollywood Cemetery. He had thus far been paid only $2,800 and was now owed $6,499 for his time and shipping expenses; a small sum for such a huge service.

Weaver needed payment quite badly. He had given almost all his savings to the deficit-ridden Hahnemann Medical College to keep it in operation. But he was confident the money due him would be forthcoming— all the other associations in the South with which he had dealt had paid him in full.

Alas, for all their good intentions, the members of the Hollywood Memorial Association encountered a crisis of their own, when in 1873 a bad investment cost the group nearly all its funds. Soon afterward, the organization, unable to meet its obligations, simply dissolved. The debt owed to Dr. Weaver was never paid. Yet, had it not been for his willingness and skill, the remains of the Confederate dead at Gettysburg might not have been recovered, never mind identified. It was rather shabby treatment of a man who deserved a great deal of gratitude.[16]

Attorney David McConaughy made something of a show of his patriotism.

After the battle, the local Republican leader who had turned *Compiler* editor Stahle in to the authorities for his alleged disloyalty and was the nemesis of the Cooperheads in town, was thinking of other ways to display his pro-Union sentiments.

On July 25, McConaughy wrote a letter to Governor Curtin. Resorting to his most flowery prose, he laid before Curtin a plan he had been entertaining for historically preserving the most significant locations on the battleground around him. Considering the event was but three weeks old, McConaughy was exhibiting rather remarkable farsightedness.

"The most interesting portions of this illustrious Battlefield" could, if protected as they were at the time of the fighting, McConaughy told the governor, serve as "the most eloquent memorials of the glorious struggles and triumphs of the Union army."[17]

As a matter of fact, McConaughy, using his own money, had already purchased sizable tracts of land on Little Round Top, Culp's Hill, and East Cemetery Hill where Federal breastworks had been built—scenes of some of the fiercest fighting. On August 14, he went public with his vision of protecting the battlefield as it was and saving it from distortion and exploitation. He called upon fellow residents of Adams County to join him in the effort to see that "the battlefield itself, with its natural and artificial defenses, is preserved and perpetuated in the exact form and condition they presented during the battle."[18]

He proposed that committees be organized in various communities throughout the state to advance the work and that shares be sold to defray the cost of land acquisitions. In order to stimulate the broadest participation, he suggested that the price of these shares be limited to $10 each.

Four days after he issued his call, twenty-six leading citizens—editor Robert G. Harper and the Rev. H. L. Baugher among them—wrote McConaughy a joint response that they "highly approved, and will cheerfully unite in the plan proposed by you" to preserve the more significant aspects of the field for the benefit "of all men who in all time shall visit them."[19]

Within 10 months, a Gettysburg Battlefield Memorial Association had been formed that not only went about buying up lands but serving as a protector of the field in general. One of its appeals published in the *Sentinel* reminded "visitors and others going upon the battlefield that the cutting of bullets from the trees and otherwise defacing the timber and woods is strictly prohibited" and, more threateningly, added, "it is hoped that this notice will be sufficient without making examples of persons guilty of acts of vandalism upon the timber and grounds."[20]

In the next three decades, the local associations, with some limited state funding, would acquire 522 acres of land which, in 1895, were transferred to the Federal government when the Gettysburg National Military Park was created. By that time, some seventeen miles of avenues had been developed on the grounds and 320 monuments erected.

David McConaughy's form of expression may have been a bit too ornate to endure for long but for all his political bluster, he had, with his sense of historical significance and his promptness of action, salvaged for posterity some of the salient features of the field before they, too, became—through avarice or indifference—part of the debris of battle.

Curiously, a number of persons who had conspicuous roles in dealing with Gettysburg's toll left the war very soon afterward. The circumstances were varied and unrelated but it nonetheless seemed rather remarkable that so many players who had figured so prominently in the drama should leave the stage within such a narrow time frame.

Herman Haupt's departure came but two months after his herculean efforts to restore the vital rail link to Gettysburg. Finding himself pressured to give up his unofficial payless status with the army and accept a brigadier general's commission (a move that would have made him subject to orders and kept him from his business and professional interests in Massachusetts), Haupt simply packed it in and went home, leaving the army to handle its own transportation problems.

Haupt regarded himself as a victim of politics, claiming it was local political opponents who were forcing the Lincoln administration to place him in a position that would keep the engineer away from Boston. But the friction—coming as soon as it did after his extraordinary Gettysburg service—found him in no mood to make concessions or bend to bureaucracy. He had shown before that he could do without the army.

Reviewing a chronology of Haupt's subsequent activities is enough to leave one breathless. In addition to publishing a library full of technical papers on bridge and railroad engineering, he served as the chief engineer and manager of a number of rail lines across the country. He was general

Cornelia Hancock and Salome Myers Stewart, attending the fiftieth-anniversary ceremony at Gettysburg. *Adams County Historical Society.*

manager of the Northern Pacific Railroad at the time of its historic completion to the Pacific in 1881. He also became interested in utilizing compressed air for mining machinery, and was a pioneer in the use of pipelines for the transportation of oil. For a time, he was even president of a nutrition company engaged in producing food from the waste products of dairies.

For a man so much identified with the growth of the railroad industry, it was rather fitting that when he suffered a fatal heart attack in 1905, it occurred while he was aboard a train en route to his home in Washington, D.C.[21]

The same September that Haupt left the army, Frederick L. Olmsted, the administrative mainstay of the U.S. Sanitary Commission, severed his relationship with that organization. Physically drained and tired of policy-wrangling within the commission, the self-willed secretary resigned to become superintendent of the Fremont Mariposa mining estates in distant California. Upon moving West, he was so taken by the beauties of the region that he was drawn back to his original interest in landscape architecture, and would make outstanding contributions in the field of preservation and public recreation.

But in the weeks before Olmsted decided to leave the Sanitary Commission and take his family to the other end of the country, far beyond Washington's sophistication and exasperation, he became deeply despondent, as he often did when he drove himself too hard. He was feeling much unappreciated and deceived by the commissioners whom, he sensed, were dissatisfied with his performance.

In one letter to President Bellows, he asserted:

> As far as the Sanitary Commission is concerned, my life in the last two years is as complete a failure as Jeff Davis's—more so—for he has yet a chance of success.
>
> I have unusual abilities, unusual, far reaching sagacity, if the Sanitary Commission had trusted me as it originally proposed to do, it would have accomplished infinitely more than it has done.[22]

In another "Dear Doctor" letter to the sympathetic Bellows, he wrote bitterly, "Promise after promise, made in the most solemn and imposing manner, has been broken with me, and all with pretence of religion & love & Friendship."[23]

Olmsted seemed obsessed with the public perception of the Christian Commission, behaving as if any recognition of its contributions must detract from popular opinion of him and the Sanitary Commission. At one point, he ventured to say of the rival relief organization that had sent more than 300 delegates to Gettysburg and distributed more than 2,500 boxes of provisions that "I believe that the Christian Commission did more harm than good, at Gettysburg . . . but I don't mean to discuss it, because I have not the ability to fully explain the grounds of my convictions, without a month's study."[24]

It was all rather odd and uncharacteristic and sounded like a man who had pushed himself too far and was losing his grip.

In approaching his new venture, "the Mariposa business," Olmsted said in his candid way, "if they will really put the management in my hands as they propose, for two or three years, I know (humbly speaking) that I can astonish them."[25]

Dr. Bellows felt he understood the antagonism some of the commissioners felt toward Olmsted.

> They think . . . him impracticable, expensive, slow, when he is only long headed with broader, deeper notions of economy than themselves and with no disposition to hurry what if done satisfactorily must be done thoroughly. My feeling is that Olmsted is an admirable governor but an uncomfortable subject.[26]

He would always maintain that Olmsted was the only one who truly grasped the purpose and objectives of the commission and recognized its potential.

It was unfair and rather tragic that someone who had forced himself to the extreme—that the frail limping Olmsted had to relieve so many of Gettysburg's survivors—should have so soon afterward given up his work in a mood of almost total dejection.

Within weeks of losing its general secretary, the Sanitary Commission suffered the further loss of the man it had so vigorously championed for surgeon general when William Hammond was suspended by Secretary of War Stanton. To the shock of everyone associated with the service, the genial giant who contributed so many lasting innovations to the office was charged with irregularities in the awarding of contracts for hospital supplies and was awaiting court martial.

Hammond apparently didn't share the surprise others felt at his situation, for his relations with the autocratic Stanton had been strained. In August, Dr. Bellows confided to General Secretary Olmsted, "Dr. Hammond tells me of the inimicalness of the Secretary of War and of his impending struggle in which he thinks it not unlikely he may lose his place."

Bellows showed his regard for Hammond by suggesting, "why might not his withdrawal or removal be the appropriate moment for ours?"[27]

It was Hammond himself, while under suspension, who appealed to President Lincoln to either have him put on trial or restored to duty. In the summer of 1864, after a court martial that went on for months, Hammond was found guilty. He was sentenced to dismissal from the army.

Left impoverished by the cost of defending himself, Hammond turned to friends in Washington for financial help in moving to New York where he set up a private practice, specializing in the new field of neurology. He soon gained a professorship of nervous and mental diseases at Bellevue Hospital Medical College, and later at the University of the City of New York. He continued his efforts to have the army's verdict against him overturned and, in 1878, the case was reviewed and the findings reversed. He was placed on the list of honorably retired generals.

In 1888, Hammond returned to Washington to resume his place in society, a man much respected for his extensive writing and lecturing, primarily in the field of neurology. One prominent neurologist regarded Hammond as the "dominant personality of the time," saying "he was a big man and had a big mind."[28]

Perhaps it was inevitable, given his strong personality, that he and the domineering Stanton would clash, but the timing of his departure only added to the list of the prominent people who joined in the post-Gettysburg exodus.

No one was more chagrined to see Hammond go than the archivist of the medical museum he had established—Dr. John H. Brinton.

Until Hammond took over, the medical department of the army "had shown almost imbecility" and "had been conducted on the basis of the army establishment of the Mexican War," Brinton recalled. While impulsive,

Hammond was "of far-reaching view and sanguine temperament" and had infused fresh life and energy throughout the department. Brinton asserted:

> Much has been said against him, heavy charges have been pressed, but from an intimate knowledge of the man, and his surroundings, I am convinced that much injustice has been done, and much undeserved obloquy has been cast upon him.
>
> He was not always wise or prudent; his ways of doing things were not always judicious but he sought to make the Medical Department of our army efficient, and to render it capable of caring for the sick and wounded, and that, too, in no niggardly or tardy spirit.[29]

The displacement of Dorothea Dix that October was not by her own choosing. After having been circumvented at Gettysburg because of her demanding ways, she found her role officially diminished by orders from the secretary of war and the surgeon general. She no longer had sole right to appoint female nurses. It was, in fact, one of General Hammond's last official acts.

Although she retained a degree of oversight, henceforth the nurses would be under the "control and direction" of the medical officers in charge. Stripped of authority, Miss Dix nevertheless remained in Washington and maintained her usual air of busyness, doing such things as carrying on extensive correspondence to locate missing soldiers.

Her war service had added little to her reputation. She had made an effort but she simply had not found a suitable way in which she could effectively express her extraordinary fervor.

October 1863 was also the month in which Jonathan Letterman married a Maryland woman, Miss Mary Lee, at whose home he had stayed the year before to recover from his exertions at Antietam. Whether or not burdened by his weighty decisions regarding Gettysburg, Letterman then gave up his post as medical director of the Army of the Potomac to become an inspector of hospitals in the Department of the Susquehanna. On December 7, 1864, he received orders from the new surgeon general to report to the Department of Missouri as medical director. Missouri? Letterman declined the reassignment. He resigned from the army and abruptly moved across the country to far away San Francisco.

Letterman at first busied himself writing his memoirs but his wife's unexpected death in 1867 was a devastating experience for him and he fell into a state of deep depression. His difficulty in dealing with his own loss, accompanied by an intestinal ailment, made him a semi-invalid and he died in 1872 at the age of 48.[30]

In recounting his career, the man who revolutionized the treatment of battlefield casualties and whose techniques served as a model for foreign armies, stoutly defended his performance at Gettysburg, expressing regret only for not having left behind some additional ambulances.

One man who was not forgiving about how the medical situation was handled at Gettysburg, and was courageous enough to convey his criticism to the highest authority was Dr. Harry M. McAbee, who served in the dual role of surgeon and minister of the 4th Ohio infantry.

In a letter of resignation to Secretary of War Stanton, the popular physician/clergyman wrote,

> After the battle of Gettysburg, with but three assistants, I was left in charge of a thousand badly wounded men, not a few of whom, I fear, absolutely died for want of appropriate and good professional care.
>
> It is my deliberate opinion, that the failure to furnish a sufficient number of medical officers on that occasion has cost the country more good men than did the charge of any rebel brigade on that severely contested field.

Having despaired of seeing the medical staff of the army "made what the country and age have a right to expect," the Second Corps physician asked that he be permitted to "retire to the quiet of private life" and he, too, joined the post-Gettysburg departure.[31]

No sooner had the disillusioned doctor's request been granted, however, than he met his own death in a railway accident.

As late as November 30, 1863, with Camp Letterman now closed, Dr. Janes informed the Surgeon General's office: "I have the honor to report that I am still on duty in this place, sending off the hospital property and completing the reports."[32]

As his next assignment, Janes was placed in charge of a hospital in Philadelphia. When the spring campaign opened in 1864, however, Janes requested a return to field duty with the Army of the Potomac, and commanded a hospital steamer on which thousands of sick and wounded men were taken from the front to hospitals in Northern port cities. That fall, the governor of Vermont, having constructed three huge wooden hospitals to provide better treatment at home for the wounded of the Green Mountain State, requested the services of Dr. Janes to direct one of them—the sprawling 1,500-bed facility at Montpelier known as the Sloan Hospital.

Janes soon demonstrated what he could accomplish with adequate resources. Of the 926 men admitted in 1865 alone, 619 were returned to duty. Following his practice of avoiding amputation if at all possible, Janes created such devices as an arm support that enabled the wearer to write with his wounded arm even though the limb might remain useless for more strenuous functions.

At Montpelier, Janes continued to maintain his journal and record his case histories, one of the last involving a man wounded not in battle but in celebration.

On April 10, 1865, while Carlos Cushman of Tunbridge was "engaged with the people of Montpelier in loading a cannon to fire a salute in honor of the capture of Lee's army, it exploded," Janes recorded. "His face, neck and arms were severely burned and his hands so severely lacerated that it was necessary to amputate the third and fourth fingers of the left hand and the fourth of the right. The wounds healed rapidly."[33]

When his war service was concluded, Dr. Janes returned to his practice in Waterbury and continued to serve that community as physician and elected official until his death at eighty-two, revered as the town's leading citizen. Eventually, his home became Waterbury's public library.[34]

The warm appreciation his neighbors expressed for his contributions to the Union army compensated in part for the lack of recognition from his army superiors for his efforts at Gettysburg.

In a sense, any acknowledgment by the Federal authorities of the extraordinary job done by the skeletal force left behind with the 21,000 wounded at Gettysburg would have been an admission that they had made inadequate provisions for caring for that great body of men.

Nevertheless, it seemed extremely odd that when it came time to file his report on the operation of the medical department in the campaign that Jonathan Letterman should not have singled out any individuals—Janes or anyone else—for plaudits. To be "mentioned in dispatches" was the traditional way in which officers received their credits.

Instead, the medical director stated simply that "the conduct of the medical officers was admirable," an all-encompassing compliment that took no specific notice of the work done at Gettysburg after he left.[35]

Whether credited or not, all those who aided in the survival of the helpless horde stranded at Gettysburg had a hand in a novel and remarkable achievement. Each of the obstacles to treating such an unprecedented number of wounded soldiers and evacuating them from the scene was formidable. There had been too few doctors, not enough attendants, woefully inadequate shelters, a dire shortage of medical supplies, and far too little transportation. For many days the town suffered a desperate shortage of food and uncertain communication with the outside world.

Thanks to an amazing groundswell of public sympathy and concern, freely expressed by generous giving and direct hands-on assistance at the scene, the problems were successively overcome.

It was apparent that the nation did not have the heart to inactively tolerate what the war-hardened generals were resigned to accept: the soldier's plight to suffer.

Few who witnessed or took part in the activities that followed the battle—particularly, as we have seen, those who had had principal roles—were untouched by the experience. For so many of them, Gettysburg marked a pivotal point in their lives. The ordeals so affected them that they could not remain on the course they had been following. It drained too much out of them, and transformed them in myriad ways.

In the process of seeking to help the victims of the battle to the extent that they were able, these men and women became wounded themselves. They went off in vastly different directions, sometimes almost irrationally, to deal privately with their hurts and frustrations, and they were never counted in the true cost of the epic struggle that continued so long after the last shot was fired.

Notes

INTRODUCTION

1. U.S. War Department. *The War of the Rebellion: Official Records of the Union and Confederate Armies,* vol. 27, part 1, 79. (Cited hereafter as *O.R.* All volumes are in Series 1 unless otherwise indicated.)
2. Sisters of Charity. St. Joseph's Provincial House Archives, 130.
3. Ibid., 117.
4. Ibid.
5. Ibid., 132.
6. Fannie J. Buehler. *Recollections of the Rebel Invasion and One Woman's Experience During the Battle of Gettysburg.* (Gettysburg, 1896), 64.
7. Mrs. Tillie (Pierce) Alleman. *At Gettysburg or What A Girl Saw and Heard of the Battle.* (New York, 1889), 63.
8. *Philadelphia Public Ledger,* July 10, 1863.
9. *O.R.* 27, part 1, 28. Report of Medical Inspector Edward P. Vollum to Surgeon General William Hammond, July 25, 1863.
10. "J. Howard Wert Series." *Harrisburg Telegraph,* August 6, 1907.

CHAPTER ONE – "WITHOUT PROPER MEANS"

1. *Dictionary of American Biography.*
2. Mary Livermore. *My Story of the War.* (Hartford, Conn., 1895), 121.
3. Ibid.

4. *O.R.* 27, part 1, 195. (Report of Medical Director Jonathan Letterman, October 3, 1863.)

5. Jonathan Letterman, M.D. *Medical Recollections of the Army of the Potomac.* (New York, 1866), 156.

6. Ibid.

7. Cornelia Hancock. *South After Gettysburg.* (Philadelphia, 1937, and New York, 1956), 5.

8. Ibid., 7–8.

9. Andrew B. Cross. *The War—The Battle of Gettysburg and the Christian Commission.* (Baltimore, 1865), 14.

10. Mary C. Fisher. *A Week of Gettysburg Field.* Grand Army Scout and Soldiers Mail 2 (1883), 2.

11. Cyrus Bacon Jr. *A Michigan Surgeon at Gettysburg 100 Years Ago—the Daily Register of Dr. Cyrus Bacon, Jr.*, entry of July 4, 1863. Cyrus Bacon Manuscript Collection, University of Michigan.

12. William Watson. *Letters of a Civil War Surgeon.* (West Lafayette, Ind., 1961), 70.

13. A. H. Nickerson. *"Personal Recollections of Two Visits to Gettysburg."* Scribner's Magazine 14 (1893), 21.

14. Louis C. Duncan. *The Medical Department of the United States Army in the Civil War.* (Washington, D.C., 1910), 22.

15. Letterman. Medical, 157.

16. "Isaac Monfort report on Indiana relief mission." *Indianapolis Daily Journal,* July 23, 1863.

17. Bacon, *Daily Register,* entry of July 2, 1863.

18. Hammond to Letterman, July 5, 1863, Office of the Surgeon General, Letters and Endorsements Sent to Medical Officers, vol. 4, Record Group 112, National Archives.

19. Watson. *Surgeon,* 72.

20. Cross. *Christian,* 14.

21. William Baird Collection, University of Michigan.

22. Hancock. *South After Gettysburg,* 8.

23. Fisher. *Week,* 6.

24. Duncan. *Department,* 16.

25. Charles S. Wainwright. *A Diary of Battle—The Personal Journals of Col. Charles S. Wainwright—1861–1865.* (New York, 1962), 253.

26. Henry S. Stevens. *Address Delivered at the Dedication of the Monument of the 14th Connecticut Volunteers at Gettysburg, Pa., July 3, 1864.* (Middletown, Conn., 1884), 36.

27. John Dooley. *John Dooley, Confederate Soldier, His War Journal.* (Washington, D.C., 1945), 110.

28. Thomas L. Livermore. *Days and Events—1860–1865.* (Boston, 1920), 258–259.

29. Nickerson. *Visits,* 22–23.

30. L. P. Brockett, M.D., and Mary C. Vaughan. *Women's Work in the Civil War.* (Philadelphia and Boston, 1868), 137.

31. The Rev. Lemuel Moss. *Annals of the United States Christian Commission.* (Philadelphia, 1868), 385.

32. T. Livermore. *Days and Events—1860–1865,* 259.

33. Mrs. Edmund A. Souder. *Leaves from the Battlefield of Gettysburg.* (Philadelphia, 1864), 23.

34. Buehler. *Invasion,* 26.

35. Charles H. Glatfelter. *A Salutary Influence: Gettysburg College, 1832–1985.* (Gettysburg, 1987), 184.

36. Second Report of the Committee of Maryland, September 1, 1863, United States Christian Commission Records, Record Group 94, National Archives.

37. *Letters of Robert Hubbard, M.D.* U.S. Army, Military History Institute, Carlisle, Pa.

38. Sisters of Charity. *Archives,* 117.

39. Liberty A. Hollinger (Mrs. L. A. Clutz). *Some Personal Recollections of the Battle of Gettysburg.* (Gettysburg, 1925), 176.

40. *Philadelphia North American,* July 4, 1909.

41. Leander H. Warren. *My Recollection of What I Saw Before, During and After the Battle of Gettysburg.* (Gettysburg, 1926), 17.

42. *Gettysburg Compiler*—125th Commemorative Edition. (1988), 31.

43. Buehler. *Invasion,* 26.

44. Moss. *Annals,* 389.

45. "Wert Series." *Harrisburg Telegraph,* August 6, 1907.

46. *Gettysburg Compiler,* July 5, 1905.

47. *Philadelphia North American,* July 4, 1909.

48. Duncan. *Department,* 8.

49. Sisters of Charity. *Archives,* 131.

50. "The Diary of Capt. George A. Bowen, 12th Regiment New Jersey Volunteers," *The Valley Forge Journal* 11 (June 1985), 135.

51. Michael Jacobs, "Later Rambles Over the Field of Gettysburg," *U.S. Service Magazine* (January, 1864), 70–71.

52. Duncan. *Department,* 19.

53. Herman Haupt. *Reminiscences of Gen. Herman Haupt.* (Milwaukee, Wis., 1901), 44.

54. *Dictionary of American Biography.*

55. Haupt. *Reminiscences of Gen. Herman Haupt,* 49.

56. Ibid., 69–70.

57. Ibid., 208 and 211.

58. Ibid., 211–212.

59. Ibid., 213.

60. Ibid.

61. Ibid., 220.

62. Ibid., 216.

63. Ibid., 221.

64. Ibid.

65. Ibid.

66. Ibid., 222.

67. Ibid., 223.

68. Ibid., 224.

69. Ibid.

70. *O.R.* 27, pt. 1, 241.

71. Charles J. Stille. *History of the United States Sanitary Commission.* (Philadelphia, 1866), 377.

72. M. Livermore. *My Story of the War,* 130.

73. Ibid., 128.

74. Marjorie Barston Greenbie. *Lincoln's Daughters of Mercy.* (New York, 1944), 72.

75. William Quentin Maxwell. *Lincoln's Fifth Wheel: The Political History of the United States Sanitary Commission.* (New York, 1956), 8.

76. Ibid., 211–212. H. W. Bellows to Frederick L. Olmsted, July 8, 1863.

CHAPTER TWO – "GOD PITY US!"

1. Francis A. Walker. *History of the Second Army Corps in the Army of the Potomac.* (New York, 1887), 134.

2. George G. Meade. "Gen. Meade on the Sanitary Commission." *Sanitary Commission Bulletin* 1 (April 1864), 368.
3. *O.R.* 27, pt. 1, 197.
4. Ibid.
5. Ibid., 198–199.
6. Letterman to Hammond, July 7, 1863, Medical Officers Files, Record Group 94, National Archives.
7. Cross. *Christian,* 16.
8. Bushrod Washington James. *Echoes of Battle.* (Philadelphia, 1895), 101.
9. Ibid.
10. Hancock. *South After Gettysburg,* 12.
11. Ibid., 8.
12. Ellen Orbison Harris. *Fifth Semi-Annual Report of the Ladies Aid Society of Philadelphia.* (Philadelphia, 1863), 13.
13. Watson. *Surgeon,* 70.
14. Ibid., 71.
15. Diary of Sarah M. Broadhead. Gettysburg National Military Park Library, Gettysburg. (cited hereafter as G.N.M.P.)
16. Second Report of the Committee of Maryland, September 1, 1863. U.S. Christian Commission Records, Record Group 94, National Archives.
17. *New York Times,* July 6, 1863.
18. Hammond to Curtin, July 5, 1863, Office of the Surgeon General, Letters and Endorsements Sent 1818–1889, General Correspondence, vol. 35, Record Group 112, National Archives.
19. Ibid., J.R. Smith to John M. Cuyler, July 6, 1863.
20. *Pittsburgh Gazette,* July 8, 1863.
21. *O.R.* 27, pt. 3, 504.
22. *Indianapolis Daily Journal,* July 23, 1863.
23. Justin Dwinell. *Manuscript Medical Report of the Second Corps Hospitals at Gettysburg.* National Library of Medicine, Bethesda, Md.
24. *O.R.* 27, pt. 1, 198.
25. Theodore Graham Lewis, compiler and editor. *History of Waterbury, Vt.* (Waterbury, 1915), 143–144.
26. Brig. Gen. W. T. H. Brooks. Commendation of Henry Janes, February 6, 1863, Medical Officers Files, Record Group 94, National Archives.
27. Duncan. *Department,* 20.

28. *Philadelphia Public Ledger,* July 15, 1863.
29. Benjamin W. Thompson Papers. John A. Thompson, Minneapolis, Minn.
30. Watson. *Surgeon,* 70.
31. *Philadelphia Weekly Times,* June 28, 1864.
32. 155th Regimental Association. *Under the Maltese Cross—155th Pennsylvania Regiment.* (Pittsburgh, Pa., 1910), 180.
33. Bacon, *Daily Register.* University of Michigan.
34. Wainwright. *Diary,* 254.
35. Ibid.
36. 155th Pennsylvania. *Maltese,* 192.
37. Ibid.
38. Duncan. *Department,* 15.
39. *Adams Sentinel,* July 28, 1863.
40. *O.R.* 27, pt. 2, 364, 557.
41. Dooley. *Journal,* 111.
42. Hancock. *South after Gettysburg,* 13.
43. Decimus et Ultimus Barziza. *Adventures of a Prisoner of War 1863–1864.* (Austin, Tex., 1964), 54.
44. Watson. *Surgeon,* 71.
45. *New York Times,* July 16, 1863.
46. John Y. Foster. "Four Days at Gettysburg." *Harper's New Monthly Magazine* 28 (February, 1864), 383.
47. Anna Holstein. *Three Years in Field Hospitals of the Army of the Potomac.* (Philadelphia, 1867), 258–259.
48. *Philadelphia North American,* June 29, 1913.
49. Simon Baruch. "A Surgeon's Story of Battle and Capture," *Confederate Veteran* 22 (1914), 545–546.
50. *O.R.* 27, pt. 1, 119.
51. Marsena R. Patrick. *Inside Lincoln's Army—The Diary of Gen. Marsena Rudolph Patrick, Provost Marshal General, Army of the Potomac.* (New York, 1964), 268.
52. Diary of William Peel. Mississippi Department of Archives and History, Jackson, Miss.
53. *New York Times,* July 16, 1863.
54. *O.R.* 27, pt. 1, 619.
55. Ibid., 69.

56. Georgeanna Woolsey. *Three Weeks at Gettysburg.* Pamphlet (New York, 1863), 5.

57. *O.R.* 27, pt. 3, 591.

58. Haupt. *Reminiscences of Gen. Herman Haupt,* 239.

59. *O.R.* 27, pt. 3, 619–620.

60. Ibid., pt. 1, 198.

61. Ibid., pt. 3, 619.

62. Ibid., pt. 1, 198.

63. Ibid., 24.

64. Dwinell Manuscript.

65. *Second Report of the Committee of Maryland,* September 1, 1863.

66. Woolsey. *Three Weeks at Gettysburg,* 5.

67. Patriot Daughters of Lancaster. *Hospital Scenes After the Battle of Gettysburg, July 1863.* (Philadelphia, 1864), 55–56.

68. Charles Muller Papers. Minnesota Historical Society, St. Paul.

69. Benjamin W. Thompson Papers.

70. Wainwright. *Diary,* 154.

71. *O.R.* 27, pt. 3, 620.

72. Acting Surgeon General J. R. Smith to Cuyler, July 9, 1863, Office of the Surgeon General, Letters and Endorsements Sent to Medical Officers, vol. 4, Record Group 112, National Archives.

73. J. W. Muffly, ed., *The Story of Our Regiment—A History of the 148th Pennsylvania Volunteers.* (Des Moines, Iowa, 1904), 467.

74. William Kepler. *History of the Three Months and Three Years Service of the Fourth Regiment Ohio Volunteer Infantry.* (Cleveland, 1886), 307.

75. Frank A. Haskell. *The Battle of Gettysburg.* (Boston, 1957), 148.

76. T. W. Herbert, "In Occupied Pennsylvania." *Georgia Review* 4 (1950), 112.

77. *New York Herald,* July 9, 1863.

78. *New York Times,* July 12, 1863.

79. Patrick. *Inside,* 268.; Diary of John B. Linn. Centre County Library and Historical Museum, Bellefonte, Pa.

80. "Wert Series," *Harrisburg Telegraph,* September 20, 1907.

81. *O.R.* 27, pt. 3, 607.

82. John H. Brinton. *Personal Memoirs of John H. Brinton.* (New York, 1914), 187.

83. Ibid., 245.
84. Hancock. *South after Gettysburg,* 7.
85. Souder. *Leaves,* 22.
86. Muffley. *Story,* 466.
87. *Gettysburg Compiler,* June 1, 1908.
88. *Diary of Sarah M. Broadhead.* G.N.M.P.
89. Nellie E. Auginbaugh. *Personal Experience of a Young Girl During the Battle of Gettysburg.* (Washington, D.C., 1926), 10.
90. Souder. *Leaves,* 23.
91. *Doylestown Daily Intelligencer,* May 30, 1959.
92. *Adams Sentinel,* July 7, 1863; *Gettysburg Star & Banner,* July 9, 1863.
93. Hancock. *South after Gettysburg,* 7.
94. *Gettysburg Compiler,* July 1863.
95. Patrick. *Inside,* 268–269.
96. Souder. *Leaves,* 18–19.
97. Hollinger. *Recollections,* 177.
98. Herbert. *In Occupied Pennsylvania,* 108.
99. John C. Wills Papers. Adams County Historical Society, Gettysburg.
100. *Gettysburg Compiler,* July 13, 1863.

CHAPTER THREE – A GREAT OUTPOURING
1. Foster. *Four,* 381.
2. Broadhead Diary. G.N.M.P.
3. Buehler. *Invasion,* 23.
4. Frederick Law Olmsted. *The Papers of Frederick Law Olmsted.* (Baltimore, 1986), 646.
5. Stille. *Sanitary,* 380.
6. *Adams Sentinel,* March 22, 1864.
7. Stille. *Sanitary,* 380–381.
8. George Templeton Strong. *Diary of the Civil War.* (New York, 1982), 425.
9. *New York Times,* July 16, 1863.
10. Maxwell. *Wheel,* 212.
11. Baruch. *Surgeon's Story,* 546.
12. Stille. *Sanitary,* 286.
13. Ibid.
14. Baruch. *Surgeon's Story,* 546.

15. Pamphlet entitled "Christian Commission for the Army and Navy of the United States of America." U.S. Christian Commission Records, Record Group 94, National Archives.
16. Maxwell. *Wheel,* 192. (H. W. Bellows to W. E. Dodge, February 12, 1863.)
17. Strong. *Diary,* 589.
18. Ibid., 311.
19. Moss. *Annals,* 381.
20. Cross. *Christian,* 17.
21. Second Report of the Committee of Maryland, September 1, 1863.
22. Ibid.
23. Ibid.
24. Cross. *Christian,* 18.
25. Ibid.
26. Ibid., 17; *New York Times,* July 16, 1863.
27. Second Report of the Committee of Maryland, September 1, 1863.
28. *Indianapolis Daily Journal,* July 23, 1863.
29. Charlotte McKay. *Stories of Hospital and Camp.* (Philadelphia, 1876), 159–160.
30. Ibid., 151–153.
31. Patriot Daughters. *Scenes,* 22–24.
32. *O.R.* 27, pt. 3, 619.
33. Ibid., pt. 1, 28.
34. Hancock. *South After Gettysburg,* 13.
35. J. A. Curran, M.D. "Billings at Gettysburg." *New England Journal of Medicine* 269 (July 4, 1963), 24.
36. Ibid., 25.
37. Ibid.
38. *The Sanitary Commission of the U.S. Army—A Succinct Narrative of its Works and Purposes.* (New York, 1864), 159.
39. Cross. *Christian* 15.
40. James. *Echoes,* 101–104.
41. *O.R.* 27, pt. 1, 25.
42. Justin Dwinell Manuscript.
43. Diary of Theodore Dimon. State University of Iowa, Iowa City.
44. *O.R.* 27, pt. 1, 197.

45. Sister Mary Denis Maher. *To Bind Up the Wounds—Catholic Sister Nurses in the Civil War.* (New York - Westport, Conn., 1989), 53.
46. *Dictionary of American Biography.*
47. Ibid.
48 Robert D. Hoffsommer and Jean O'Brien. "Dorothea Dix—A Personality Profile." *Civil War Times Illustrated* 4 (August 1965), 40.
49. Strong. *Diary,* 173–174.
50. M. Livermore. *Story,* 247.
51. Maher. *Bind,* 52.
52. M. Livermore. *My Story of the War,* 246.
53. Donald Dale Jackson and the editors of Time-Life Books. *The Civil War—Twenty Million Yankees.* (Alexandria, Va., 1985), 128.
54. Hancock. *South After Gettysburg,* 6.
55. Sophronia E. Bucklin. *In Hospital and Camp.* (Philadelphia, 1869), 138.
56. Maxwell. *Wheel,* 65.
57. Barziza. *Adventures,* 57–58.
58. "Wert Series," *Harrisburg Telegraph,* July 27, 1907.
59. Dooley. *Journal,* 119–120.
60. Nickerson. *Two Visits,* 23–24.
61. *O.R.* 27, pt. 1, 27.
62. *O.R.* 6, series 2, 102.
63. *New York Times,* July 16, 1863.
64. Dooley. *Journal,* 123.
65. Barziza. *Adventures,* 63–64.
66. *O.R.* 27, pt. 3, 521.
67. Ibid.
68. Georgeanna (Woolsey) Bacon and Eliza Newton (Woolsey) Howland. *Letters of a Family During the War, 1861–1865.* (New York, 1899), vol. 2, 535.
69. Woolsey. *Three Weeks at Gettysburg.* 7–10.
70. Woolsey. *Letters,* vol. 2, 528–529.
71. Moss. *Annals,* 384.

CHAPTER FOUR – A SECOND INVASION

1. Broadhead Diary. G.N.M.P.
2. Leander H. Warren. *My Recollections of What I Saw Before, During and After the Battle of Gettysburg.* (Gettysburg, 1926), 17.

3. *New York Times,* July 9, 1863.

4. *Philadelphia Public Ledger,* July 15, 1863.

5. Woolsey. *Three Weeks at Gettysburg,* 13.

6. Buehler. *Invasion,* 27.

7. Ibid., 23.

8. Dimon Diary.

9. Patriot Daughters. *Scenes,* 21.

10. *Philadelphia Weekly Press,* November 16, 1887.

11. Robert M. Powell. *Recollections of a Texas Colonel at Gettysburg.* (Gettysburg, 1990), 21.

12. *Philadelphia Weekly Press,* November 16, 1887.

13. Hancock. *South After Gettysburg,* 18.

14. Bucklin. *In Hospital and Camp,* 155–156.

15. Copy of advertisement at Kean Archives, Philadelphia.

16. Albertus McCreary. "Gettysburg: A Boy's Experience of the Battle." *McClure's Magazine* 33 (July 1909).

17. Letters of Justus M. Silliman. New Canaan Historical Society, New Canaan, Conn.

18. Souder. *Leaves,* 63.

19. *Adams Sentinel,* July 20, 1863.

20. Gregory A. Coco. *On the Bloodstained Field II.* (Gettysburg, 1989), 108.

21. Evelyn Page. "After Gettysburg—Frederick Law Olmsted on the Escape of Lee." *Pennsylvania Magazine* 72, (October 1951), 442.

22. Daniel A. Skelley. *A Boy's Experience During the Battle of Gettysburg.* (Gettysburg, 1932), 24.

23. Wills Papers. Adams County Historical Society, Gettysburg.

24. *O.R.* 27, pt. 3, 699.

25. Acting Surgeon General J. R. Smith to Cuyler, July 13, 1863. Office of the Surgeon General, Letters and Endorsements Sent to Medical Officers, vol. 4, Record Group 112, National Archives.

26. Ibid., Smith to Surgeon Eben Swift, July 15, 1863.

27. Hammond to Stanton, July 17, 1863. Office of the Surgeon General, Letters and Endorsements Sent to the Secretary of War, April 1863–April 1864, vol. 4, Record Group 112, National Archives.

28. *O.R.* 27, pt. 3, 568.

29. Brinton, *Memoirs,* 244.

30. Diary of Henry B. Blood. Library of Congress, Washington, D.C.

31. Office of the Quartermaster General, Reports of Capt. W. W. Smith, Record Group 92, National Archives.

32. Ibid.

33. "Wert Series." *Harrisburg Telegraph,* September 20, 1907; David McConaughy to Maj. Gen. D. N. Couch, November 7, 1863, copy at G.N.M.P.

34. Smith Reports, Record Group 92, National Archives.

35. *Gettysburg Compiler,* July 6, 1910.

36. Warren. *Recollections,* 17.

37. "Wert Series." *Harrisburg Telegraph,* September 20, 1907.

38. Alleman. *What a Girl Saw,* 106.

39. Smith Reports, Record Group 92, National Archives.

40. McCreary. *Boy's Experience.*

41. Ibid.

42. *O.R.* 27, pt. 1, 225–226. (Report of Lt. John R. Edie, Acting Chief Ordnance Officer.)

43. Samuel Bates. *History of the Pennsylvania Volunteers.* (Harrisburg, 1871), vol. 10, 1229.

44. Col. J. G. Benton. *A Course of Instruction in Ordnance and Gunnery.* (New York, 1875), 341.

45. Cross. *Christian,* 27.

46. Hollinger. *Recollections,* 175.

47. Souder. *Leaves,* 59.

48. *Philadelphia Weekly Press,* November 16, 1887.

49. James R. Crocker. "Prison Reminiscences." *Southern Historical Society Papers* 34 (1906), 28–29.

50. Baruch. *Surgeon,* 546.

51. Ibid.

52. Barziza. *Adventures,* 61.

53. Capt. W. C. Ward. "Incidents and Personal Experiences on the Battlefield of Gettysburg." *Confederate Veteran* 8 (1900), 349.

54. "College Hospital in Gettysburg," writer unidentified. *Land We Love* 2 (February 1867), 290–294.

55. E. F. Conklin. *Women at Gettysburg 1863.* (Gettysburg 1993), 354.

56. Ward. *Incidents,* 349.

57. Powell. *Texas,* 34.

58. Henry Kyd Douglas. *I Rode With Stonewall.* (Chapel Hill, N.C., 1940), 257.

59. Crocker. *Prison,* 29.

60. Henry Janes file, U.S. Army, Military History Institute, Carlisle, Pa.

61. Patrick. *Inside,* 269.

62. Gregory A. Coco. *A Vast Sea of Misery.* (Gettysburg, 1988), 36.

63. *O.R.* 27, pt. 3, 646.

64. *O.R.* 6, Series 2, 102.

65. Ibid., 103.

66. Powell. *Texas,* 31.

67. Souder. *Leaves,* 59.

68. Gen. Isaac R. Trimble. "The Civil War Diary of . . ." *Maryland Historical Magazine* 17 (March 1922), 13.

69. Patriot Daughters. *Scenes,* 49–50.

70. Hollinger. *Recollections,* 174.

71. Souder. *Leaves,* 63.

72. Hollinger, *Recollections,* 173.

73. Woolsey. *Three Weeks at Gettysburg,* 15.

74. Hancock. *South After Gettysburg,* 14.

75. Ibid.

76. Ibid., 21.

77. "Wert Series." *Harrisburg Telegraph,* July 27, 1907.

78. *Gettysburg Compiler,* July 13, 1863.

79. *Adams Sentinel,* July 28, 1863.

80. Ibid.

81. Ibid.

82. Ibid., July 21, 1863.

83. Hancock. *South After Gettysburg,* 11.

84. Hubbard Letters.

85. *Adams Sentinel,* August 11, 1863.

86. *New York Times,* July 9, 1863.

87. Second Report of the Committee of Maryland, September 1, 1983.

88. Michael Jacobs. *Notes on the Rebel Invasion of Maryland and Pennsylvania and the Battle of Gettysburg.* (Philadelphia, 1864), 29–30.

89. McKay. *Stories of Hospital and Camp,* 53–56.

90. Ibid.

91. Henry Janes file.

92. J. R. Smith to Janes, August 25, 1863, Office of the Surgeon General, Letters and Endorsements Sent to Medical Officers, vol. 4, Record Group 112, National Archives.

CHAPTER FIVE – "ALL WERE GONE"
1. Bucklin, *In Hospital and Camp,* 143–144.
2. Ibid., 142.
3. *The Sanitary Commission of the U.S. Army—A Succinct Narrative of its Works and Purposes.* 145.
4. James P. Ludlow letter, *Rochester, N.Y., Democrat & American,* August 15, 1863.
5. Broadhead Diary. G.N.M.P.
6. Hancock. *South After Gettysburg,* 19.
7. Ibid., 16.
8. Woolsey. *Three Weeks at Gettysburg,* 10.
9. H. H. Cunningham. *Doctors in Gray.* (Baton Rouge, 1958), 131.
10. Baruch. *Surgeon,* 546.
11. L. P. Warren obituary. *Confederate Veteran* 22 (1914), 472.
12. Baruch. *Surgeon,* 546.
13. *Adams Sentinel,* August 11, 1863.
14. At McHenry, Baruch said he was confined with 110 surgeons and 10 chaplains and, if all the doctors had come from Gettysburg, it would indicate that the total number of Southern physicians left there actually had exceeded the number Jonathan Letterman had assigned from the Army of the Potomac for nearly twice as many Union wounded.

   One Union medical officer said—mistakenly as to the timing—that "all of the *eighty* Confederates who were left with their wounded at Gettysburg were promptly sent home as soon as we could dispense with their services." (S. Weir Mitchell, M.D. "The Medical Department in the Civil War," *Journal of the American Medical Association* 62, May 1914, 1450.)
15. *O.R.* 27, pt. 3, 730.
16. Ibid., pt. 1, 196.
17. J. R. Smith to W. S. King, July 18, 1863, Office of the Surgeon General, Letters and Endorsements Sent to Medical Officers, vol. 4, Record Group 112, National Archives.

18. Ibid., E. S. Dunster to King, July 28, 1863.
19. *Christian Advocate,* August 1, 1863.
20. *Dictionary of American Biography.*
21. J. R. Smith to Janes, September 2, 1863, Office of the Surgeon General, Letters and Endorsements Sent to Medical Officers, vol. 5, Record Group 112, National Archives.
22. Duncan. *Department, 22.*
23. F. M. Stoke letter, October 26, 1863, Gettysburg College, Gettysburg.
24. Second Report of the Committee of Maryland, September 1, 1863.
25. Hancock. *South After Gettysburg,* 24.
26. Bucklin. *In Hospital and Camp,* 146.
27. Ibid., 181.
28. Hancock. *South After Gettysburg,* 21.
29. Bucklin. *In Hospital and Camp,* 161.
30. Ibid.
31. Henry Janes file.
32. Bucklin. *In Hospital and Camp,* 174–175.
33. Ibid.
34. Holstein pension records, Private Act 141, 52nd Congress.
35. Hancock. *South After Gettysburg,* 21.
36. *O.R.* 27, pt. 3, 263.
37. Henry Janes file.
38. Mrs. R. P. McCormick. *"The Banishment of Miss Euphemia Goldsborough,"* a journal composition by a sister of Miss Goldsborough. Typescript at G.N.M.P.; original held by descendants.
39. Howard Coffin. "Blood, Sweat and Tears—The Journal of a Civil War Surgeon," *Vermont Sunday Magazine of the Sunday Rutland,* Vt., *Herald* and the *Sunday Times Argus,* May 7, 1989.
40. Holstein. *Three Years,* 50.
41. *Adams Sentinel,* September 29, 1863.
42. Holstein. *Three Years,* 50.
43. Justus M. Silliman Letters. New Canaan Historical Society, New Canaan, Conn.
44. Bucklin. *In Hospital and Camp,* 183–184.
45. Holstein. *Three Years,* 51.
46. *"Revised Report of the Select Committee Relative to the Soldiers' National Cemetery,"* Pennsylvania House of Representatives, 149.

47. Ibid., 8.

48. Ibid., 151.

49. Ibid., 148.

50. Olmsted. *Papers,* 649.

51. Henry W. Bellows Papers. Massachusetts Historical Society. (Bellows to J. Miller McKim, August 18, 1865.)

52. "Supplies Distributed During and Immediately After the Battles at Gettysburg." *Sanitary Commission Bulletin* 1 (February 1864), 229.

53. Ibid., 229–230.

54. McCreary. *Boy's Experience.*

55. Sisters of Charity. *Archives,* 133.

56. Brockett and Vaughan. *Women's Work,* 286.

57. Hancock. *South After Gettysburg,* 27.

58. Ibid.

59. Ibid., 21.

60. Ibid., 28–29.

61. McCormick. *Banishment.*

62. Conklin. *Women at Gettysburg 1863,* 351.

63. Ibid., 417.

64. Hancock. *South After Gettysburg,* 140.

65. John G. Nicolay and John Hay. *Abraham Lincoln, A History* 8 (New York, 1890), 190.

66. Carl Sandburg. *Abraham Lincoln—The Prairie Years and the War Years.* One-volume edition. (New York, 1954), 441.

67. Bucklin. *Hospital,* 192.

68. Ibid., 192–193.

69. Skelly. *Experiences,* 27.

70. Bucklin. *Hospital,* 193–194.

71. Ibid., 195.

72. Nickerson. *Visits,* 28.

73. Skelly. *Experiences,* 27.

74. Bucklin. *In Hospital and Camp,* 196.

75. Holstein. *Three Years,* 54.

CHAPTER SIX – THE UNCOUNTED CASUALTIES

1. *O.R.* 27, pt. 1, 24–25.

2. Sanitary Commission Bulletin 1 (April 1864), 368.

3. Duncan. *Department,* 27.

4. *O.R.* 27, pt. 1, 196.

5. Ibid., 28.

6. Stille. *Sanitary,* 388.

7. How individuals respond to disaster situations is analyzed in detail in Beverley Raphael's *When Disaster Strikes* (New York, 1986).

8. Virginia Walcott Beauchamp. "The Sisters and the Soldiers," *Maryland Historical Magazine* 81 (Summer 1986), 132.

9. Baruch. *Surgeon,* 548.

10. *Dictionary of American Biography.*

11. Curran. *Billings,* 23.

12. *Adams Sentinel,* February 2, 1864.

13. James K. P. Scott. *The Story of the Battles of Gettysburg.* (Harrisburg, 1927), 35.

14. "The Golden Jubilee of Rufus Benjamin Weaver, Master Anatomist," *The Hahnemannian Monthly* (June 1915).

15. Mary H. Mitchell. *Hollywood Cemetery—The History of a Southern Shrine.* (Richmond, 1985), 84–92.

16. Kathleen Georg Harrison. "A Fitting and Expressive Memorial—The Development of Gettysburg National Military Park." *Gettysburg Compiler*—125 Commemorative Edition (1988).

17. Ibid.

18. *Adams Sentinel,* August 14, 1863.

19. Ibid., September 15, 1863.

20. Ibid., March 1, 1864.

21. *Dictionary of American Biography.*

22. Olmsted. *Papers,* 697.

23. Ibid., 680–681.

24. Ibid., 672.

25. Ibid., 697.

26. Henry W. Bellows Papers. Massachusetts Historical Society, Bellows to J. Miller McKim, August 18, 1865.

27. Ibid., 221.

28. *Dictionary of American Biography.*

29. Brinton. *Memoirs,* 170–171.

30. Jonathan Letterman. Medical Officers Files, Record Group 94, National Archives; *Dictionary of American Biography.*

31. Kepler. *Ohio,* 193.

32. Janes to Surgeon General's Office, November 30, 1863, Office of the Surgeon General, Medical Officers Files, Record Group 94, National Archives.

33. *Sunday Rutland, Vermont, Herald and Sunday Times Argus,* May 7, 1989.

34. Theodore G. Lewis. *History of Waterbury, Vermont.* (Waterbury, 1915), 144–146.

35. *O.R.* 27, pt. 1, 199.

Bibliography

MANUSCRIPT SOURCES

Adams County Historical Society, Gettysburg, Pennsylvania, John C. Wills Papers.

Centre County Library and Historical Museum, Bellefonte, Pennsylvania, John B. Linn Diary.

Gettysburg College, Gettysburg, F. M. Stoke Letter.

Gettysburg National Military Park, Gettysburg, Sarah M. Broadhead Diary.

State University of Iowa, Iowa City, Dr. Theodore Dimon Diary.

Library of Congress, Washington, District of Columbia, Henry B. Blood Diary.

Massachusetts Historical Society, Boston, Massachusetts, Henry W. Bellows Papers.

National Archives, Washington, D.C.
    Record Group 92
        Office of the Quartermaster General
            Capt. W. W. Smith Reports.
    Record Group 94
        Medical Officers Files
            John M. Cuyler, Henry Janes, Jonathan Letterman, Edward P. Vollum.
        United States Christian Commission Records
            Second Report of the Committee of Maryland, Christian Commission for the Army and Navy of the U.S.A. (pamphlet).

Record Group 112
> Office of the Surgeon General
>> Letters and Endorsements Sent (General Correspondence), vol., 35; Letters and Endorsements Sent to Medical Officers, vols. 4 and 5; Letters and Endorsements Sent to the Secretary of War, vol. 4.

National Library of Medicine, Bethesda, Maryland, Justin Dwinell Manuscript.

University of Michigan, Ann Arbor, Cyrus Bacon Manuscript, William Baird Collection.

Minnesota Historical Society, St. Paul, Charles Muller Papers.

Mississippi Department of Archives and History, Jackson, William Peel Diary.

New Canaan Historical Society, New Canaan, Connecticut, Justus M. Silliman Letters.

Sisters of Charity, Emmitsburg, Maryland, Archives of St. Joseph's Provincial House.

John A. Thompson, Minneapolis, Minnesota, Benjamin W. Thompson Papers.

United States Army, Military History Institute, Carlisle, Pennsylvania, Dr. Robert Hubbard Letters.

NEWSPAPERS

Adams Sentinel, (Gettysburg, Pa.), 1863, 1864.

Doylestown Daily Intelligencer, (Pa.) 1959.

Gettysburg Compiler, (Pa.), 1863, 1905, 1908, 1910, 1988.

Gettysburg Star & Banner, (Pa.), 1863.

Harrisburg Telegraph, (Pa.), 1907.

Indianapolis Daily Journal, 1863.

Lancaster Daily Express, (Pa.), 1863.

Lutheran Observer, (Baltimore).

New York Herald, 1863.

New York Times, 1863.

Philadelphia North American, 1909, 1913.

Philadelphia Public Ledger, 1863.

Philadelphia Weekly Press, 1887.

Philadelphia Weekly Times, 1884.

Pittsburgh Evening Chronicle, (Pa.), 1863.
Pittsburgh Gazette, (Pa.), 1863.
Rochester Democrat & American, (N.Y.), 1863.
Sunday Rutland Herald and Sunday Times Argus, (Vt.), 1989.

OFFICIAL PUBLICATIONS

Pennsylvania House of Representatives. *Revised Report of the Select Committee Relative to the Soldiers National Cemetery.* Harrisburg, 1865.
United States War Department. *War of the Rebellion: Official Records of the Union and Confederate Armies.* 128 vols. Washington, D.C., 1880–1901.

BOOKS

Alleman, Tillie (Pierce). *At Gettysburg or What a Girl Saw and Heard of the Battle.* New York, 1889.
Auginbaugh, Nellie E. *Personal Experience of a Young Girl During the Battle of Gettysburg.* Washington, D.C., 1926.
Baruch, Bernard M. *Baruch—My Own Story.* New York, 1957.
Barziza, Decimus et Ultimus. *Adventures of a Prisoner of War 1863–1864.* Austin, TX, 1964.
Bates, Samuel. *History of the Pennsylvania Volunteers.* Harrisburg, PA, 1871.
Benedict, George G. *Army Life in Virginia.* Burlington, VT., 1895.
Benton, James G. *A Course of Instruction in Ordnance and Gunnery.* New York, 1875.
Billings, John D. *Hardtack and Coffee.* Williamstown, MA, 1980.
Brinton, John H. *Personal Memoirs of John H. Brinton.* New York, 1914.
Brockett, L. P., M.D., and Mary C. Vaughan. *Women's Work in the Civil War.* Philadelphia and Boston, 1868.
Bucklin, Sophronia E. *In Hospital & Camp.* Philadelphia, 1869.
Buehler, Fannie J. *Recollections of the Rebel Invasion and One Woman's Experience During the Battle of Gettysburg.* Gettysburg, PA, 1896.
Coco, Gregory A. *A Strange and Blighted Land—Gettysburg: The Aftermath of a Battle.* Gettysburg, PA, 1995.
———— *A Vast Sea of Misery.* Gettysburg, PA, 1988.
———— *On the Bloodstained Field II.* Gettysburg, PA, 1989.
Coffin, Howard. *Full Duty—Vermonters in the Civil War.* Woodstock, VT, 1993.

Conklin, E. F. *Women at Gettysburg 1863*. Gettysburg, PA, 1993.

Cross, Andrew B. *The War—the Battle of Gettysburg and the Christian Commission*. Baltimore, MD, 1865.

Cunningham, H. H. *Doctors in Gray*. Baton Rouge, LA, 1958.

Dooley, John. *John Dooley, Confederate Soldier, His War Journal*. Joseph T. Durkin, editor. Washington, D.C., 1945.

Douglas, Henry Kyd. *I Rode With Stonewall*. Chapel Hill, NC, 1940.

Duncan, Louis C. *The Medical Department of the U.S. Army in the Civil War*. Washington, D.C., 1910.

Glatfelter, Charles H. *A Salutary Influence: Gettysburg College, 1832–1985*. Gettysburg, PA, 1987.

Greenbie, Marjorie Barstow. *Lincoln's Daughters of Mercy*. New York, 1944.

Hancock, Cornelia. *South After Gettysburg: Letters of Cornelia Hancock*. Edited by Henrietta Stratton Jaquette. Philadelphia, 1937, and New York, 1956.

Harris, Ellen Orbison. *Fifth Semi-Annual Report of the Ladies Aid Society of Philadelphia*. Philadelphia, 1863.

Haskell, Frank A. *The Battle of Gettysburg*. Boston, 1957.

Haupt, Herman. *Reminiscences of General Herman Haupt*. Milwaukee, WI, 1901.

Holland, Mary A. Gardner. *Our Army Nurses*. Boston, 1897.

Hollinger, Liberty (Mrs. L. A. Clutz). *Some Personal Recollections of the Battle of Gettysburg*. Gettysburg, PA, 1925.

Holstein, Anna. *Three Years in Field Hospitals of the Army of the Potomac*. Philadelphia, 1867.

Jackson, Donald Dale, and the editors of Time-Life Books. *The Civil War—Twenty Million Yankees*. Alexandria, VA, 1985.

Jacobs, Michael. *Notes on the Rebel Invasion of Maryland and Pennsylvania and the Battle of Gettysburg*. Philadelphia, 1864.

James, Bushrod Washington. *Echoes of Battle*. Philadelphia, 1895.

Kepler, William. *History of the Three Months and Three Years Service of the Fourth Regiment, Ohio Volunteer Infantry*. Cleveland, OH, 1886.

Letterman, Jonathan, M.D. *Medical Recollections of the Army of the Potomac*. New York, 1866.

Lewis, Theodore Graham, compiler and editor. *History of Waterbury, Vermont*. Waterbury, VT, 1915.

Livermore, Mary. *My Story of the War.* Hartford, CT.

Livermore, Thomas L. *Days and Events, 1860–1866.* Boston, 1920.

McKay, Charlotte. *Stories of Hospital and Camp.* Philadelphia, 1876.

McLaughlin, Jack. *Gettysburg: The Long Encampment.* New York, 1963.

Maher, Sister Mary Denis. *To Bind Up the Wounds—Catholic Sister Nurses in the Civil War.* New York-Westport, CT, 1989.

Maxwell, William Quentin. *Lincoln's Fifth Wheel: The Political History of the United States Sanitary Commission.* New York, 1956.

Mitchell, Mary H. *Hollywood Cemetery—The History of a Southern Shrine.* Richmond, VA, 1985.

Moss, The Rev. Lemuel. *Annals of the U.S. Christian Commission.* Philadelphia, 1868.

Muffly, J. W., editor. *The Story of Our Regiment (A History of the 148th Pennsylvania Volunteers).* Des Moines, IA, 1904.

Nicolay, John G., and John Hay. *Abraham Lincoln—A History.* 10 vols. New York, 1890.

Olmsted, Frederick Law. *The Papers of Frederick Law Olmsted.* Jane Turner Censer, editor. Baltimore, MD, 1986.

155th Regimental Association. *Under the Maltese Cross (155th Pennsylvania Regiment).* Pittsburgh, PA, 1910.

Patrick, Marsena Rudolph. *Inside Lincoln's Army (The Diary of Gen. Marsena Rudolph Patrick, Provost Marshal General, Army of the Potomac).* Edited by David S. Sparks. New York, 1964.

Patriot Daughters of Lancaster. *Hospital Scenes After the Battle of Gettysburg.* Philadelphia, 1864.

Powell, Robert M. *Recollections of a Texas Colonel at Gettysburg.* Gettysburg, PA, 1990.

Raphael, Beverley. *When Disaster Strikes.* New York, 1986.

Sandburg, Carl. *Abraham Lincoln—The Prairie Years and the War Years.* One volume edition. New York, 1954.

The Sanitary Commission of the U.S. Army—A Succinct Narrative of its Works and Purposes. New York, 1864.

Scott, James K. P. *The Story of the Battles of Gettysburg.* Harrisburg, PA, 1927.

Skelly, Daniel Alexander. *A Boy's Experiences During the Battles of Gettysburg.* Gettysburg, PA, 1932.

Souder, Mrs. Edmund A. *Leaves from the Battlefield of Gettysburg.* Philadelphia, 1864.

Stevens, Henry S. *Address Delivered at the Dedication of the Monument of the 14th Connecticut Volunteers at Gettysburg, Pa., July 3, 1884.* Middletown, CT, 1884.

Stille, Charles J. *History of the United States Sanitary Commission.* Philadelphia, 1866.

Storrick, W. C. *Gettysburg: The Place, The Battles, The Outcome.* Harrisburg, PA, 1932.

Strong, George Templeton. *Diary of the Civil War.* New York, 1982.

Wainwright, Charles S. *A Diary of Battle—The Personal Journals of Col. Charles S. Wainwright—1861–1865.* Edited by Allan Nevins. New York, 1962.

Walker, Francis A. *History of the Second Army Corps in the Army of the Potomac.* New York, 1887.

Warren, Leander H. *My Recollections of What I Saw Before, During and After the Battle of Gettysburg.* Gettysburg, PA, 1926.

Watson, William. *Letters of a Civil War Surgeon.* Edited by Paul Fatout. West Lafayette, IN, 1961.

Woolsey, Georgeanna (Woolsey) Bacon and Eliza Newton (Woolsey) Howland. *Letters of a Family During the War, 1861–1865.* New York, 1899. Two vols.

Wormeley, Katherine Prescott. *With the Army of the Potomac.* Boston, 1889.

ARTICLES

Baruch, Simon. "A Surgeon's Story of Battle and Capture." *Confederate Veteran* 22 (1914), 545–546.

Beauchamp, Virginia Walcott. "The Sisters and the Soldiers." *Maryland Historical Magazine* 81 (Summer 1986), 117–133.

Bowen, George A. "The Diary of Capt. George A. Bowen, 12th Regiment, New Jersey Volunteers." *The Valley Forge Journal* 2 (June 1985).

Coates, Earl J. "A Quartermaster's Battle of Gettysburg." *North South Trader* 5 (November-December 1977), 17–40.

Crocker, James R. "Prison Reminiscences." *Southern Historical Society Papers* 34 (1906), 28–31.

Curran, J. A., M.D. "Billings at Gettysburg." *New England Journal of Medicine* 269 (July 1963), 23–27.

Davis, Curtis Carroll. "Effie Goldsborough—Confederate Courier." *Civil War Times Illustrated* 7 (April 1968), 29–31.

Fisher, Mary C. "A Week on Gettysburg Field." *Grand Army Scout and Soldiers Mail* 2 (1883).

Foster, John Y. "Four Days at Gettysburg." *Harper's New Monthly Magazine* 28 (February 1864), 381–388.

Herbert, T. W. "In Occupied Pennsylvania." *Georgia Review* 4 (1950), 103–113.

Hoffsommer, Robert D. and Jean O'Brien. "Dorothea Dix—A Personality Profile." *Civil War Times Illustrated* 4 (August 1965), 39–44.

Jacobs, Michael. "Later Rambles Over the Field of Gettysburg." *U. S. Service Magazine* (January 1864), 70–71.

McCreary, Albertus. "Gettysburg: A Boy's Experience of the Battle." *McClure's Magazine* 33 (July 1909), 243–253.

Meade, George Gordon. "Gen. Meade on the Sanitary Commission." *Sanitary Commission Bulletin* 1 (April 1864), 69.

Mitchell S. Weir, M.D. "The Medical Department in the Civil War." *Journal of the American Medical Association* 62 (May 1914), 1445–1450.

Nickerson, A. H. "Personal Recollections of Two Visits to Gettysburg." *Scribner's Magazine* 14 (1893), 18–28.

Page, Evelyn. "After Gettysburg—Frederick Law Olmsted on the Escape of Lee." *Pennsylvania Magazine* 72 (October 1951), 436–446.

"The Golden Jubilee of Rufus Benjamin Weaver, Master Anatomist." *The Hahnemannian Monthly* (June 1915), 401–413.

Trimble, Gen. Isaac R. "The Civil War Diary of . . ." *Maryland Historical Magazine* 17 (March 1922), 1–20.

Ward, Capt. W. C. "Incidents and Personal Experiences on the Battlefield at Gettysburg." *Confederate Veteran* 8 (1900), 345–349.

Warren, L. P. Obituary. *Confederate Veteran* 22 (1914), 472.

Woolsey, Georgeanna. "Three Weeks at Gettysburg." Pamphlet (1863), 24 pp.

"College Hospital in Gettysburg." Writer unidentified. *Land We Love* 2 (February 1867), 290–294.

Index